IN THE NEW COUNTRY

David Foster is the author of the highly acclaimed novel *The Glade Within The Grove* and eleven preceding works of fiction. He was born in 1944 and spent his early childhood in the Blue Mountains of New South Wales, Australia. He achieved academic distinction as a scientist but soon turned to writing, first as a poet and subsequently as an award-winning novelist.

David Foster lives with his wife in the Southern Highlands of New South Wales.

In the New Country

David Foster

FOURTH ESTATE • *London*

First published in Great Britain in 1999 by
Fourth Estate Limited
6 Salem Road
London W2 4BU

1 3 5 7 9 10 8 6 4 2

A catalogue record for this book is available from
the British Library.

ISBN 1–85702–452–4

Typeset by Avon Dataset Ltd, Bidford on Avon B50 4JH
Printed and bound in Great Britain by
Clays Ltd, St Ives plc

For Michael Duffy

Acknowledgements

This project has been assisted by the Commonwealth Government through the Australia Council, its arts funding and advisory body. I wish to thank Raymond Plank and the UCross Foundation, Wyoming, for making possible a residency at the Kocur Writers' Retreat. Particular thanks to Bruce Pryor (ceramic detail and books – thanks, Bruce), Frank and Steve Davenport, Roger Robinson, the late Dave Quinlivan, Josh Shepherd and Kit Guyatt, Gerda Foster, Vince Nicholls, Jim Barrett, Samantha Wright, Rose Creswell, Jane Palfreyman, Paul Sheehan, Annie Proulx and Christopher Potter.

The anecdote of the Gucci 'roo is an Australian urban myth, which I have adapted here, to my own purpose.

To my part-aboriginal grandsons, Michael, Caleb and Willem Foster, in the hope that Australians may learn to see them, so that they may be permitted to see themselves, as Australians, rather than as aboriginal Australians.

Important Note:
The surname 'Leahey' is pronounced throughout, Australian style, as 'Lay'; not Irish style, as 'Law-hee' or 'Lee-hee'.

1

Gorillas, as is well known, run the City to Surf in teams of three. Any properly alert official should have suspected something amiss when, of five distinct gorilla congeries contesting last year's event, one consisted of two, rather than the customary three, gorillas. It often happens a man opting to run a race in a gorilla suit will collect his bib with his number on it already dressed in his suit. It was here race organisers felt lay the best chance of identifying the first gorilla home, who ran off shortly after crossing the line in the direction of the Jewish Social Club, Hakoah. Runners hoping to better their previous times are nervous before an event, and a gesture serving to put them at their ease is welcomed by race organisers. A runner dressed as a convict, say, who carries a heavy ball and chain, will serve a purpose in de-emphasising the competitive nature of the contest, for such is the tragic character of the male ego someone usually dies. One year, three runners died of heart attacks, none of whom was suffering a coronary disease.

The bibs, with their detachable tag for your medal, for this is a democratic event, are mailed to you, if you get in early; handed out, in the Water Board basement, by the Wilmot Street entrance, if you don't. But of fourteen gorillas identified, from video clip, as having lined up for the start, only six collected their bibs in their suits, according to race officials. The remainder either donned suits having collected the bib, or had the bib already with them, having received it by mail. Officials were thus unable to ascertain who these gorillas had been. When an appeal was later made asking all gorillas to step forward, no fewer than four hundred and ten runners claimed they had been running as gorillas.

The second Sunday in the month of August was a fine, clear, sunny day, as the cold winter gales that sweep the Great Divide are breezes by the time they reach Big Syd; welcome breezes, on Heartbreak Hill, to runners soaked in perspiration. Forty-five minutes before a start the precincts of Park and College Streets and Hyde Park are filled with the largely lightly clad, some attempting to push down plane trees, others apparently striving to scratch the smalls of their backs with the toes of their feet, a few, marginally less lightly clad, drifting home from dance parties. Queues in front of the sentry box unisex portable toilets are twenty deep: here no false modesty, but frank acceptance of the flesh and her dejecta. Music purloined from an aerobics class fills the linament-scented air, interrupted by exhortations from the starter that runners should remove themselves from garden beds, interspersed with cheer in the form of messages of goodwill from illustrious newsreaders.

Red Bibs best to begin. Fifteen thousand or so red bibbers. These back up, behind the start, down Park Street towards the Town Hall. Red bibbers have previously run a City to Surf, and will finish the course, most of them, at that sixty- to ninety-minute mark that constitutes a bottleneck of the moderately fit. In front of the red bibbers start purple bibbers, the preferred harriers, and even before these purple bibbers, green bibbers, the seeded runners, élite runners, Olympians, national champions, lithe Ethiopians and the like. Green bibbers sprint off at the start unimpeded by the pack and are entering the tunnel under Darlinghurst Road at the very top of William Street, while red bibbers at the back of their pack, who maybe needed to visit the loo, are still uncertain as to whether to walk or jog across the College Street intersection, as they make a tentative way over discarded complimentary copies of the sponsor's rag. Keeping cautious eyes to the ground, if, on occasion they glance up, it is to see before them an undulating wave, shopfront to shopfront up William Street, of a kind unique to late twentieth-century civilisation. Whereupon they whoop and holla.

To the right of the red bibbers, in front of the Museum and

up past Sydney Grammer School, stand blue bibbers, fifteen thousand or more. These are runners who require, to their discredit, more than one hundred minutes to run fourteen ks, or runners, however capable, who have never before run a City to Surf. It is here you will find the jovial, elderly Brits in their Boston Marathon caps; indeed, all moderns for whom to know a city is to run, swim or cycle, and preferably all three, through it. A chastening sight, to many a red bibber puffing past South Head cemetery and hearing, on someone's radio, that the first female is home, is a nimble, diminutive blue bibber, who cannot be more than eight years of age, scooting and darting her way through a pack of wheezing, overweight has-beens. The blue bibber finishing under an hour has run an exceptional race, as he must run an extra lateral kilometre, just to get through the red bibs. Blue bibbers start at the second gun but their times are accordingly adjusted.

And last, but by no means least in the Land Down Under, is the Back of the Pack. Yellow bibbers stand on the opposite side of College Street from blue bibbers, outside the Bowling Club. They have nothing to prove. Yellow bibbers turn left into William Street, after blue bibbers have turned right. Among the yellow bibbers are many who will walk the course and many who don't even know if they can walk it. It is here you will find, not so much wheelchair athletes with their sturdy upper arms, or soldiers running in their army boots, wearing full battledress with sixty-pound packs, for these take pride in a respectable time – rather old women, children in strollers, the terminally ill, the fantastically attired. Fifteen thousand yellow bibbers. Here are they who secrete the characteristic choice of blue sixpack under, say, a dufflecoat, sneaking, with a cackle, a surreptitious swig, while smoking cigarette upon cigarette. Here are your Phantoms, your Supermen, your Batmen, your Humpty Dumpties, your Wonderwomen, your Gorillas. First novelty team across the line gets a rousing reception all the way, from the multitude that lines the route, some, perhaps, merely waiting to cross the road, others playing bongos on their balconies, or spraying water at the grateful half-dead. Three triathletes from Newcastle, with pink wings and tutus and bestarred wands, are a sure thing here, as they wear red bibs and have pushed their way well among the purple by the start, but gorillas are often close to last to finish, if indeed they finish the run. By the time gorillas cross the line the barbecues have all but vanished from Bondi. The joke tends to wear thin as the day warms up and you can't slurp a Gatorade in your gorilla mask. You would first have to remove the mask, which would spoil the entire effect. They don't supply straws to you at drink stations and you've no pockets in your black gorilla suit and you can't carry straws in your grey gorilla hands.

Ten minutes before the start green bibbers are called to the line. As befits their celestial status on the day, they are not obliged to queue with *hoi polloi*. Red bibbers standing in Hyde Park garden beds slip into the unyielding mob on the road below, as the first items of cast-off clothing start to land on unsuspecting heads. Careful scrutiny of overhead shots at this juncture indicates fourteen gorillas, in four groups of three and one of two, limbering up at the back of the Back of the Pack.

Three minutes before the start red bibbers begin to press forward, heart rates rise and, in order to curtail an instinct that could turn tragic were things to go badly wrong, the starter steps up his inane palaver, making no mention whatsoever of the time. A video shot, taken three minutes to ten from high above the starting banners, reveals a crucial development, in that all four packs of three gorillas are still to be seen well back from the start, while one gorilla, from the brace of two, is beginning to force his way forward. As he shoves and elbows himself through the serried ranks, contrary to the spirit of the event, the resentment of those he displaces can be seen from the height of the helicopter. He is seen copping a good one to the kidneys, one to the neck, but it doesn't slow him down. Some way back, now forced to contend with an irate and mobilised resistance, his hapless colleague attempts to pursue him, in a futile effort to hose him down.

Bang! The gun for the first start fires as the irate gorilla, aggrieved, no doubt, by some aspersion, pushes his way to the front row of the third start. He is wearing no bib. What ensues is surely familiar to every human being on earth with TV, but to recapitulate, green bibbers sprint off, purple bibbers following, along with some pushier red bibbers, while in contravention of every regulation of the *Sun-Herald* City to Surf Fun Run, a bibless gorilla, running from the yellow start, joins them, going like a chimney fire in a gale.

Streakers at the cricket, throwing eggs at politicians, refusing to stand for 'God Save the Queen' – we have always among us the hooligan. Such disruption at the start of a City to Surf is not unprecedented; indeed, it is normal. With nigh on fifty thousand runners in motion, however, no official can much protest. The delinquent may well be detained and lectured, when he burns out and drops off in a block or two, by some altruistic red bibber who's pulled a hamstring at the start, say, and a proscription against him entering next year's run may well be contemplated. Blue bibbers, standing under the banner at the second start, are rooting for this outlaw, and the joke is, he's going well, which can't be easy, so laid-back and upright, in a gorilla suit. He's wearing a brand-new pair of Nike joggers, which seem spotless, as though never before worn.

By the time frontrunners, in that crucial opening sprint, have entered the Darlinghurst tunnel, the gorilla is no longer copping cuffs and curses from red bibs whose progress he impedes. To the contrary; he has made up ground, to the delight of spectators. As to the expressions on the faces of preferred and seeded runners as they are overtaken, so recurrent a staple of credit sequences on TV Sports Shows have these become, no more need here be said. Suffice it to remark, when, at the four-kilometre mark and proceeding down New South Head Road, traffic has thinned to the point where three burly officials dash out to apprehend the interloper, the chorus of outrage, the booing and hissing ensuing from spectators, gives way to a roar of delight when the ape, now running in fourteenth position, shows a step off both feet, and a change of pace and a fend, would do credit to any Black Pearl in the centres and freezes the grins on the faces of such Rugby

League coaches as watch a replay. And when, at the five-kilometre mark, the ape having moved up into twelfth place, a fourth official moves out, with a net, he is promptly restrained by a fifth, who attends, with a free hand, the mobile phone, for a Word has come down from The Man. The Man, in whose mind's eye projected advertising revenue is swelling, like an inflamed carbuncle.

Leave him alone. Let him contend.

The frontrunner, a South African junior ten-thousand-metre representative, is outside where Jack Davy's wife used to have the dress shop there in Rose Bay, but the leader is by now of little interest. Analysts later insist the besuited contender is a cross-country man, as he's losing ground on the long flat from Doyle's Seafood Restaurant to where the Wintergarden was, and likes to jump up and down off the kerbing and guttering as he hastens. Heartbreak Hill, where the concrete winds up past the Convent of the Sacred Heart, is, as a rule, where the race is won or lost, and a must-show sequence on the nightly news. Something about this hill brings out the best in the besuited contender. Commentators suspect he is a man, not through sexism, which far be it from them, but simply because the winning time of forty-one minutes twenty-seven seconds is seven minutes faster than the first woman's time, and it would unduly stretch the imagination to suppose a woman, however dressed, could run a City to Surf in forty-one minutes.

Running in only twenty-seventh place at the foot of Heartbreak Hill, the besuited contender ascends the next two kilometres in under five minutes. Never, perhaps, in the City to Surf has such a hill climb been witnessed, a commendable charge. Along Military Road, no doubt mistaking the ape for one of those drunk and disruptive clowns intent on spoiling every sporting event in the Land Down Under, and supposing him to have just crashed in around the block, certain spectators run out in an effort to grab and tackle the ape, which only makes him prop to the preternatural extent of his agility. Other spectators, to the contrary aware, from listening to a commentary, of the true situation, and deranged with excitement on apprehending that an underdog has a chance of getting up, commence interfering with the three lean leaders, throwing cans at their feet and spraying them with water. The last few kilometres, that welcome downhill off Dover Heights, are pandemonium. Later, the official victor – and of course, a bibless gorilla cannot, strictly speaking, win – will claim, at a press conference poorly attended, he would have won outright, had he not been hit on the head with a banjo, but who so much as remembers his name? He is forgotten, and how unsporting to complain, given the besuited contender was brought down twice off his feet, only to recover and hasten on.

To recover and hasten on; nay, to sprint down onto Campbell Parade thirty seconds in front of the field. But he doesn't beat his breast as he breaks the tape a kilometre down the track, and to their credit they let him break the tape: they had a full minute to reconstitute it; nor does he punch the cloudless sky, as he leaps, clicking heels, with an Oh What a Feeling. No, he looks about, analysts later claiming he doesn't seem to know where he is, as though he has never before been on Bondi Beach. So we know he can't be English.

He picks up speed as he breasts the tape, and then he's down into the sand, and up and down the beach, confused. He pauses at a barbecue outside a corporate tent, to poke with a grey hand at a T-bone. The real race is become the side-show, notwithstanding the tens of thousands pouring down Campbell Parade. Then up and over the skateboard ramp, and once he's among those side-streets off the main drag, who can keep up? Anyone in Sydney who can run a bit is running still or quite exhausted. And when the helicopter pilot lost him, it's off with the suit and the joggers – he discarded a right Nike jogger, we think it was him, size twelve – and he's become another runner. He's just another runner. He may have caught a bus or walked up Bondi Road, like everyone else, to sit on a subway train with the other runners, all blissed out in their shorts and singlets, enjoying the runners' high, among those elderly Eastern Suburbs Eastern European refugees in their gloves, coats and scarves, because, remember,

7

this is winter, and winters are cold. They found a gorilla suit not far from the Hakoah Club, which, we contend, proves nothing, along with the joggers, although one had been taken, perhaps by a passer-by with a pegleg. They don't cost much to confect in Indonesia but they're worth a motza in the West. Or perhaps he just went off, wearing the one shoe, ay.

Word spread fast. It got back to the back of the Back of the Pack, conveyed there by those with breath still to speak. All fourteen hirsute and supernumerary suits were found abandoned. If they hadn't already been ditched – it was an unseasonably hot day – then on hearing of their confrère's success, the remaining gorillas reacted spontaneously. Three suits were found in blue portaloos, three in telephone booths, one down by the old flying-boat base, a couple in bunkers on the Royal Sydney Golf Course and, of course, they're identical. One size fits all. Indistinguishable, one from another, all made by the same Taiwanese company.

Where to start? Sydney Two Thousand Olympics coming up, and a medal certainty for the men's marathon or steeplechase, gone to ground. Disappeared.

Most people hire gorilla suits. So every party hire and novelty shop in the whole of this country was checked out, but none overseas; you see, if he wasn't Australian, we didn't want to know him. Fair enough?

8

2

The Irish New Country, as it was known in the early eighteen hundreds, stretches down the open western slopes of the Australian Great Divide, on the New South Wales Central and Southern Tableland, from Mudgee to Boorowa. There are still fiddlers about to give you 'Clementine' for a mazurka. In a good year, the New Country makes a fine sight, in spring, to the cattleman or beekeeper, ryegrass tall and Paterson's Curse (Salvation Jame) in flower, but by mid-June you could flog a flea across it and the Alpine winds will rock your vehicle most anyplace you park. Here and there, in the south of this Irish New Country, you cross the Great Divide, but you wouldn't feel you were crossing it, were the sign not there to inform. For the Great Divide here is no Wilderness, clad in evergreen, flammable forest, as it is on the eastern slopes of the Blue Mountains, upon which it abuts.

In order to feel more at home, in an emerald landscape on a stony outcrop, the settlers poisoned, burnt or ringbarked all the remaining timber, sparing only that dense, dry woodland towards The Hole, Mount Nerong, and a tall, wet forest of manna gum and brown barrel eucalypt above Blanket Flat. To the north, Kanangra Tops and the Murruin Plateau rise to over four thousand feet, to constitute a wilderness of sclerophyll forest, the most impressive on the planet, and the most intractable massif in the whole Australian Great Divide. Known as the 'Blue Mountains' – for flammable mountains, from a distance, are 'blue' to the eye – this massif, seen from the colony of Sydney to its east, formed, providentially, a barricade to the wandering mobs of cattle that decamped from the colony. These mobs, a valuable resource, along with the convicts who depastured and rustled them, form a significant chapter in the European history of the Blue Mountains. It was twenty-five years after settlement before the first official crossing was made, up a central ridge by what is now the town of Katoomba, with its world-renowned Three Sisters, a beguiling rock formation, though no doubt the odd scrub bull, and the odd scrub convict, was already through to the West. We now boast a city of four million people encroaching on the Wilderness of the eastern slopes. Fifteen minutes into a flight from Sydney to Perth and watch the passengers' eyes drift from the windows. West of the Blue Mountains, Australia is all but featureless to the shores of the Indian Ocean.

Despite being farmland, specialising, from a school-project-book perspective, in seed potato and superfine fleeces, fat lambs and beef cattle, like Hibernia, the Argentine pampas, the US Pacific Coast and the South African Cape, the New Country was occupied by hunters, not farmers, when Irish-men arrived. Today, tropics and sub-tropics hold more appeal, to the antipodean, than ancestral climes, and the family farm is on the way out the world over. Not all the New Country is doing so brilliant. Indeed, there is a moeity of the New Country where no money has trickled down to the people since the late nineteen fifties, and if you drive down the dusty road takes you from the two-pub town of Knocklofty – where, if you're driving a green Mazda Ricebubble, say, you're sure to get a wave, but not because they welcome strangers; more because they're short-sighted and impatient, and cannot imagine there could be more than one green Mazda Rice-bubble – till you reach Crooked Corner, what, in May, resembles a top cotton crop will prove, on closer inspection, to be thistles. Chipping out saffron thistles is hard work and pointless, as they always grow back, such a task as a young man never undertakes, except to curry favour. In the late nineteen nineties there is no money for sprays here, no money to hire hands, and no farmer's son who much cares if he inherits a farm he cannot profit from. Divide and rule then subdivide, and piss off.

Patrick MacPeatrick, nonagenarian younger brother of nonagenarian Joe and scion of the pioneer, stands, with a horn-handled blackthorn stick, outside a hut like the one to be seen in Herberton Museum, except the roof here is of corrugated iron. Still has an ant-nest floor, though, and the walls are well-ventilated ironbark slabs. Patrick and Joseph no longer live in this obdurate tribute to the adze, although they did when they were boys. It is presently a storeroom, but not for much longer, if they have their wicked way. When Pat and Joe were boys there was no such thing as a Holden vehicle, in fact there was no such thing as a petrol pump, but the Crooked Corner was a thriving village, with a parish school, a butchery, a general store, and a church, the Fane of St Fiacre. Today, it is more of a district, for the purpose of the telephone code. It retains, in state of disrepair, the Fane of St Fiacre, an ant-nest tennis court and the new Fire Brigade Shed. The road through is sealed, for a bit, but if you miss the white and black bullet-perforated signpost announcing Crooked Corner, you mightn't guess you were in Crooked Corner, or rather, you wouldn't know which Crooked Corner you were in, because it stands to rural reason there would have to be at least three. She's crooked all right: fencers round here still think light travels in straight lines; they're not quite up to speed.

Joseph MacPeatrick, a man wearing a crooked, orange-fibre wig, appears, with a sneeze that could fracture a rib, in a doorway of one of the two occupied dwellings of the modern Crooked Corner, which is not the one near Binda: that's another Crooked Corner. Scattering geese ('Orville' grey; 'Wilbur' grey and white – these head downhill like lyrebirds, the flying fishes of our forest floor) Joe calls on his brother for wood, a large, weathered heap of which is better than money in the bank, to the non-shareholder in the bank. He holds, in his hand, as he has all winter, two foxed Ansett Airline tickets, but the hand that holds them is presently slackened by his side, not threatening the flight-paths.

'Come see the fire in the front room, Bubba,' says Joe. 'Bit of action there. Large log just fell off a fire dog. I was tippin that might happen.'

'What's happening on the fire in your own room, then?'

'Oh, it's borin me to death. I feel I've seen it before.'

'Why you up so early, Joe? Haven't wet your bed, I hope? If so, let me take out the mattress this time, for the love of Mary, Brigid and Therese. Draggin a mattress up and down a yard is a job for a man who milks a herd by hand.'

'Which you don't. What you doin there, Bubba?'

'Checkin out this beet. Pat's High School Class of Sixty-One Reunion's comin up an Shorn's doin the caterin. Wants me beetroot. Buyin the n-tyre crop.'

'That Shorn himself went to that school is a disgrace to his mother and the Church.'

'Why's that?'

'Because all the boys and girls was in the one class, with no proper religious instruction.'

'You're thinkin of somewhere else. Wasn't it Sister Patrick and Father Carney give 'em instruction at Pat's? Oh, here's Shorn now. Looks like he broke an accelerator cable. That's the third this year.'

'Don't sound like it, even if I am deaf.'

'Shoulda worn muffs feedin pigs. Not to mention blind as a beetle and dribble night and day. Why else would a man drive holdin his fist clenched outside the window of his vehicle? I guarantee there's a piece of string in that hand, attached to the carbyretta.'

'Why don't he buy himself a decent vehicle, Bubba? Sixty-six Haitch Ar when he could afford a Suzuki.'

'I best go 'n tell him pick this crop 'fore the geese get into 'em.'

'Here's a mean-lookin man,' affirms Pat, limping out to greet Shorn MacEwe, a rubicund battler of fifty-five winters with a sleeper in his earlobe and a fortuitous Irish tonsure and known as 'Blue', not because of his hair, which as it happens is red, but because his arms are blue, a faded, navy blue, from each shoulder to every fingertip, for there are no temporary tattoos in the New Oireland. 'Here's the meanest-lookin man I ever seen. Here's a man too mean to respond when a neighbour sent him a card of con-gratulation, followin his win.'

Shorn known as 'Blue' appeals, smiling, to the unseen

angels over the two-tone Haitch Ar. He wears, as always, a pair of blue socks half swallowed by safety boots, blue singlet and blue shorts.

'Pat,' he says, 'you're like a bloody old gramophone record stuck in a groove. Yours, as you know, was the four hundred and first card of congratulation I received and I was fresh out of envelopes and tirin of the attention. Had yours been the first, even the one hundred and first, things would have been different. I guarantee I'd have sent you a letter as long and as warm as the first I composed, now what's goin on? What's with this swede turnip in your mitt? Is that what she got in that back paddock up Killaarney feedin them dairy steers? She be getting the same for them as what she paid, fat or thin. It oughta be mine, that place, you know. I'm descended from Carmel O'Roy and MacEwe o' The Hole, Mount Nerong.'

'So you say. This is no turnip, Shorn. When you asked me to grow you a crop of finest beet, for the Pat's School Reunion, I recalled I had some seed left of a special white which money cannot buy. Now this is not a sugar beet, although it'd give you diabetes. Taste this, Shorn. Go on! Take a bite outta that. Sweet's not the word.'

'And purple's not the colour, Pat. Can't you see it's the wrong colour? Food for a champ, and we're all winners here, must be the colour of a championship sash, at least on top. You go and wash this under the tap at your tank, your geese have been on it.'

'No, you do it for me, your hand's already frozen. I couldn't help it I was away in hospital, when you had the win.'

'Oh? You wasn't unconscious when they took you up to that hospital, was you, Pat? Heard you marched in under your own steam. Waste o'money, givin expensive hospital treatments to a man your age. There oughta be a cut-off point. Three-score years and ten'd make sense. If you was a horse I'd shoot ya.'

'You'll never get to my age, Shorn.'

'No. There'll be no pension or expensive hospital treatments for the generation of Sixty-One.'

'Your generation never fought in the war and you're all on drugs.'

'Ever heard o' Vietnam? And you like a cuppa. Now you tellin me the meat inside this beet is cream? 'Cause that's no good to me.'

'Taste it, 'fore you complain of it, boy! You'd like a fair go, I'd like a fair go. Dare say the Vietnamese would have liked a fair go. Give this beetroot a fair go.'

'This is no beetroot. This is what they used to call mangel wurzel, only fit for cattle. I can't serve a thing like this to the Pat's School Reunion.'

'You dunno the first bloody thing about croppin, Shorn. When was you a farmer?'

'I do know, thanks to you it's now too late to plant real beet, and I am determined to serve up nothin but fresh-picked local produce. That's what I'm about, Pat. That's what wins me these big contracts.'

'Heard Dud Leahey could be comin out.'

'We're hopin Dud'll be there.'

'Fine thing for the district, Shorn, if Dud Leahey was to come. God knows, he can afford it and we need a boost, what with cattle fetchin what they don't, yet you ask for a steak at a butchery and see what you pay. Someone's makin money and I think I know his name. I guarantee we've more Dud Leaheys out here, if the truth were known. See, you could have a photo taken for the local paper, give us all some heart.'

'Oh, we will, Pat. We will. That's our strategy, see. Now what you want is to get into superfine wool, once this Ovine Johnes Disease is conquered. I want to offer Dudley a meal he can't get in New York.'

'You'd be doin that with this, Shorn.'

'No, I won't. My Hamburger from Hell is purple, Pat. It's an Australian burger, although conceived in Wandsworth. You won't see beet in a Big Mac and that's what's given me the edge.'

'They reckon Oh Jay Dee come out here with these Heartier Rowans. All these Maori shearers, usin the wide comb, put an end to Mike Hock.'

'I wouldn't know.'

★　★　★

Most of the fences in Crooked Corner are post and rail with the rails long gone and replaced by droppers, stand-offs for the electrics and the posts at twenty degrees. The characteristic shape of the shed in Crooked Corner is a parallelogram, owing to the turbulent winter wind never blew two sheds down at the same angle. The trees in Crooked Corner are predominantly snowgum, which is always crooked, and twisted basket willows that grow on the sinuous banks of the creek. The cows have crumpled horns, the road describes a scimitar, and the safety chain, or tailgate, is secured here by means of a pigtail.

Later that morning, passing by Blue MacEwe's neglected orchard, where Blue, a chef at Ballymeaner Sportsman's Club in Ballymeaner – the place you would need to go, if you want any item of new hardware – is relaxing before he retires, as he keeps late hours on account of the job, by sitting on an upturned camp oven shooting starlings with a pea rifle, Patrick MacPeatrick walks to the top of the hill overlooking the High Plain. Cold now, under a slow-moving mantle of winter-grey cloud, it stretches, far as an eye can see, beyond Killaarney, a station extending from Blanket Flat – swampy sedgeland, covered in ti tree, first place a fogpatch forms, take your blanket – to The Hole, Mount Nerong, a sheer rocky gorge, much prone to lightning strike and often supporting a thread of smoke. The Hole, Mount Nerong, a Dreaming Site, a sacred site to local aborigines (who, in the main, were tribal outcasts, lacking the numbers to hunt 'roo), was a place where a monitor, a big kind of lizard, made a hole in the ground in pursuit of a black bream. Before they became fierce black men, the local aborigines were reptiles and fish.

Normally a sheep station, Killaarney, like many a station hereabout but bigger than most, is officially destocked for two clips, on the recommendation of the Ovine Johnes Disease (OJD) Steering Committee. There are dams, half frozen and now surrounded by Friesian steers, head down between the granite rocks, caterpillars of Monterey pine, winding in corners to form windbreaks, and by the road, occasional leafless hawthorns, the ground beneath them denuded. Free-standing dead gums act as sentry boxes for the white cockatoos, over thistles and burrs and tussock, with a far-distant, bright-blue tractor the only primary colour to be seen, apart from the red cat's-eye reflectors on the white guideposts that descend the hill. You can understand the hunger here for beet and chilli sauces.

On a dead fox, a luxuriant fur by the roadside ripples in the wind. Woulda been worth a bob, that skin, once upon a time.

The fane, which stands atop the hill, lichen peeling off its green wooden walls, has four side windows and two back windows, but no glass; all shut up with iron. The porch is secured with a rusty chain and a lock no intruder need pick, because there is a room, an annexe with a chimney, at the rear of the fane, with no door to it. A fane should stand always open, but then, a pope should never have surgery. Making his way towards the wooden fane annexe, and crossing himself as he enters, Patrick MacPeatrick seizes, from the floor, a biscuit of oaten hay, and is turning to inspect the contents of a polythene sack of wheaten chaff for mildew when he hears, in trepidation, the cessation of the purr of a passing C Two Hundred Classic. Fearing, perhaps, the appearance of a self-righteous cleric with beetroot-coloured nose or shirt, the devout man hastily kicks aside the ashes of the fireplace that serves him, on a Sabbath, for an altar, and stands affrighted, tremulously holding his hay and blackthorn stick. The Merc door slams shut and a pair of well-shod feet approach, scrunching over the yet unthawed frost in shadow of the fane. They don't sound like Father Carney's feet. More like high-heeled stock boots. Not so peremptory.

Poisonous cigarette smoke and shortly thereafter, the belly of a big-bellied man, who wears a pale-blue short-sleeved shirt from the retailer R. M. Williams, with a tie of agricultural brown, over a pair of cream moleskins and no coat and no hat. The moleskins hang precariously off an all-but-arseless pair of hips.

You would need to go to Ballymeaner to buy any item of rural clothing now, unless you were content with a hand-knitted beanie, of the kind sold in Knocklofty craft shops.

Dark in the fane, ay. The stout New Countryman peers in, and is turning to walk off, when Pat, obliged to clear his throat, precipitates a paroxysm of expectoration.

'Oh. Someone there? Is there a sick old wombat in there?'

'Just gettin this bit of hay.'

'No worries. Patrick MacPeatrick! Old Paddy MacPeatrick. Pat, is there much doin here? I see from the board, reconciliation is held before mass each third Sunday of the month.'

'Not since the war. Do I know you?'

Out shoots, with speed and purpose would please a warrant officer and frighten a horse, a hand.

'Adam Hock. Stock and station agent. Wool broker. Cattle futures. Feedlot consultant. Your godson. I think you knew my mother. Smoke? No? Mind if I do? Ta. I'm visitin Shorn MacEwe. Would you know if he's about, Pat?'

'Be asleep.'

'I'll wake him. I'll put on me CB radio loud and his horses'll think they're racin. That'll bring him out. Not right, a man sleepin on such a lovely day. So this is the "Fane of St Fiacre", Pat. This is the famous fane. I don't think I have been here since the day I was baptised here. Oh yes, I was baptised here. It's a bloody beautiful song that, too, I think it's my favourite on the n-tyre album. I find I hum it, any time of day. I need somethin to cheer me up, what with the dive in the Hang Seng and the Nikkei. What's wrong with this local Council, Pat? Here we have a Living National Treasure, a Crooked Corner boy who wins a Grammy for a CD that goes platinum, I think it went platinum in the States, I know it went gold in the UK. What an incomparable opportunity we have to boost tourism to the district, and not a thing has been done. Not one job has been created.'

'Hear the man could be comin back.'

'Yes, we suspect so, Pat. I'm pretty sure you're right. Well I know you are, because I know what you don't, I am Chairperson of the Steerin Committee that steered Dud to the Reunion. I am Chairperson of this Committee what is organising the Pat's School Reunion, which I set up, pure and simple, in order to lure Dud. Now you didn't hear me say that. So you've given up the fags, Pat? Can't tempt you with one of these? Supermild.'

'Who can afford a smoke today, Ad. Ta.'

'Tobacco, Pat. There's a crop you wouldn't want futures in. They grow it at Mareeba on the Atherton, you know, where they got that big rodeo goin up there for the Japs? What do you make of this Asian downturn? Can't see it hurtin tourism, can you? I know the worse things get for me, the more I want to drink and travel and smoke. Yes, every day a rodeo. They're on the ball up there. You get in the bus at Cairns, or rather – picture this for a TV ad, swandive off your luxury liner, swim in to the drop-off, Pat, discard your flippers, spit your snorkel, hop in the Quicksilver cat on the Outer Reef, head due west. First up you have the mangroves and the wonderful birdlife on those Cairns mudflats to admire, the Casino, stop to watch the Corroboree, all day every day, perhaps a Bungy Jump, then the Range, with its beautiful blue butterflies, Kuranda, with the magnificent Tropical Rainforest, World Heritage listed, shop at the local markets there, open all day every day, and by lunch-time you're in the outback, mate, or near enough. Mareeba Rodeo. Dry as a nun's tit, Mareeba. Sure, you can do the entire North Aussie experience in a single day. They don't have a lot of time, these Japs. They have only the three days here. Three days only! We're mission out on their yen. Well, what would you expect. Our market's once a month and our rodeo's once a bloody year. Anyway, I'm gonna do something about that, I'm not waitin for this Council. I'm off to Japan shortly, Pat. Japan, then on to New York, my purpose bein to change a few Mickey Mouse dollars into greenbacks and to visit Dud Leahey in Greenwich Village, where he resides. Of course, he remains fiercely and proudly Australian, as we read. I'm goin to press in the man's slide hand a return ticket to Knocklofty, compliments of our Countrywoman's Association, proceeds of the market-day Devonshire teas.'

'Not before time. This district is goin to the dogs. Why, look across there on that far hill, Adam. Someone put up a war cemetery, but never got round to completin it. No crosspiece on the headstones.'

'That is a vineyard, Paddy. What you see are the white, polythene cylinders guidin the young vines. See, I sold that block for a vineyard block. Well, I read anywhere you can grow an apple, you can grow a grape. They had apples there, didn't they? Would have grown apples there, wouldn't they, in the old days, like?'

'Never. That was the orchard, on that hill over there.'

'Oh well. No harm done.'

'Blue Commodore with a young German couple come through here th'other mornin.'

'Oh?'

'They was wantin directions. Terrified, they was.'

'Oh?'

'Dirt road. Never driven a car on a dirt road.'

'Oh. Did yez ask what they was doin out here, Pat, and where they'd heard of us? Always ask. I put that very question to a couple of young Israelis I found in a campervan of late. They'd been everywhere. Everywhere about Asia. Reckoned Australia was a Great Place to Come Down. I presume they meant Come Down Under.'

'I did. I was hitchin to Knocklofty. Scored two flats in the Sierra and couldn't find a beadbreaker. I won't jack a vehicle on rubber. So she didn't want to shift her luggage from the boot, to make way for me wheel. Speakin in German, she was, but she understood every word I said. He insisted. Threw her bags out on the road. Well, we couldn't see what she was worried over. Avis car. Plenty of room in the back seat of a V six Commodore.'

'Good on him. He didn't want to see an old farmer stuck by the side of the road, in what could have been, for all he knew, a life or death situation. He took an appropriate measure. He knows that, in his heart. So what was they doin out here, Pat?'

'Hired a car in Sydney to go down to Can-berra, then choose a route through the Blue Mountains, give 'emselves a night out of Sydney. Couldn't read a map. Must have come up through Porter's Retreat. Don't think they realised what they was doin, till it was too late. No turnin round there. Joe had trouble gettin the six-wheel-drive Studebaker up. Shoulda seen their white faces. He was grippin that wheel like he was tryin to fart, for a cash prize.'

'Everyone goes to the blessed Blue Mountains. They get more tourists there than Mareeba. What have the Blue Mountains got, this shire cannot offer? That's the Blue Mountains right there, Pat. Your Three Sisters are the other side o' that. Why, this property, Killaarney, goes all the way to The Hole, Mount Nerong. Mount Nerong's Blue Mountains. Did they enjoy our scenery?'

'Wasn't lookin at it. When he got on the tar outside Knock-lofty, she laughed like a cat and he cried.'

'Well there you go. A Wilderness experience, by German standards, within a day's drive o' Kingsford Smith. I'm not in favour o' sealin the roads at all. But supposin they wanted a bite to eat in Knocklofty, Pat, where would they find it? Supposin they wanted accommodation for the night, with a spa, or at least a bath. Supposin they wanted champagne, as you or I might, after such an experience. Supposin she wanted to freshen up. We cannot expect a modern German to walk a muddy oval to a toilet block, which, in all likelihood, is locked, or squat beside a road. See, that's where we come unstuck. Our infrastructure lets us down. People want a Wilderness experience but no one wants to spend a night in the Wilderness. I hope you told them it's tar all the way to Canberra? Two-lane highway from Goulburn?'

'They was gonna spend a whole day in Can-berra.'

'Well there's another problem, Pat. Misinformation.'

'I have to go feed me cows now.'

'Course you do. Of course you do. You know, this place of yours here would make an excellent wind farm? Wind farm, like they got at Pejar, near Crookwell, and the Rosses on Donegal? Big, clean, attractive windmills, make a tourist attraction. You'd have a layby off the road, see, a viewin area. I got to get goin too. I want to be sure Friend MacEwe has the prawns organised for the prawn cocktails. He was dead against the notion o' prawn cocktails, then talkin of buyin prawn farm prawn; I says, buy real ones and serve'm in champagne tulips.

Go for the doctor. I'll think about what you've said to me, though, and iceberg lettuce. I'll think of that young German couple. I may even mention them at the next Council meeting, to make a point. I guarantee pickin you up was the high point of their visit to Australia. Did yez get on? Did they take a photo of ya?'

'He was all right. Turned out he don't like Nazis either.'

'Well that's what it's about, Pat. Education goes both ways. Oh, I feel positive about this district, with these Olympics comin up. I know that's not a common view, but I feel we have barely begun to tap our tourist potential here. We have talent aplenty. This is not the first Dud Leahey we've produced, nor will it be the last. Trouble is, we have somehow managed to create the wrong impression, it's like those signs you see above the chains that stop the trains that say "Penalty for Improper Use Not Exceeding", are you with me, Pat? Naturally tourists want to see a place no one's ever heard of, who wouldn't, but we cannot have them stumbling upon us like this, Pat. What's in it for us?'

3

The Western Slopes of New South Wales, of which the New Country is but one small component, range in width from 250 to 450km, and slope away to the Western Plains and the arid Western Division of the state. While grassland, fully cured, will burn, the whole of the Eastern Fall of the Divide, outside the urban regions, is afforested, mostly with wet or dry sclerophyll (eucalypt: hardly any rainforest left, rainforest being easier to clear as it won't resucker after being burnt), setting aside some extensive clearing north of Newcastle to the Queensland border. The Great Divide in New South Wales is never more than 150km from the coast. Inland of the Central Coastal region much of the plain has been cleared for housing, but timbered gorges invade many of the outer suburbs of Sydney. In the Blue Mountains proper, dwellings are often crassly arranged as to maximise a view (often as not from a wooden deck) along a ridge set above a sharply ascending afforested slope. Unsurprisingly, fire poses a periodic menace here, given Australia is the driest and the least populous of all continents. Moreover, many Australian eucalypts are not so much fire resistant as fire adapted: candlebark and stringybark eucalypts, in particular, seemed designed to coax surface fires into the crown, or promote spotfiring, by flaking off bark, in the form of firebrands. Given such potentially perilous conditions, in time of drought and antisocial arson, that well-trained body of citizen fire-fighters known as the 'Bush Fire Brigade' is indispensable to the welfare of any antipodean hamlet. Volunteers – it gives them an interest, and would cost too much to pay them – supervised by the shire Fire Control Officer (FCO), who superintend the mitigation of wildfires, through a judicious programme of selective hazard reduction.

The objective is to reduce fuel load, and thus, fire intensity, by prescribed burns, so making the inevitable fires, when they occur, more manageable. And of course if a car, or structural fire, does occur in a hamlet, there's no one else to fight it, or more generally, stand by, then 'black out' (mop up) the embers.

Wednesday night is the night Bush Fire Brigades meet in Yarrawongamullee Shire, to catch up on gossip, to make sure the trucks, and the pumps on those trucks, start, to take the appropriate measures if they don't, and to run radio and pager checks, one of the bees in Ad Hock's bonnet being the need to change the name of this shire to something travel agents can spell, while giving a clearer indication of the district's geographical location. When he proposed 'Shire of the Mid-Western Slopes: Bushranger Country' as a cogent orthographical alternative, and called for debate, or plebiscite, in the *Ballymeaner Examiner*, seven of eight letters received by the editor in consequence put the kybosh on, one correspondent (a blow-in) noting the suggestion could only be construed as racism, given the shire's otherwise blithe contempt for its aboriginal toponymy, others, locally born, weighing cost, which was certain, against potential advantage, which was moot, and noting the cost would have to be borne by the ratepayer, as per usual. Shaking his head disconsolately as he read these feckless epistles while mopping up residual syrup on his styrene trencher with his McHash Brown, Ad Hock returned the rag to the rack forthwith.

Knocklofty Fire Brigade sheds, like most, are of galvanised iron over a concrete slab, with a couple of big white rendered concrete tanks, to collect roof runoff. The object of the water supply is to provide water to fill the tankers, both red trucks with a tank and a pump on the back, and fitted with hoses and tools. Unlike Crooked Corner, Knocklofty, as befits a village of substance, has the water, but copperhead and yellow-bellied black snakes hibernate in the hydrant holes, and shipping a standpipe to a hydrant, in order to fill a tanker, or blast away, with a canvas sixty-five hose to remove degreasers from the shed floor, has so frequently muddied Thursday nappy wash in neighbouring streets, the process is now discountenanced, except in the rare event of structural fire, when overprecipitate opening of the standpipe can cause a hammer that blows the mains. For this reason, the task of shipping a standpipe is sagaciously assigned to the most junior member of crew; that is, Billy, the person with least to lose in way of reputation should flood follow fire.

As the sun sinks on the horizon, the doors of the tanker shed are brutally raised by means of sturdy chains, on which pull men, both bending at the waist. Either would dismantle a gearbox as soon as looking at it. The exhalations from their exertions condense and drift from the shed like smoke. Both wear a pair of yellow overalls, with 'Yarrawongamullee Shire' written on the back, in reflective tape, which is fine, except that cotton overalls burn in fire, whereas plastic tends to melt. The loyal O'Mara, last member of Knocklofty Brigade to die fighting a bushfire, went to his grave with 'Yarrawongamullee Shire' poignantly branded across his shoulders.

Before the doors are fully raised, an air compression warning buzzer sounds, as Billy Minogue turns the key, never removed from the ignition switch, on Knocklofty One, an antique Bedford with a mere seven thousand klicks on the clock, and an Isuzu badge on the grille, for a joke. Affixed before the last Parade to celebrate Fire Prevention Week – held, the world over, in October, to commemorate the Chicago fire of 1871, which burnt eighteen thousand buildings, four thousand more than the Great Fire of London – a joke it remains, for the sad fact is, the new Isuzu Category One, with micro-switched lights in every storage area, and a huge pump, with round-the-pump foam proportioner, and twenty-four-volt electric pump crew protection spray unit, went to Ballymeaner, despite there being a Town Brigade in Ballymeaner, who get paid for turning out.

One of his freckled, pudgy hands on the key, the other pulling at the choke, Billy Minogue starts Knocklofty One. Too young to hold a driver's licence, he loves to start the tankers, and beams with pleasure as Knocklofty One groans to life, albeit under protest. Unless, at this juncture, ordered out, Billy will proceed to drive both tankers from the shed, for the satisfaction that hearing the hiss of the air as he applies the handbrakes affords.

'What's on tonight?' inquires Keyring MacHugh, a thin man, rubbing together abraded hands. 'Might see if we'd get a burn on, ay. Frosts'lla dried things a bit. Might make a start on some 'azard reduction.'

Without waiting for an answer – the chain of command is perforce tenuous in a brigade of Australian rural volunteers – Keyring, a self-employed carpet cleaner these days, walks to tanker Knocklofty Two, takes down a 'Firebug' driptorch from the rack, a driptorch being a metal container that trickles fuel down a metal line, through a pigtail. He knows it's full, as he filled them all last week with his premium driptorch mix, which gives an almighty 'Whoomph' when ignited. He inverts the torch, opens the valve, strikes and tosses a match at the business end – Whoomph! – and soon has a nearby patch of scrub satisfactorily ablaze. The recommended seventy per cent diesel can barely be kept alight, he finds. A Molotov cocktail'd do better.

'Wastin fuel,' observes World Wide Webb, Brigade Senior Deputy Captain. World Wide, who sports a dark Viva Zapata mo and a ziff with a pair of muttonchops, was slaughterman at the abattoir – twenty-two magnum for bulls, bolts for the cows, belt sheep on the head – till it closed last June, giving a week's notice and leaving half Knocklofty unemployed. The other half was already unemployed.

'Give it another week, mate. Won't spread. Too cold. We're gettin a visit from the DFCO, then we'll head out and fill MacPeatrick's house tanks. Runnin low on water in the Corner.'

'Will we fill at the hydrant, World Wide?' Young Billy Minogue wears the yellow duds his mother Molly made for him, on a sewing machine in a private room at the Top Pub, Minogue's. Minogue's is your typical Irish watering hole, with empty kegs and canisters of gas, in an outside lane oddly visible from all doors and most windows of the premises, lined by a wall that is darker towards the bottom than

25

towards the top. The carpets are threadbare, the floorboards in the bedrooms creak, as you make your nocturnal way to and from the loo, on which the seat won't remain upright, for, let's face it, you're an alcoholic. You wouldn't live here, unless you were an alco, and you wouldn't know how the floorboards creaked, unless you were living here. No lady visitors.

'Sure. Fill up at the hydrant on the edge o' town on the way back in an stuff 'em.'

'Takin both tankers?'

'Only got one tanker driver 'ere,' observes Keyring. Scorning use of the knapsack spray – a force-fed, hand-held water pump fitted to a tank, carried on the back and diabolically heavy – he will watch the fire burn itself out. 'Where's our so-call Cap'n?'

'God knows,' admits World Wide. 'Man's a law unto himself. Rung me at home this afternoon, said he said somepin comin up.'

'Probly gone to throw 'is pots. Someone oughta throw 'em back.'

'Dunno, mate. Carn work 'im out. Billy! Start the pump on number one 'n make sure the lights is workin.'

'Want me to take the troopie outta the shed first, World Wide?'

'No thanks. Where's Willco? Willco comin tonight?'

'Said he might be along later.'

'Bullshit. What, is it State of Origin Football on tele? Christ All Bloody Mighty, this is the worst turnout all winter. Looks good for the DFCO.'

'Someone shootin round town last night. You blokes hear it? Shotgun. Coupla shots.'

'Nup. Get that pump started please, Billy, and don't flood it, like you did when Johnson's house burnt down.'

Piling into Knocklofty Two – which, while only two-wheel drive, of the two Knocklofty Bedfords is the more easy to control as it doesn't stall when cold if you take your foot from the accelerator to double shuffle, and has a further advantage in being able to hold more than three crew – World Wide Webb, Keyring MacHugh and young Billy Minogue head off down Ballymeaner Road, the principal thoroughfare of Knocklofty. Many smaller premises, including both banks and a pharmacy, have recently closed doors, and between one group of painted shells and the next are vacant blocks, with ratty fences, on which graze, amid thistles, Merino wethers and Hereford steers. There is a man, a suit, in the telephone booth outside the Post Office, unknown to all three crew, which induces in Keyring a sense of unease, in World Wide a sense of foreboding. They never saw a stranger after dark here, let alone one so inappropriately attired. World Wide drives, while Keyring fiddles with the squelch control on the radio, before placing the mouthpiece, which resembles an electric razor, to his cheek.

'Bushfire Control, 'sss Knocklofty Two.'

'Go ahead, Knocklofty Two.'

'We're been hangin round our shed an hour, waitin for this DFCO.'

'Deputy Fire Control Officer is taken ill and won't be coming out.'

'Thank you very little. OK, we're headin out to Crooked Corner, with a crew of six, for a joint trainin exercise.'

'Thank you, Knocklofty Two, copy that. Control clear.'

As so often on a winter's evening the cloud obscuring the sky all day has gone and the stars are out, twinkling, as they will, when a winter wind is blowing. There wouldn't be a man in this whole New Country could name you one constellation, as he'd need to twist his head right upside down to recognise the zodiac. Negotiating the narrow dirt road as fast as a water-laden tanker will hike, World Wide wonders, aloud, if Keyring, who has brought along a mobile phone, would like to ring ahead.

'What, talk to Blue MacEwe? I doubt he'd talk to the likes o' me. He's that fuckin up 'imself since he 'ad that win, I think he's grown an inch. 'Nother coupla wins he be as tall as Billy 'ere.'

'Mum said he was in the bar th' other night and picked up someone's change.'

'That'd be right. Always bin mean, all mean, these MacEwes. Blue couldn't cut it in London, ay. Wouldn't mind bettin it was him didn't flash his lights when I got nabbed for speedin th' other day, though I see the target for the month is helmetless cyclists and skateboards on footpaths.'

'I don't think I'm related to Shorn. We don't spell our name the same.'

'Dangerous man on a burn. Shouldn't be wearin a red 'elmet. Smelt his skin? I reckon he washes in diesel. Smells to me like diesel. Gets rid of 'is crabs, ay. Wooo! Fark!! Feel that tank swing? Never thought I'd get a drift in this shitbox.'

'Settle down, Websta! Someone sprintin up the road ahead there, see?'

'Ah yeah, I see 'em now. Struth, is that Mike Hock? Have to be. Gawd, it's Mike. Hoi! Michael! What chup to? Where y'off to?'

No reply, no inclination of the grizzled head from the backpacker, although he raises a muscular right arm in tacit greeting, as if to halt the tanker. It doesn't stop, although it does decelerate. As it draws level, World Wide Webb winds down the driver's side window. An attempt at conversation faltering, the window is again wound up, and the tanker moves off at a snail's pace, designed to minimise exhaust, dust and wake. Mike Hock sprints on, barefoot, neat, upright style. Sprints on towards Knocklofty.

'Looks like he had the anglegrinder out,' observes Keyring, not before the tanker is back in fifth.

'No way, mate,' replies World Wide. 'Seems he went grey overnight last week. Hear he's losin it. Walked outta the Bottom Pub last Thursdey, shoutin, "That's right, Boys, I'm a Wuss!" '

'Tragic, ay.'

'Shockin. I was there. But shackin up with Breda Looney at his age, his balls are bigger'n his brains. Ya gotta feel sorry for Billy here and Molly. Miss your stepfather, do you, Billy? I could say more but I better not. Just wish he'd turn up at the shed, once in a bloody blue moon, an do 'is job.'

'Ar, he's all right, World Wide. Dad's doin all right.'

'It's good you're still a fan, Billy. Reckon that's more'n he deserves. Thick as thieves with that cousin of his, too, that mongrel of a Deputy Mayor. 'Member the time Billy here shook hands with the Prince of Wales, Keyring? Prince looks down at his hand, and it's like, Wow! Kung Fu chicken beak. Pulls a face, calls for an ambulance officer, and that big fat cousin o' Mike's, I think he was Mayor at the time, he puts the arm round Billy's shoulder 'n says, as pleased as Punch, "He was taught to shake hands by Mike Hock, Yer Royal Highness, have ya met Mike Hock? He's a cousin o' mine, a gun shearer, who swears by the hand clippers." Now who was it tellin me Mike Hock and Dud Leahey was like two peas in a pod? Musta been me missus.'

Leaving their brigade captain sprinting down the road, Knocklofty Two proceeds to Crooked Corner. There are forty-five members in Knocklofty Brigade and they all turn out for the Annual General Meeting. In yellow overalls they formed a Guard of Honour at O'Mara's funeral.

Turning into Crooked Corner, past the ant-nest tennis court, so popular, in its heyday, no one ever got more than one set, and with its rusty umpire's chair, upon which, back in sixty-one, Blue MacEwe commenced a science project, incompleted, assessing the rate at which a tennis net falls to pieces when exposed to the elements – World Wide Webb notes, disapprovingly, the side door to the Crooked Corner shed open and, from the jumper leads lying by the roller door, he deduces the tanker is out. Indeed, Crooked Corner One, a World War Two Ford Blitz, donated by a defunct mill and fitted with tank and centrifugal pump by Tubbercurry Steel and Welding of Tubbercurry, is soon discovered parked across the road, blocking it completely, outside MacPeatricks'. Feeling for the shift, World Wide engages both siren and red flashing light, as he inadvisedly drives off the road, clear down the left-side bank. Feeling the drive wheels spin as he attempts an ascent, he decides to park the tanker and orders out the crew. He leaves the headlights on full beam and the red light rotating on the roof.

'Thought we might try a closed relay,' says Websta, as the crew clambers up the steep bank. 'Billy, can you explain to Keyring the advantage of a closed relay? Hello, Keyring, here's your cousin come down to greet us. Hey there, Blue!'

'Whatcha done now, Webbie? You're never gonna get up outta there.'

'I'll get out when I've emptied my water. We wanta do a closed relay. Billy, if we was to use a suction lift, what's the maximum height we could lift our water?'

'Seven metres?'

'No. Because, for all practical purposes, we're not at sea level, more like a thousand metres here, so call that three metres, and we're down the bank further'n three metres. OK, let's *go*! I wanta see what *speeeed*'s about.'

'What's with this closed relay, mate?'

'How long since you done your training, Blue? All you MacEwes and MacHughs is good for is lightin friggin fires. We'll hook up from our pump straight to your pump, mate, while you're pumpin into MacPeatricks' tank. What ya gotta watch for, Billy, is that Blue don't pump faster'n us, so keep your eye on the incomin line. Watch for any flutter. You might man Blue's pump here, that's if that's all right with Blue.'

'We're got somepin more important on tonight. I wanted that truck up here. I blocked the road so's yez wouldn't drive past. Talk to the group captain, here he comes.'

The group captain is the fireboss, who oversees a number of brigades. He is recognised, in the field, by his, or nowadays her, orange plastic helmet. Footsoldiers like Billy wear a white helmet, captains like Shorn a red helmet. Webbie, brigade senior deputy captain, should wear a red helmet with a white flash, but in point of fact, he won't wear a helmet and can't be made to wear one, being a volunteer. No FCO would dare inquire where was Webbie's helmet, for fear he might retort (as certainly he would), 'Get fucked!' and resign from the brigade on the spot.

'Ar Christ, has he still got them Ansett tickets in his mitt? I can see 'em.'

'He's wearin his orange helmet. Shape up or ship out, World Wide.'

'That's his wig, ay. Ever seen inside their kitchen, Billy? Looks like someone's bin in there with a sandblaster. All the grease is covered with this fine dust.'

Joseph MacPeatrick, a non-driver since the age of eighty-six, but still a district group captain and possibly the world's most experienced dry forest dry fire-fighter, deaf, to the left, from exposure to tractor engine noises while looking over his right shoulder while ploughing, hooks a wire rope tow line, with a D shackle, to the capacious 'roo bar (modified cow-catcher) of Crooked Corner One, then directs Keyring MacHugh, a distant cousin of Blue MacEwe, to assist old Paddy, who is somewhere on the opposite side of the slab hut, attaching a hook to a cornerpost.

'We're bin lookin forward to this,' admits Blue, standing on the deaf side of his groupie, although there is none so deaf as them as don't want to hear. 'Wind's bin comin from the wrong direction. We spent the last two days takin all the stores from the hut up to the fane. We was waitin for your tow rope.'

'I won't be towin nothin, Cob, till I get rid o' me water. You'll be towin me.'

'Argue with old Joe, Webbie. Keyring and me better go burn a break round that fane, seein as it's all full o' hay. Then at least, yez can see what yez are doin, with the flames we create. Whatta ya say, Cuz?'

'Good thinkin, Blue. Has Roger been in touch? Roger Willco? He's got them onions ready for the Reunion. I think he said they're ready.'

Blue lights a rollie, as he complacently contemplates the prospect of fresh onions on the Hamburger from Hell, while World Wide squats, which he can do with his heels on the ground and pointing uphill.

'Seen our captain on the way here, Shorn. He was runnin along the road in fear 'n dread. Didn't like the look of him, actually. Looked like he'd just seen a ghost. Bit worried, he's been doin funny things. Someone saw him readin a book in the main street. Thought he wasn't speakin with old Joe. Musta been visitin Kerry up Killaarney.'

'Never been easy talkin with Joe, Webbie, and not because he's deaf to the left. He only takes in what's bein said on his right, when it suits him. Thinks he's heard it all.'

'Alzheimers, mate. Incipient Alzheimers. I was alludin to the time he went round tapin up all the instructions in the sheds. "If you need to read instructions," he says, "yez are not proper fire-fighters." Thought Mike'd have a fit. Charges out to the nearest tree and says to old Joe, "Tell me, Joe, what tree is that?" After makin like he doesn't hear, Joe comes up with, "That's a white gum." So Mike rattles off its proper botanical name, somepin like "Eucalyptus baloneyaloxylon", and says, "You've spent your entire life in the bush, Joe, and you still don't know the first fuckin thing about it." Don't think they've spoken since. Found our McArthur metre taped up the other day, when Billy cleaned the shed. We never use one.'

'Naa, we never use ours. Too complicated. Ya gotta factor in the number of days since rain and the rainfall at the time, the drought index, the air temperature, the relative humidity, the wind speed, and then it's only good for flat ground and we haven't got any flat ground. Come on, Keyring, grab a torch and let's go burn that cemetery.'

' 'Fore you do, Blue!'

'Careful o' the persimmon, mate. It's the only one in the district. Wouldn't want our currawongs starvin.'

'What was Mike doin out here, mate? As a matter of interest.'

'We're got him makin the plates and goblets for this Pat's School Reunion. Figure if he put on a commemorative stamp, we could take 'em home for souvenirs.'

'Was this Ad Hock's idea?'

'All of us on the Steerin Committee thought it was a good idea, mate, 'cause he's gettin good on the pots. Actually, Mike's been out here quite a bit. I think he is knockin the Gurney witch. Always runnin, you know what he's like. When first he come out here, he was strollin. Then he started joggin. Now he's runnin flat out.'

'No demand for him these days, Blue. No demand for his services. The days of hand shearin and cuttin fencin timber with saws and axes is over. And frankly, so's pottin. Who buys pots? I think he made one move too many with Breda Looney, but that's just my view. Me and Billy pull down this hut, while you and Keyring burn a break around the fane. Is that the go?'

'Yeah. The roof, bein iron, should come off easy. Not so sure about them slabs. We'll drain your tank, then we'll drag your tanker up. Might need two tankers on the hut. See how we go.'

Two hours later both tankers are emptied of water and back on the blacktop, and the fane yard and much of the graveyard is black and the slab hut at a strange angle. Joseph and Patrick MacPeatrick invite the Knocklofty Brigade for tea. Although he would rather be home watching tele, World Wide wants Billy to see the house.

'They got open fires in every room o' this house, Billy. Move among 'em night and day, just starin into 'em. Never let 'em die.'

'See these tickets,' says old Joseph, as brother Patrick refuels the stove, with its four huge ovens, using for the purpose a slab column drum sawn off by Billy, with the Stihl saw, 'I bought these tickets, Ansett tickets, from Ballymeaner Travel Agency. I won't say what they cost. Brother and me was meanin to go down to Melbourne, to visit a sick aunt. Now they told us to pay the full amount on both these tickets within fourteen days. Brother! May have been fifteen. Any rate, I pays 'em the full amount a day before it was due, and lo and behold, two weeks later I sees in the paper that Qantas and Ansett are offerin deals, at discount prices, for their winter sale. Hundreds of dollars at a discount price, for the same flight on the same day. Now is that right?'

'No.'

'You can't tell me it's right.'

'We can't.'

'So I goes back to the Travel Agency, and I says to the

33

woman there, not that girl, the woman there, what's her name again? Brother! Beverley. I says to Beverley, I says, get onto Ansett, we've paid too much for these tickets. Now would you believe, they won't refund our money? Won't give us our blessed money back. Beverley says, your fares was already discounted, and you were sold them in good faith. Good Faith! This is the airline for Sydney Two Thousand. Official Olympic Airline! I says, I'll take the matter further, so I wrote to the Minister for Transportation. He's a National Party member. But he says nothin he can do, it's my stupid fault for buyin the tickets early. I was taught to do things early. Pay what you owe early. Bring in your hay early. It seems like I was wrong all these years, it seems like you wait till the last moment, you get yourself a discount. It's got me beat. I says to Beverley, you should have told us the score. You should have warned us. Don't tell me this is the first time an airline pulled a stunt like this. But she says, we knew nothin of it, read it in the paper, same as you. I says to Patrick at the time, I says, it's strange they want the money now. Very strange. Why do they need our money now? Flight's a good month off yet. Well of course, as soon as they had our money, they discounted the fares. And we've lost hundreds of dollars, Brother and me. Hundreds of dollars.'

'Poor old buggers. And are ya still goin down to Melbourne, Joe? Still gonna visit the old aunt? She must be a great age if you're ninety-seven.'

'No, she's younger'n me. We're not goin. No fear, we're not goin. No way in the world would we go.'

'Rupert Murdoch owns Ansett Airlines.'

'Don't talk to me about Rupert Murdoch! I been readin up on him. He's a disgrace to this country. He owns newspapers. He owns film companies, he owns television stations. Got a place at Yass. He's the man ruined the Rugby League, and yet he's American. He was born in Australia.'

'What can we say? He don't love his country like you, Joe. It's simple as that. He loves but one thing, and that's cash, and you can justify anything you love enough.'

'Oh, it's not just Rupert Murdoch. What about these banks

34

today? Farmers payin fifteen per cent and pensioners gettin two, if they're lucky. What about the customer?'

'He don't count. Only bloke counts is the shareholder. You had a few shares in Ansett, Joe, I guarantee you'd be laughin. You'd be sittin in the Goldwing Lounge clockin up yer Frequent Flier points.'

'So you won't use the tickets on principle, Joe?'

'Don't encourage him!' says Patrick. He pours out a brew, into chipped enamel mugs, from a kettle that some day might interest Rupert's rels, were they to spot it, on some damp morning, in a Knocklofty craft shop.

'Plenty of ash for a damper,' says Patrick. 'Would yez like me to make yez a damper?'

World Wide frowns. He'd like young Billy to see this all-but-vanished bit of bush lore, but time is a'gettin on.

'No thanks, Paddy. Thanks for the thought, but young Billy has to go to school.'

'I still maintain it's a terrible thing we didn't get our discount. It's not as though we had the flight. I says to Beverley, this is a disgraceful breach of corporate trust. I'll take the matter higher.'

Blue MacEwe splutters and chokes.

'How much higher could you go, Joe, than Mr Twentieth Century Fox? He makes and breaks them pollies.'

'And to think he's an American citizen, Shorn. He was born in Australia.'

'Well thanks for your brew,' says World Wide, pushing back a chair to reassert authority. He would like to rinse his cup under the tap, but it won't fit; the dishes are piled too high. Billy must get to school and Keyring has a job, or a job of a sort: it entails, for the most part, ringing housewives, to give them a piece of great news. They just won a free carpet cleaning, in any one room of the house.

'Thanks for yer help and the water, boys. We got a big fire year comin. And when we get that old hut down, we'll see some early light in the garden.'

'Terrible thing about them tickets.' World Wide's eyes have a

35

far-off look. He hates injustice, how he hates it. Knocklofty men hate injustice. Pigeons are born with little magnets in their brains and Knocklofty men with small injustice meters. Knocklofty men hate injustice, and Knocklofty women hate listening to Knocklofty men complaining of their unjust lot.

World Wide's in no hurry. Though empty of water, he drives back in third. He wouldn't bother filling at the hydrant. It's as though a realisation he has nothing to do all day tomorrow has crippled his right foot.

'Council clean-up next week. Might go round and needle the heaps. Already grabbed that big galvanised water tank with the top and bottom rusted out – girls could get in that and roll it along, it'd be just perfect for pickin blackberries – and I scored that thing last year, you know, with the angle iron feet and the macramé battery grips and the Geiger counter? Still haven't worked out what it's for, but it's never been used, ay. Yeah, pretty sad, Rupert rippin off a pair of old pensioners, Keyring. Wouldn't ya say so, Billy? I must get you to gimme a trim, Billy. 'Bout due for a haircut.'

'He's asleep, mate. Don't wake him. Didn't he give you a trim last week? Ask Molly what she thinks of Alan Bond. And if my missus was to buy some item at a sale, and it was discounted next day, well that's tough.'

'Yeah, but they never got the service they paid for, Keyring. Ar, I dunno. The more I see of this fuckin world, the more I wish I was out of it. I never got one cent the Meatworks owed me, mate. Not one bloody penny.'

'That's because unions are a thing of the past and the days of communism is over.'

'Remember our Pat's school motto? "To Them That Hath Shall Be Given"? Farkin hell . . . Oh, you're awake, young Billy Boy. Learn anything tonight?'

'Joe reckons there's a big fire season comin, on account of the sunspot activity. He reckons it comes every ten or fifteen years. That's when you get the bigger fires.'

'Billy, eight hundred thousand hectares burnt out in this state in ninety-three, so how's that tally? How'd ya go with your burn up the graveyard, Keyring? Didn't hurt that persimmon?'

'No way, mate. Plenty of tussock up there. Made heaps o' thick white smoke, ay. Fumigated the fane. Shoulda seen the rats runnin.'

'Evil spirits put to the sword. Ar, the lights of Knocklofty, mates, don't she look a treat? Only one street light in the whole of Crooked Corner and it shines right inta Shorn's bedroom.'

WorldWide must be half thinking of leaving town. He hates Carol earning more than him. Of course, he prefers to drink with men he has known from Playgroup, who wouldn't. On the one occasion he worked in Sydney, driving a meat truck in a cream beret, he got so terribly homesick he had to return home inside the month. It's a town exacts a big degree of fealty to its realty from its residents, Knocklofty. Why, 'I Still Calls Knocklofty Home' is the title of Dud Leahey's Grammy-winning CD.

No one can love a dying town, although dead ones often look quite smart. Many a passing traveller admires the bluestone buildings of Knocklofty.

Slowing down at the fire shed, WorldWide, to Billy's delight, misses second gear, and while he's swearing and crunching about the box, he feels an urgent hand upon his non-sword arm.

'Look, mate! Sittin in that car over there, it's that geezer was outside the PO. The suit. See him, Billy? That's his car, that Statesman, oo, I don't like this at all. Somepin funny goin on here.'

'Settle down, Keyring. Take it steady. Probly just the Council meter reader clockin up some overtime.'

'Hangin round a fire shed, though. Whattaya reckon. Could be a pyromaniac? Didn't like the way he was lookin at our tanker when we drove off earlier, did you? Could be a pyromaniac. Probly him with that shotgun. Wonder if he wets the bed and murders cats? Those are the signs of the serial killer.'

'Ar, for Chrissake, give us a break! Open the door to the shed, Billy. I'll back the tanker in.'

'Can't I do it, World Wide?'

'No! I'm doin it. You open the door.'

Backing the tanker into the shed is a delicate operation, for the shed's too small, and a two-inch clearance to either side has put scratches aplenty on the mirrors. Billy, giving delicate hand signals, beckons, as World Wide, a study in concentration, jumps her up.

' 'Ey there,' says Keyring, swaggering over to the suit, who coolly emerges from the vehicle. Keyring's built like a stick insect while the suit could be a South Sea Islander.

' 'Ey there, Cob!' The door to the shed rattles down. 'You Mike Hock, by any chance?'

'You better talk with our Senior Deputy. He'll be out in a minute. So what's your prob?'

'No prob, Cob. I'm trying to locate a man by the name of Mike Hock. You know him?'

'Maybe. Webbie! Man here's lookin for Michael.'

'Yeah? Why? With what porpoise? Willco's been here tonight, mate. Radio's on in the troopie. Never took the troopie out of the shed. Just sits there and listens to who's doin what. I logged us up forty-eight man hours.'

'I was informed Mike Hock was captain of this brigade, so I thought I'd find him in the shed Wednesday night. But when I noticed the tanker drive off, I thought I'd wait till you returned.'

'We're been gone hours. Christ, if it's about money or an Apprehended Violence Order . . .'

'Nothing like that. Actually, I tend to have a soft spot for any man who takes his responsibilities seriously. I guess I was lucky. We had a father gave the whole family firm discipline. Withhold not correction from the child, for if thou beatest him with the rod, he shall not die. Proverbs twenty-three, thirteen. He had to keep my mother in line, too. She was a headstrong woman, although the head of every man is Christ, and the head of the woman is the man, and the head of Christ is God, one Corinthians eleven, three. You recall strange events attended the recent City to Surf?'

'What, that foot race? That bloke in the gorilla suit

winnin? Yeah, that was a bit of a hoot.'

'Two gorilla suits, as distinct from the more normal three, went out a week before the run, from Ballymeaner Party Hire. Neither one came back. Both were hired out in the name of Mike Hock. What's his shoe size?'

'Aha! So you assume . . . ah no, mate, it couldn't been Mike Hock.'

'Why not?'

'Because he's old. He'd have to be fifty years old. Besides, he got no sense of humour. Mike'd never run in a gorilla suit.'

'Even so, I need to speak to him. Does he leave his fireboots here? I understand he has no fixed address.'

'Tell me, mate, have you a card or somepin? A contact number? And if so, and if I should stumble on Mike Hock . . .'

'But, World Wide, what about . . .'

'Shut up, Billy! It's time young men were in bed. Keyring, could you please run Billy home? Molly will not be overjoyed.'

'You appreciate the implication here for a medal at Sydney Two Thousand?'

'Yeah, we understand, mate. We're not stupid. We're not all boofheads in the bush. We're not all rednecks with goitres and rifles, like the cartoons in the city papers draw us. Naturally, we want to see the host country doin the best it can, and should it prove Mike is the man you're after, which I doubt, we'll be in touch, for sure. Unfortunately, Mike is in age denial. How you approach him'd be crucial. Ya wouldn't wanta rub him up the wrong way. Give us your card, and we'll see what we can do. What are you, a dick or somepin?'

'Federal Police. I have a feeling you know where he is. I just wish I could gain your confidence. Be assured, so far as we're concerned, no crime has been committed. Indeed, I am authorised, by my superiors, to remit the cost of both gorilla suits. My number.'

'This the number of some police station?'

'No, that is the number of my private mobile.'

'OK, mate, leave it with us. We'll see what we can come up with.'

39

'I should like to believe you could come up with Mike Hock.
I really would. Good-evening, boys.'

'Good-evening, mate.'

The suit, who could probably run out of sight on a dark
night and probably fight his way out of a wet paper bag,
returns to the Statesman, which settles on its springs as though
harbouring two hundred kilograms of Semtex. Starting the
engine, the suit opens the window and proffers a final after-
thought.

'I am trained to find people. That's all it is, boys. Swear to
you there's no crime involved. Can't you forget I'm a policeman? Like you, I want to see this country kick ass.'

'That'll be the fuckin day. And why should I forget you're a
copper? You got me picked for a villain.'

'You don't seem comfortable in my police presence. Oh
well, I guess I can live with that.'

'It's your black hair and your tan face. Some people are
sayin the world will end in the year two thousand and there
won't be any Olympics.'

Two big open palms are raised, wrists bedecked with
bracelets. Two big open palms, honest, huge, smooth, brown
at the web.

'Bullshit. For who is worthy to open the book and to loose
the seals thereof? Give this country a break, boys. Marathon
runners peak later.'

The suit drives off, slowly at first, gaining speed as he
departs Knocklofty. He passes the sign that says 'Police Target
This Month', the target for the month being helmetless cyclists
and skateboards on footpaths. The suit makes a point of
exceeding the speed limit, indicating impunity? Solidarity?
No doubt he watches the three men, in their yellow overalls,
in his rear-vision mirror, but not before they can no longer
hear the Statesman can the three, overall, feel comfortable.

'Where'd Mike get to?' inquires World Wide, mulling up a
small marihuana joint. 'He should be back by now. I just can't
help meself when I'm talkin to a copper. Besides, if Mike
wanted to pay for them missin gorilla suits, he's had the time
to do it.'

'You're not wrong, World Wide. Plenty of runners in contention there. They'll never know who won that race.'

'I think it was him. Dad could win us a gold medal!'

'Bullshit. Go home with Keyring and don't, I beg you, whatever you do, don't say nothin to yer mother. As you may appreciate, it's most important we alert Mike to the fact he's being sought here. Hunted, mates! Hunted down. I feel I've seen that phone number before. I suspect this is a dummy operation. I reckon they're after him for somepin big. And they know we know where he is, or at least, they suspect we know where he is, which we don't. They'll be watchin us. Billy, you go to school like normal and don't say nothin to no one. Keyring, you got a job on tomorrow?'

'Ah, yeah. If they don't cancel.'

'Act normal, mate. Just act normal. Leave this one to me. I have the time to look into it. I have the time to locate Mike Hock and clue him in, and then it's up to him, although frankly, if I was Mike Hock, I'd be out of here fast as me legs'd carry me.'

'Yeah, but . . .'

'No buts, Billy! Never trust a copper, that's the first thing to remember. The second is, a talebearer revealeth secrets, but he that is of a faithful nature concealeth the matter. The third thing is, Mike may not be interested. Not every person is cut out to be a star. It has nothin to do with talent. Look at it this way. Supposin it was Mike won that race, he run it incognito, right? Now why would a man with no sense of humour run a race in a gorilla suit? There'd be no future for the camera-shy athlete. Mind you, I don't believe, for one minute, it was Mike Hock won that race. He never went to Sydney in his life. No, it might take me a few days to work things out, but I will suss out what this suit's after. Got a name on the card here, what's his name I wonder? – Harley Christian – then I'll locate Mike Hock, and we'll have a heart to heart. Leave it with me, boys. Of a sudden, I feel quite energised. Wonder where I've seen that phone number before? I shall have to go home and search my documents.'

4

In gross misjudgement of future trends, the huge, cathedral-like Church of St Patrick, in bluestone, next to the Boys' High School, with a Romanesque window, intended to seat, in holy discomfort, a congregation of five hundred, was built, on the outskirts of Knocklofty, as recently as nineteen thirty-two. The sandstone wheel, for the Romanesque window, arrived, embedded in sand, on a five-ton Fiat, and seventeen men were required to lift it off. Sixteen men would have been too few, eighteen men too many. The only addition, since the laying of the foundation stone, has been a much-needed wheelchair ramp, for access through a side door. The stained-glass windows, donated by the pious Gurney family, who own Killaarney, feature a shamrock, and the Saints Francis, Patrick, Joseph and Therese, as do the niches. Nowadays, the four or five geriatrics who attend, on a regular basis, mass, can just about hear the beating of the Sacred Heart in the plaster, so brilliant the acoustics. Hauling himself to the pulpit, old Father Carney need not raise his voice above a whisper, while the sunlight beating on his threadbare soutane illuminates a multifarious dust. The fact is his faithful, unpaid retainer is past it, while he himself lives alone in the vast adjoining presbytery, demarked from the quasi-cathedral by a rusty cyclone gate. It is through this squeaky, decrepit gate Ad Hock makes his way, eleven a.m. Thursday.

'Father! Are you in there, Father?'

'I'm always in here, Adam. You will hear my mower start any time. I want to collect the leaves off the lawn. These plastic rakes, they don't last.'

'Father, can I let myself in?'

'Let yourself in and put a kettle on. If you're here to buy

some memento from my mission field days, save your breath. As I've told you before, and many's the time, they're not for sale to you, Adam. They were given me, as artefacts of Satan, when their owners, accepting Christ, had no further use for them, and I find they serve to keep in my mind the most God-fearin people.'

'It's just they're worth money now, these artworks of yours from the Central Desert. All these spears and clappin sticks and sacred stones and didgeridoos and ceremonial feathers. I'm concerned for their security and yours, in this ramshackle dump of a presbytery. And frankly, it's just a matter of time before the people who gave them to you want them back again. *Demand* them back, Father! It won't help the shire's reputation, you grabbed these sacred tribal objects. Can't you see what I'm sayin to you? The cultural climate has changed in this country since you was workin the Central Desert. There's more respect for indigenous culture, since the rogue Keating made his Redfern Park address. But if you won't part with them, you might display them, for the education of our youth. Council, I assure you, would be more than happy to co-operate, in this regard. We've several local buildings could be suitable. Selfish and dangerous to keep them to yourself. Did you remember I made an appointment? I made an appoint-ment to see you, Father, about some other matter, as it happens, but I made it on my mobile from the saleyard, and what with all the bellowin goin on down there, I wondered if you'd heard what I said.'

'You got a bit o' dung on your boot there, Adam. Mind where you're puttin your foot. You're wrong about the desert people. They don't regret takin Christ into their hearts, they get more people in their church than what I get in mine. In fact, I'm due to receive a young colleague, Father Ignatius, any day. He's black as soot, and the last priest to be ordained in this whole country.'

'Forgive me, Father. I apologise. I knew not what I said.'

'Supposed to be a coir mat by the door. Wonder what become of it?'

'Would you like me to use the bootscraper down at the

school, Father, put your mind at ease? I could take off me boots, but I'm not quite sure about the socks I have on. You see, I was in a hurry.'

'You're always in a hurry.'

'It's true. How I envy the contemplative life. I just wish I could get to mass more often, for you see, I do believe in a God.'

'Oh, don't let's talk about that. What did you want to see me about? There's iced Vo Vos in that tin up there. No, the one with the kookaburra lid.'

'I suppose you knew Arnott's biscuits was taken over by Campbell's Soups?'

'I don't mind a bit of biscuit in a soup.'

'We lost an Australian icon. But speakin of American take-overs, Father, I see you bought yourself a satellite dish.'

'When can we finish this small talk, Adam? I've no patience for it. What with the state of the world, on the dish, I'd rather say me prayers.'

'I was only tryin to be civil. All right, I'll lay it on the line. You know that church at Crooked Corner, the Fane of St Fiacre? Would you like to see it done up?'

'What do you mean "done up"?'

'Restored. Rectified. I was out there, when was it? God help me, I'm losin track of time, Father. I've that much to do before I fly off to Japan and America, I don't know whether I'm Arthur or Martha.'

'Flyin off to America, eh? I wish I'd gone to America.'

'I thought I told you over the phone I was visitin America. I prefer America to Japan. Don't like being styled a barbarian. What these Japs don't seem to realise is we have our own valid culture here. You can't pick it up in three days. Have you given any more thought, by the way, to conducting these Japanese weddings? The Japanese wedding market is worth a lot to our economy. It is every young Japanese woman's dream to be married as a bride in an old Australian church, to the point where 5880 Japanese couples married here last year. That's an increase of seven per cent over ninety-six, notwithstandin the downturn. It's worth a hundred and fifty million a year to

44

the local economy, of which this shire gets not one cent. You're sure you won't reconsider, Father?'

'I've one question and it's this. Are they Christian, Adam?'

'Well, you could certainly brief them on Christian values before they entered your church. I could provide a translator.'

'We might leave that to the Proddos. Which part of America you off to?'

'I should have to check that out with Beverley. You know, you disappoint me. I think we fly in to San Fran.'

'We should all be part of America. San Francisco. That's American for St Francis, Adam.'

'I never knew that.'

'Yes, you did. You knew, because I taught it you.'

'I know I had a good education, Father. I know the education I had, at St Patrick's, was the best I could have had. I still remember some things you taught us. I recall August thirty is the Feast Day of St Fiacre. Or was it Finian the Leper? No, I been sendin out these invitations for the Class of Sixty-One Reunion, as you know, and by God, we've some distinguished alumni. A Living National Treasure. Doctors, dentists, managers of banks. Judges. Professors at the university.'

'Why would you want to do up the old fane? There's no one out Crooked Corner now. If you wanted to put your money to a good cause, there's a heap of work needs doin here.'

'Yes, I know there is, Father, but the thing is, you could see a result for your efforts, out there. I feel that a workin bee, for one weekend, could see that fane lookin a million dollars US.'

'Seems a funny thing to want to do.'

'Let me remind you that fane commands the best aspect in Yarrawongamullee. You can see all the way from Blanket Flat to The Hole, Mount Nerong, from the porch. I'm not sayin here's not a wonderful church, but call me sentimental, if not God-fearin, we have to start somewhere. You know if that fane is still consecrated, Father? Do you ever go out there now?'

'Does it have a cross, Adam? If it has a cross, it may be consecrated, if it doesn't, well it's not.'

'Are there no church records, Father?'

'I can't do everything, Adam. I'm all alone here, and there are twenty-seven churches in this parish now. I turn seventy-eight next year.'

'Twenty-seven! What a waste, when a weddin in Japan costs forty grand. I could offer one here for less than five. I wouldn't mind havin a look at them records. That's if you can point me in the right direction. I'll have my secretary sort them out. You see, I been thinkin that if all these boys that remember you with so much affection, if they could just see what can be done – and let's not forget we're dealin with wealthy men, Double Bay, St Ives, Gymea, these are the postcodes I been lookin up – if all these boys could only see what can be done in a single working bee, well, who's to say they won't decide, on the night, to pledge you all the money you need? Need and deserve. I must say St Joseph's House of Prayer, up on the hill, is lookin very shabby. Who put the alpacas in that paddock, Father? That paddock is vastly overstocked. I can make out the cross on the roof, through the pines, and the Shrine to the Blessed Virgin, but never any cars do I see parked outside. I never see anyone goin in or out. The place fairly bristles with brick chimneys, but never any smoke comin from 'em.'

'All right. You could have a look at the records. There's records here go back a hundred and fifty years. I haven't had time to put them in order.'

'As you say, a man can't do everything. And where might I find these records, Father?'

'All over the place. I don't remember where.'

'A hundred and fifty years, you say. That's a long time, Father.'

'No, it's not. But a hundred and fifty miles, Adam. That's a long way, in the Old Country.'

Fanging back in the white Merc in which no one could sit behind him unless they'd a pair of legs no thicker than those on a folding card table, Ad Hock enjoys the view, the black Angus cattle, the white cockatoos, the red soil hills lightly wooded with box, the sun upon a sky of grey-blue cumulonimbus cloud, and suddenly, impulsively, he seizes from the glovebox a red McDonalds French Fries container and assumes it for a coronet. Though it lacks the elasticised piece of string for the chin it looks as though it should have, Ad Hock determines to keep it on his head, through sheer concentration, for a half-hour. He has been aware, since his days at Pat's, of the social need to send himself up, and exhibits, on the cupboard in his office, an otherwise highly sober affair, which stands next to the Auto Barn in Ballymeaner, a Mexican sombrero. This, he finds, never fails to break the ice when he meets with a new client.

He is pretty pleased with the outcome of this morning's meeting with Father Carney and the smile on his face contrasts with the scowl he will presently discern on the face of World Wide Webb. Webbie is kicking at the chassis of his Ford Cortina, in a futile effort to rectify the damage, sustained earlier, when struck by a kangaroo. Ad Hock hits the anchors on the Merc so hard he all but inflates an airbag, but demonstrating the fine physical poise that has made him such an adept on the dance floor, contrives to retain the coronet upon his head, as he operates the fast glass to commiserate, while at the same time igniting a supermild cigarette.

'Good God, you've done a front end.'

'I spun the wheel but she kept goin! Worst handlin car ever built, this. Bloody missus'll kill me.'

'What do you want to do?'

'Can't leave her here, Ad. Someone'll strip her. Those are brand-new retreads. Wouldn't read about it. I never seen a 'roo here in all the years I been drivin. Bastard come over that fence right there and almost landed in me lap. One hop and he was on me, mate. Spun round and I musta hit that bank, and here's a funny thing, Ad. Believe it or not, that 'roo was wearin dark glasses and a jacket.'

'Marvellous animals, these 'roos. Don't you think so, Duncan? Takin off, in that act of faith, they never know where they're gonna land. They just have to deal with what comes up. What time was this then, Duncan?'

'Dark. Early. Listen, I need to talk to you.'

'Let's get this mess sorted out first. Where's the kangaroo now?'

'Took off. You must think I'm crazy, Adam, but he left behind his dark glasses. These are they.'

'Hmm. You hit the Gucci kangaroo, that bastard must have nine lives. See, a couple of young Israelis come through here, this would have been, oh, a month ago. They hit a grey 'roo, right about here, but he didn't damage their vehicle. They was rentin one o' them big campervans, with the Desert Duellers and 'roo bar. Anyway, the 'roo was flat on his flank, so conceivin a photo opportunity, one of the Israelis took off his glasses and jacket, while the other popped a flash in the camera. With much hilarity, they rigged up the 'roo in the dark glasses and jacket, and propped him against a door, but as it turns out he wasn't dead at all, only stunned, so he comes to and hops off. Well these are Versace glasses all right. Could you see was the jacket a Gucci?'

'I wouldn't know what a Gucci jacket looks like. I'm an unemployed slaughterman, remember? What is more, I'm an unemployed slaughterman whose wife won't be gettin to work this afternoon.'

'I'll take you in to Ballymeaner now.'

'No! I don't wanta go to Ballymeaner now. Listen, Ad, I need to talk to you about Mike Hock.'

'Why?'

'It's a long story. I'm very tired. I never got any sleep last night.'

'Well now you know how I'm gonna feel when I get back from my world tour.'

'World tour, eh? It's all right for some.'

'I'm goin for you, for your wife and children's sake, for the sake of every citizen of Yarrawongamullee. I'm goin to do some Outreach. And the fact you can still call yourself an unemployed slaughterman indicates your backward thinkin. There'll never be a meatworks here again, you'll have to come to terms with that, Duncan. Live cattle markets for our Asian trade and feedlots; those are the options now. To be sure, Java's bankrupt, but I sold a big consignment to Vietnam just last week. And why be circumcised by animals? Why let animals rule our lives? Why can't we think of them as scenic features of a landscape, rather than as creatures to be knocked? By Jove, there's more money in service industries than ever come out of an abattoir. I could see you in a white ruffled shirt, with a black bow tie and pink cummerbund. Try on them Versace glasses.'

'No! They're all cracked and dusty.'

'Duncan, if you're not prepared to change your views, the world is going to pass you by.'

'I don't want to open doors and serve cocktails to foreigners.'

'Then starve to bloody death. Look at you! Look at the state you're in! Your eyes are pink, you've smashed up your vehicle. You won't get a hundred dollars for that wreck.'

'I'll have her goin again, don't you worry.'

'Yeah? And who's gonna run you round, lookin for a front end?'

'Sittin up there in your Mackas crown, who do you think you are?'

'Irrespective of who I am, I know you caper, boy. I'm awake up to you. I may not expect thanks for shakin young men from their torpor, but watch your tongue. I can't imagine Mike Hock would like to hear you insultin me.'

'Sorry, mate. If you could just drop me off a pinch bar. You comin back this way? I'm tired, Adam, and very concerned to think what Carol will say.'

'It wasn't your fault. And it wasn't really the fault of the 'roo, he couldn't see at night in them dark glasses. I am comin back this way, as it happens. I need to go out to Crooked Corner. But instead of broodin over what's gone wrong here, why not concentrate on positives? You can make Carol a fine gift. Those glasses are worth more than your vehicle.'

'Ar Christ, what a rotten world we live in, where a pair o' dark glasses is worth more'n a car.'

'What a stupid opinion. Gianni Versace had a genius. That's the problem with this country. You're a negative man, Duncan Webb. All right, I'll be back in a couple of hours. I'll bring you a pinch bar, a burger and a shake, and while I'm gone, you think about the truth of what I've been sayin to you.'

'Here you go, Ad, here's sixteen cents. That's the cost o' the ingredients in a Big Mac and a medium Coke.'

5

'Could you speak right into the microphone, sir? Thank you, Mr Deputy Mayor. This won't take long.'

'I have the house, "Stillorgan", on the market. Handyman special now. He's ruined it. I have the key from my agency, the girl said someone should clean it up, I said I'm not doin it. I shall have to rent it to another potter, another potter won't care. They're messy bastards, spend their lives puddling mud, but you never saw an ex-potter. Well, not in the New Country. We're stickers here.

'Luckily, I know a bit about pottery. In recent times, he spoke of little else.

'It's an old dilapidated weatherboard cottage, with a lean-to he must have flung up himself, opposite the railway yard there, next to the Central Hotel in Ballymeaner. As I say, he's ruined the place, muddified it to suit his muddy purposes. Under the lean-to he's erected gas kilns and blunger, and his big potter's gas bottles. A loo at the end of the hall filled with the styrofoam broccoli boxes that potters use to transport pots. Which he never would have used, as he never sold a pot, the Vincent van Gogh of Knocklofty. Copies of *Craft Australia* on the shelf beside the loo, but I know if I dug deeper I'd find a *Penthouse* magazine. My cousin was deeply ashamed of this inexplicable need to throw pots, which only come upon him when he was fifty-three years of age, so he kept the location of the pottery a secret. I don't suppose more than two or three hundred people knew where it was.

'There's a study. The room in which he slept, with his bed, its cotton doona and sheets unmade. I could see him in there, through the window, lying with his back towards me, curled up under a pillow. He was wearing a Pat's High School jumper, I recall, grey, with the green and white V neck. It was starting to rain, only light, but he must have been in for a swim, at some stage, at the indoor pool. His togs was hangin off the doorknob. Opalescent turquoise togs.

'Affixed to the wall over his bed, on rice paper, calligraphy. All his own work and he often told me what it said, "No form better than dead form." Well, it could have said anything to me. No language better than a foreign language.

'The window overlooking the views of Ballymeaner he has shut out, using a bamboo blind that admits light. The window was broken, the blind too. Too few sluts, as a Maori might say. Oh, Michael hated Maoris. Some of his ugly big iron-glazed mugs sat on a battered desk, filled with pencils and brushes. The first five thousand of those he made went straight back into the waste-clay bin. There was half a bundle of cane of the type he used to make teapot handles sitting on his wedging table in the studio, the potting studio. I don't know what he did at that desk, he never worked out his finances. He never responded to mail. When ladies' men are disappointed in life they withdraw from it.

'On a shelf were the books my cousin would read, when he wasn't perving on nudes. Bernard Leach's *Potter's Book*, *The Unknown Craftsman*, *Living Crafts of Okinawa*. A couple of books on Druids, too, and the *History of St Kevin*. A certificate, registering the name of his shearing business, was up on the wall, along with a photo of him from the old days, winning the woodcut at the Show.

'A photo of him in the next room, too, on a drawing-board for designing pots, but strange to say, none of his umpteen kids, or any of his myriad women. A cupboard full of varnishes, and professional artists' acrylic colours, mars black, titanium white. On a wall, photocopies of the shells he used to inspire design. He often claimed the intuition for pattern-making is lost in modern ceramic wear, as melody is in music. That would have come from some book he'd read, he tended to exaggerate. I see shapes of spiriferid and pentamerid brachiopods over boxes filled with invoices, globes, double adaptors, discarded sketches of shells.

'In what had been the lounge room of Michael's last abode, by the window, his electric wheel, above it a blackboard, still with a last, chalk-written note to himself ("blue slip for cobalt ware, fane with prepared persimmon glaze stain, slip cast torsos") and everywhere clay scrap, tins of rampant kaolin, green dolomite, giffen grips, bags of premium potash feldspar, boxes of glaze-testing tiles, boxes of pyrometric cones.

'All through Stillorgan, broken bowls, broken goblets, broken platters. He's been through, the night before, smashing all the pots. The little showroom describes his faience, that pit-fired stuff he would persist in throwing, but he was never open to the public.

' "These pots are coated ten times in a microfine white stoneware clay slip," he declares, in his tiny spidery hand, "then decorated with an orange terracotta slip, before being dried then fired to one thousand degrees centigrade in a gas-fired kiln." He must have planned to open his showroom, at some stage, but he never got round to it.

'Somewhere out in the backyard there would be a pit. He'd have dug a pit there. Mike Hock couldn't keep himself from digging holes and causing trouble, the bed of sawdust under the timber to the depth of half a metre, the pots, the lid. Fire away, burn down from the top, nine hundred degrees, the clay absorbs the carbon, the beautiful cloudy, smoky glaze that results, but the pots emerging from the pit are porous and they don't hold water. You can't wash them. That was his speciality. Pots you might admire but pots you could never use.

'I can say now what I couldn't before. His finest work was that stoneware produced from the big wood-fired climbing kiln he built out back of Tubbercurry, that took thirty-five hours to fire up and five full days to cool. Breda Looney's place. All very functional ware back then. Big, chunky pilgrim bottles and salt pigs and cheese bells with an iron and wood-ash glaze, very sixties.

'So I knocks on the door. No answer. I shouts through the bamboo blind at the window, "Michael," I says, "could you lend me your pinch bar, please?" No reply. This would have been, I suppose, midday? He must have been working all night there. Every single goblet, every single platter he has made for the Reunion he has smashed. But he had the pugmill ready to go and he's been potting like a demon. The profile cutter's in three pieces and the cutting harp broken in two and everywhere, all about the floor, discarded plastic packets off clay blocks.

'He's fired up a kiln for a bisque firing. Four burners. Haven't opened it. Scared of what I might find, ay. Didn't realise he was dead, you see, not sleeping, till I forced entry. Well, I had no choice. There was a tin of something on the stove, boiled dry. Might have started a fire.'

'Thank you, Mr Deputy Mayor. We've just had the coroner's report. There are no suspicious circumstances. Your cousin died of an infarction.'

6

In winter, when Knocklofty hawthorn hedges and basket willows are bare, so many are the vacant blocks about the town and so parsimonious the town centre, you can see who's visiting whom, and what they're up to, from who's parked where, and who's not home, sussing it out through cleaning your venetians in every compass direction. Only someone deafer than old Joe MacPeatrick and blinder than the Gucci 'roo could have failed to apprehend something momentous, from the vehicles, that Friday, approaching the church, from every road and lane out of Knocklofty, even those lowered and fitted with spoilers and breathers creeping along at the speed limit. And all the men and women emerging from these vehicles, who face a fair walk by ten twenty, are as neatly attired, and as weary and thoughtful in appearance, as seasick tourists.

Bob Dylan's 'Everything is Broken', a favourite song of the deceased, blares forth from the PA, to indicate the Church is willing to come to terms with the modern world.

Ad Hock, next of kin to the deceased, greets mourners at the church porch, but he puts an arm round Blue's shoulder, and turns Blue aside for a quick word.

'Thank you so for bringin in the old boys, Shorn. I intended to pick 'em up myself, but as you may appreciate, it's been a long week, and a terrible shock to me, this.'

'Sorry, Adam.'

'Yes, but don't feel sorry for Mike Hock. Rather, feel sorry for yourself.'

'I do. I am.'

'I didn't want Carney officiatin, but he would, of course, insist, and I couldn't have Mike Hock laid to rest in

Ballymeaner, he loved Knocklofty so. You must excuse me, I see Snidely, our local member and his lady, I'll catch up with you later. I expect we'll all be meeting at Molly Minogue's for a quiet drink.'

'Molly Minogue's! Is that wise, Adam? Molly's an old squeeze of his!'

'To her credit, it was her suggestion. We can't have it down that other place. They barred him from there last week. I hear he walked out with tears in his eyes and his hair went grey overnight. Now make sure old Joe sits by a door. Can't have him wettin himself. Snidely! How very good of you to come. Can you give us a bell, Shorn, if I miss you at the wake? There are ramifications we must discuss. He smashed all the platters and goblets.'

'What!'

'God knows what was going through his mind, poor soul, but he's in peace now, which is a comfort. Snidely!'

'This is the biggest funeral I have attended in years, Adam.'

'Yes, he was much loved.'

Father Carney decides, on the spur of the moment, to abuse his congregation. 'Saint Patrick,' he invokes, 'keep the Light of the True Faith ever brightly burning in the hearts of our people.' He then castigates their neglect of their souls, he deplores their contempt for their ancestry, he contrasts the God-fearing world he knew with the *Gay Mardi Gras* on Channel Two. He reviles abortion and contraception, condemns fornication and divorce, but when he starts to lapse into the Latin, World Wide leaps to his feet. Webbie's been getting a hard time from Carol, which may explain his behaviour.

' 'Ow much longer do we listen to this? What a borefest. You've had your say, Old Boy. We didn't come here to listen to you, we're come to farewell a good friend. And if you got nothin to say about Mike Hock, let someone speak who has. I'll do it, if no one else will.'

'You'll do it, will you? And who are you? Have I seen your face before? You're not the boy won the Canberra–Goulburn

Bible prize? Ah yes, I recall now, you were married here. I haven't seen you since. I tell a lie, I baptised those three children. I don't expect to see you again, as I dare say you wear a condom, until such time as, like your friend, you're lying before me in a box.'

'God Struth! And they wonder why no one listens to their boring sermons.'

'Very well, Duncan. I'll take your point. I won't bore you further. I do get a bit carried away when I see this church full of sinners. I will say a few words about the deceased; as it happens, he was known to me. But it's not something I have been looking forward to, so perhaps I have been avoiding it.

'Mike Hock. I do feel for him. Don't think I don't feel for Mike Hock. There was never a morning, since I made his acquaintance, I didn't wake feeling for Mike Hock. I am appalled he was never contented and led a life of such frustration.

'I recall him, in the playground of St Patrick's, hard, strong and determined. Though never the biggest of fellows, he carried himself erect. I recall him throbbing with vitality, in those days it positively oozed from him.

'Now I'm going to confess to you, a thing which may surprise you. I am one of many here today was led astray by Mike Hock. He was never more happy as when he was feeling his strength in some kind of rough play and indeed, it was only when he had exhausted himself I felt I had the better of him. I wasted too much time on Mike Hock, to the neglect of my higher duties, but keeping him under control back then was virtually a full-time job. I suppose he felt the weight of my hand more often than he should have, were the truth known.

'However, there were indications, towards the end, he had seen the error of his ways and it was actually possible to go for some weeks unaware of his appetites. He come to see me, not a week back, to borrow my books on ancient Irish churches. Adam, could I have them back please? Mike Hock was a friend to Satan, a bad influence on everyone else, but when he showed us his softer side, when he seemed more relaxed and subdued, when he was less concerned with making a big fellow of himself, he did, I think, serve a vital role. Can we now survive without him? Or will the poisons he served to eliminate build within us, till we burst?

'You will notice his hand clippers have been placed in the casket beside the body. In the modern spirit of ecumenism, I call upon the congregation to join me in singing "My God is a Trail Bike". '

Mike Hock is sent on his way with the Irish blessing, the one about the light rain falling on your fields and the Lord God holding you in His palm. Then with ash-white, hard-faced World Wide Webb and a weeping Billy Minogue among the bearers, the coffin is loaded in a flower-filled hearse, and the cortège proceeds to the cemetery. Many a hay-strewn Suzuki ute, and many a squeaking Ford Fairlane, are among the more than one hundred bleary-eyed vehicles following the woody.

Knocklofty cemetery stands on the edge of Knocklofty town, in view of the House of Prayer. There's a pine-covered hill in the far distance. Always a partially uncleared or pine-covered mountain in the distance. Always a windbreak of Monterey pine in the middle distance, and always a solitary snowgum, with a broken crown, by the roadside. The coffin is lowered in the fresh-dug grave marked with a simple wooden cross and it's clear there'll always be a glass bottle here, or two, containing plastic roses. Billy and Molly, his mother, Breda and Jacqui, Kelly and Sally, Deidree and Jacen and all the rest of the deceased's *de factos*, misbegotten bastards and long-suffering stepchildren, seize and toss, or hurl in some instances, lumps of clay upon the coffin. Someone lobs in a crosscut saw that wouldn't fit into the casket. But Knocklofty men won't cry at a funeral till they see some woman cry. They're only glad it wasn't them, or sorry it wasn't them.

At the gate, in a suit, stands Harley Christian, the Fed, wearing a gorilla mask. He thought it worth a try. Ignored by all he turns up later, minus mask, at the Top Pub, Minogue's. In track-suit pants and flannelette shirt, he could pass for a Maori shearer, one of the deceased's rivals, but seeks out

Adam, to make clear he wants to ramp Stillorgan in search of footwear.

Blue MacEwe, with World Wide idly watching this exchange over a glass canoe, smiles to see Adam, normally a man of peace, turn his tormentor towards the door. Both big men, they resemble a pair of lightweight Sumo wrestlers. The suitless suit smiles, as he departs, to indicate unrelenting goodwill, but Adam returns in such a state he is slopping his whiskey and soda.

'What nerve, what insensitivity. Standing at the gate in a gorilla mask. He said he was looking for reaction. As if he wouldn't get a reaction. I gather he thought a bar an appropriate place to interrogate me. Had the idea a wake is a place to interrogate a grieving rel. I showed him the door.'

'Well done.'

'He says he wants the key to the Hock pottery, Stillorgan. I says, there's no way you're gettin it. You could be anyone at all, I says. I wouldn't know who you were.'

'That's true.'

'He says it's to the greater glory of Michael's memory. He wants a shoe. I says, that may well be, but now is neither the time nor the place. You're an ill-mannered beast, I told him. He saith a man hath no pre-eminence over a beast, but that which befalleth a man befalleth a beast, and as the one dieth so dieth the other, yea, they have all one breath, for all is vanity. What's this about, Duncan? Somepin about a prize-winnin run? Michael was more of a boxer. I says to him, have you a warrant? He says, I don't need one. I says, yes you do. I haven't time to escort you about, I'm off on a world tour shortly. He says there's no question of crime, he's actin for the Ministry for Sport. The Ministry for Sport! Since when did sport need a ministry? What's this about, Duncan? You did say something to me, but the mind's gone blank. I must be in shock. I feel as though I'm jetlagged and I'm not off the ground.'

'Drink your whiskey, Adam,' says Blue MacEwe. 'Just drink and forget. You found the body, you organised the funeral and you'll receive sympathy cards by the dozen.'

'I give Carol a sympathy card for Mother's Day. Shoulda

looked inside, ay. Only noticed the rose on the front.'

'No, I have to carry on, lads. I can't relax now. There'll be no rest for me. The coconut'll find the pottery. Half Ballymeaner know where it is. How much you had to drink, Duncan?'

' 'Coupla schooners.'

'How bout you hold your horses and drive Shorn and me to Ballymeaner? I must have a drink or two to be sociable. I can't get out of it. Here. Take the key to the Mercedes and switch to low-alcohol Mickey Mouse beer. It's a nuisance, Shorn, but we shall have to go in and check the pottery. Damn! I've written on every invitation there would be a commemorative platter.'

'Ad Hock!'

'Aidan MacHugh.'

Aidan, a former garbage collector, is well known to Adam, as Deputy Mayor, for having set up a waste-disposal outfit, in opposition to Council, using a Council truck.

'Is it drinks on the house, ole Buddy? Molly says to ask you if the drinks is on the house.'

'Well I told her there'd be a time limit.'

'He was a cunt, your cousin, Ad, but what will life be without Mike Hock? I feel as if a light is both goin out 'n comin on, and I know I speak for every member of Knocklofty Gang, Yarrawongamullee Yard.'

'It's always been the way with a man like that, he has to wait to die. And had he lived, he would a been nice as pie when he got older. Men like Mike are always nice as pie when they get older.'

'They're gotta be. They get vulnerable. I was with yez both at Pat's, so I, too, must come to the death o' the terms of the, what the . . . Farkin Ell! Mind where you're puttin your elbow, cunt, or I'll farkin . . .'

'Settle down! Settle down, Aidan. That lad's only tryin to order a drink. Molly! We might close the bar, and move family and close friends only, to the snug, for tea and cakes.'

'I might run the old boys home.'

'That's a great idea, Duncan. Paddy's up there drinkin

60

like a fish and Joe's holdin forth on Rupert. See if they need help gettin undressed when they get home and don't drive that vehicle too fast. I couldn't tolerate another tragedy today.'

'No worries, Ad. I will be back in well over an hour.'

Joe, clutching his Ansett tickets, and Pat with his blackthorn stick, are guided gingerly by World Wide Webb, who pulls forward the driver's seat on the Merc, so he can stuff them both in the back. This takes a full five minutes of shoving and lifting and groaning and swearing, as Patrick, in particular, is a handful, being broad-shouldered but bent almost double. The brothers are then conveyed, sedately, to their home at Crooked Corner.

A wind is whipping up from the west now, an unseasonable nor'wester.

'Hard to believe it was just two nights back I was drivin a tanker here. I don't think I ever recall a funeral followin a death so fast, but Adam says he couldn't bear to see the way the body was laid out and the grey hair gone white. What a lot has happened since Wednesdey, what with Mike Hock dyin of infarction, and me smashin up me vehicle. I suppose I'm Knocklofty captain now. Must be hard at your age, Patrick, copin with endless change. Seein young men and middle-aged men dyin, wonderin why you're still alive.'

But to Webbie's surprise it is Joe responds, as Patrick is fast asleep.

'You never mopped up that burn properly.'

'What?'

'Burn up the fane. You never mopped up. And whoever scratched round that fane with the McLeod tool never got down to mineral earth.'

'But that wasn't my burn, that was Blue's burn! I was pullin down your slab hut, or tryin to. I don't like them McLeod tools, Joe. Nothin but a bloody rake hoe, ay. Gimme an American Pulaski tool, which incorporates an axehead.'

'What you really need is four heavy-duty mower blades, welded to angle iron. I've been tellin 'em that for years. But it don't matter. Duncan, whose burn it was, if you're captain now, you had a right to be up there. Not enough water went on the grass, and a piece o' manure musta blown back. Someone shoulda rolled that persimmon stump, too. That stump was smoulderin.'

'Keyring says they never burnt the persimmon!'

'It was ablaze when I got there. I says to Shorn, cut if off at the base, which he done, but he never mopped up properly. He never extinguishes a fire. As a result, much of the hay we had stored in the fane has been spoiled. We had a hundred bales of hay up that fane and a bag or two of chaff. When moppin up a grass fire, Duncan, all logs must be rolled, to ensure penetration.'

'What about the fane itself, Joe? Fane itself all right?'

'Fane has been somewhat charred, where the tussock burnt up against the walls. Brother and me dragged out the hay and the chaff. Shorn was at work.'

'Maybe the fire got down in the roots of the tussock, Joe, and went under.'

'That's possible. Grass is growin all through that fane. It never gets maintained.'

'When was this?'

'Thursdey arvo. Must have been smoulderin all Wednesdey night, and when I went out to take to the slab hut with an axe, I noticed smoke on the hill. So I says to Patrick, quick! Give us a hand! But he's frail and I'm gettin old. I can't get the door up in the fire shed and Pat should be on medications. Thing is, he don't feel confident drivin on tar and they closed Knocklofty pharmacy.'

'Why couldn't you have rung for assistance? I got a pager here in me pocket. I could have had a crew out there.'

'No great harm done. We lost a few bales of hay. We lost a bit of surplus lumber. I can handle any fire situation, Duncan, I was fightin fires 'fore you was born. We will call by, though, 'fore we get home, so you can look at it, with your good eyes. Then we can load the hay back in. My eyes aren't what they were.'

'Yeah, but I see you often hear when you want to.'

'I don't often hear what's bein said, though, Duncan. I think I lip-read.'

'Gotcha! I never move me lips.'

'It may have to do with smell. I may smell your breath, as you mumble. If you want my view, I read minds. I know I'm a mystery to medicine. When I went back to Beersheba in Palestine, where I fought in the World War, the doctor asked me what medications I was on. I said I'm not on any medications. The main thing is, I know what's bein said. You tell me if I'm wrong.'

'Ar, you been gossipin a hundred years, Joseph. You just put two and two together.'

'Well it's true nothin much changes here, or not since I was weaned. People are always sayin the same things, in the same order. First up, they'll talk about the weather. Then they'll bemoan a commodity price. I been to that many funerals, Duncan, I could tell you what Adam is sayin right now. In fact, I think funerals is the one thing I enjoy more as I get older.'

'Ah yeah, I see the fane. Christ, as you say, it's gone black and the woodwork has been charred. The big persimmon tree is down. I don't see any smoke, though.'

'Here's the key to the fire shed, Duncan. Jump the tanker battery off this car, then drench and saturate the Fane of St Fiacre with foam. All them posts need a good wettin. It may be, as you say, the fire's gone under and could spring up any day. I've seen a fire in a sawdust heap at a mill burn, smoulderin, two years. It's warm, for the time of year. Very mild. Only had a couple o' frosts, and no frost at all this morning, although the sky was clear last night. Winter oats failed again.'

' 'Cordin to the Southern Oscillation Index, we're in for another El Ninyo. All the water went into your house tank, old mate.'

'Then suck it out and drench them graves and give the fane a good soakin.'

'All right. You're the boss. But I'm gonna have to be quick about it. You got a pair o' yellow overalls? Don't wanta wreck me jean jacket.'

7

'How do you regard the prospects for Ballymeaner, Shorn? Think the new K-Mart will make a difference?'

Ad Hock has a myriad keys on his ring and since forcing the door to Stillorgan has had the lock changed, and now can't recognise the key.

'Sportsman's Club's doin all right, since Buzzacott joined Blenkinsop.'

'Yeah? Many in the dining-room at night?'

'Gets a bit quiet early in the week, but weekends are always busy.'

'Given any more thought, Shorn, to sellin the rest o' that place o' yours to Kerry Gurney?'

'Buzzacott reckons I'm a fool, Adam, for sellin what I did.'

'Oh? Why's that?'

'Because, actin on your advice, we changed my title to pastoral leasehold and that means that I am now open to a Native Title claim. There's nothin to prevent some bunch of abos forcin me off me place!'

'Any claimant would have to demonstrate ongoin connection with the land, so I don't think you've any worries there, Shorn.'

'I still don't understand this Native Title legislation.'

'No one does. That's the beauty of it. Each claim must go to court to be individually adjudicated. Try to see it from a legal viewpoint. They'll be appealin every decision.'

'Why'd we change my title to pastoral leasehold in the first place? Buzzacott never heard of pastoral leasehold this far east.'

'You've a short memory. I told you why at the time. Killaarney is pastoral leasehold. It facilitated the transfer.'

'But how could Killaarney be pastoral leasehold, when everything else round here is crown land or freehold or national park or state forest?'

'As I told ya, the Gurneys come from the other side of Balranald. Now the Patriarch always wanted to build a Queen Anne-style mansion, see, but every time he started to build, it didn't look quite right. He always thought it would look a bit better, a little further to the east, and who could argue? Nothin looks worse than a Queen Anne-style mansion in the middle of a desert. So he bought out the neighbour's property, see, money being no object. Now the original holdin, which was out in the Western Division, bein pastoral leasehold, the initial expansion of that border was deemed to fall under the same title. You could argue here a mistake was made, but don't waste money on a court case. There's a statute of limitations. Suffice it to say that no sooner had your man got up his foundations, than he'd glance east or north-east and pull 'em down. The grass was always greener, see, on the other side of the fence. I understand, at one point, the Gurneys had an empire stretched all the way from the back of Balranald to Mount Nerong.'

'Well, he finally got up the Queen Anne-style mansion. Still don't look right.'

'Yes, but he couldn't venture any further east, because of the Blue Mountains. Any psychiatrist could tell ya, Shorn, he was tryin, unbeknownst to himself, to get back home to the Emerald Isle. However, beyond Mount Nerong, he found himself hard up against a massif, and having overreached himself financially in the process, he had to break the property up. It was sold off, west of Blanket Flat, but Killaarney, to this day, remains pastoral leasehold.'

'Well that explains how we MacEwes have lost our home and hearth. See, I'm descended from Carmel O'Roy and MacEwe o' The Hole, Mount Nerong'.

'You cannot take it on board. No matter how many times you are told, you cannot accept it, on some fundamental level. As I understand, it was sold for a song, too. I just hope the pocket money you got for that paddock was useful at the time.'

'Pocket money's about right. I can't explain to anyone the

way I feel about The Hole. You wouldn't understand, that's for sure. Ain't you found that key yet?'

'I won't detain you much longer. I'm about to make me fifth sweep through these keys. Stop interruptin! Let me concentrate. I dare say things have improved for you, Shorn, have they, since you had the win?'

'I did notice a big increase in me sexual energies at first, but that's gone.'

'Sounds as though that could have been more of a nuisance than a . . . Ah! Found the right key. God, what a mess he made of this place! Will you look at the floor? Mind where you step.'

'Pity about the crockery, Adam. Pity about the design.'

'Oh, he had a wonderful eye for design. I can't imagine what you mean. Now I'm goin through here with a fine-tooth comb. At least I think we're first in. The thought of a policeman comin through here and findin *Penthouse* magazines. I couldn't bear it.'

'Nothin illegal about 'em, Adam. You buy 'em at the newsagency.'

'Oh no, these were the black-label ones. You can't get them over a counter. Which reminds me, I shall have to cancel the subscription. I shall have to go up to the PO. I can't have my secretary doin it. God help me! As if I haven't enough to do. It's a question of shame to our family name. I dare say you understand. Well no, you probably don't.'

'What do you want me to do, then?'

'Keep me company. I'm distraught. That dreadful Harley Christian, then Duncan Webb come back to Minogue's lookin wet and dirty and covered in hay, and I felt I was under the limit, or close, and as you had to go to work this afternoon in Ballymeaner, it made sense for you to drive your own vehicle here, and so it was that I drove meself to Ballymeaner, and you come in in your Haitch Ar, and Duncan went home, without havin said one word to either one of us, sulkin because I wouldn't let him drive the Merc, all covered in hay. But neither you nor me wanted him here. He knew that. He could sense it. Because he was never a member of the Steerin Committee for the Pat's School Reunion. Too young. We may have to rethink those invitations. That's if we can't come up with somethin here. Shorn, why not see if you could find a platter, or goblet, unbroken, as I go through these drawers? I have to find the books he took from Carney, too. Remind me of that. Is it possible to stick shards together? Is there a glue, as efficacious as Christianity proved for the colonisers and the colonised?'

'Get real, Ad. Look at the size of these plates! Here's one with just a bit chipped off the side. See, me Hamburger from Hell is nouvelle. It's a very compact burger. It's small but it's tall, if you know what I mean, it goes up, rather than spreadin out? Now the whole idea of havin plates this size was to admire the pattern while you ate? When I discussed it with Mike he agreed to put the fane to one side, but he hasn't done it. He's got the fane fair square in the middle of the plate. See? Right where the burger should go.'

'It could just as easily fit to one side. There's plenty of room here. Why can't it go on the persimmon?'

'Doesn't really matter now, ay. 'Cause even if we could piece these pieces together, they'd still look shithouse, glued. Make a travesty of the whole function, servin up tucker on glued-together plates. What would Dud Leahey think?'

'Who knows what Dud Leahey thinks? I see where he's callin on the Governor-General not to extinguish Native Title, but apart from that I haven't a clue what Dud Leahey thinks about anything. And that is the principal reason I must visit New York City.'

'Here you go, Ad. Here's that magazine with Dud's interview and the picture of Dud in his black Stetson, black preacher's frock-coat and black granny glasses.'

'They was inseparable at school, you know, Mike Hock and Dud Leahey.'

'Listen to what it says here. "When first he arrived in Nashville from an outback town in the Wide Brown Land, Dud Leahey wore lovebeads and a leather coat with nailheads on the back that spelt out 'Born to Lose'. Who could have guessed that, thirty years on, this fun-loving bushman, with the magic slide guitar, would so captivate the Hamptons by singing, in his high, distinctive reedy voice, on his début album as singer-songwriter, these heart-rending paeans to a world the Boy from Oz knew that not just he, but time itself, had left behind. Today, looking out on Greenwich Village from his loft, hearing sirens screaming down Sixth Avenue, Leahey says that distance lends him perspective and helps him see Australia more clearly. 'I cannot return to Australia,' he complains, 'because of my high profile there. I hate to be recognised in a street, as I am not an egotistical person. Unlike Nashville, in Manhattan I can live without the burden of fame and recognition, with which I am so uncomfortable. But when I says "I still calls Knocklofty Home", why, I speaks from the heart.' " Now we can't ask a Manhattan resident, who still calls Knocklofty home, to eat off a glued-up plate.'

'You're right. I wonder is it too late to get some other potter to make us up somethin bigger? I'll have a poke round in the rooms down the hall while you see what you can find here. But even if you found just the one platter, the one goblet, Shorn, unbroken, that would be a start. That would provide us a template we could take to some other potter and say, make us somethin along these lines. Oh, what a blue, this platter. God, is that a cobalt blue? Did you ever see in your whole life, Shorn, a more deep and brilliant blue?'

'Nice, ay.'

'Nice? It's majestic. It's heavenly. It's gorgeous. Poor Michael, he was always in a blue. He may well be sayin to everyone here, "Look. See how I loved a blue." '

'I gotta get goin.'

'Yes, I know. But I couldn't have come here alone, Shorn. Not here. Not today. Not on the day of the funeral. I'll be right tomorrow, now you start rakin round in there and don't cut yourself, will ya. I'll go down the hall. I mean to find every one of those filthy magazines and burn them, out the back.'

'No need for that, Ad. Anyway, they don't burn all that good. You'd have bits of tits and bums floatin everywhere.'

'All right, you take them home with you. Just so long as they're out of here.'

'Fair enough.'

'Someone broke a side window. Must have been Mike.'

Watching the big boy furiously rummaging through crannies where no magazine or book could fit, Shorn cannot but conclude that something more illegal is being sought for. Oh well, the big boy must be close to a nervous shakedown, and keen to avert family disgrace in the form of a cousin's posthumous bust, but will he recognise what he is searching out? Having abandoned the task assigned him by Ad as pointless and futile – the platter his eye was first drawn towards proves to be the only one chipped not shattered, while the goblets have all been decollated, their stems having been wrought overthin – Blue, his chef's attire of shorts, singlet and safety boots in part concealed by the Harris tweed coat he donned for the funeral service, is browsing through a *Penthouse* when he hears a cry from the lean-to.

'Shorn!'

'What ho.'

'Out here, mate. Out the back! The oven, Shorn. The gas oven! The kiln was on but the gas has run out, and there's a deathly silence. God, is it safe to open?'

'Search me.'

'I should have recollected. I should have come in and monitored the firing. I forgot all about it. 'Struth! I've a mind like a sieve these days. Too much on. I suppose what he had in here is ruined? How long you s'posed to fire these things? Oh what to do. Is it like a cake, do you think? If I open this door and it's not ready, will I ruin it?'

'Hit the button on the pyrometer. See how hot it is inside.'

'Of course. You're right. Twenty-five degrees.'

'OK. Now look in the spyhole.'

'Of course. The spyhole. Let me . . . ah yes. I see the pyrometric cone. I recognise it from Mike's description. They stand up straight to begin with but they droop, when the kiln's up to temperature.'

'Is it droopin or standin up straight?'

'It's droopin. It's droopin right over.'

69

'Then the firing is done. Should be cool enough to open now. OK, open the door, Ad.'

'I guess I have no choice. All right, keep your fingers crossed. Whatever he threw, in his dying moments, I would be sure proud to own. All I have, as a memento of his work, is that marvellous garden sculpture he created, when the brick stitts supportin the kiln shelving collapsed under the weight of fifty pilgrim bottles. I hope you like this, he says, when he give it me. Had to bring it round on the box trailer. Look, I says, if you're happy with it, then I'm happy for you. On the other hand, if what's in here's ruined and black, does it really matter? He never sold a pot in his life. We did him a great favour with this commission, but bein Mike Hock, he blew it. Oh well, I'll just . . . is this where . . .'

'Here let me do it, Ad. I'm used to openin freezers.'

As Blue MacEwe opens the door, there is no perceived rush of heat from within. The gas bottles are all empty, but through some quirk of providence the bisque firing has been a success. It was neither too long nor too brief. The baked clay vessels are porous, but firm to the touch and none cracked or blackened. A vast selection of platters and goblets, all most beautifully constructed, sit on the shelves in the kiln, to greet the grateful eyes of the two members of the Steering Committee.

'Shorn, we're in with a chance. I think he did 'em again. Michael! I knew you wouldn't let us down, wherever it is you may now be.'

And the tears, at last, come flowing from Ad Hock's eyes, as he sinks to his knees, popping buttons. Blue rests a hand, briefly, on the shoulder of the R. M. Williams shirt, then, selecting a proximate platter, holds it to the light for inspection. The platter is very beautifully wrought, if light blue, the same colour as Ad's shirt.

'Count 'em,' says Adam, rising to his feet. 'Count every platter and goblet. I guarantee there's forty-four of each, or a few more, if he made spares. This is very satisfactory, Shorn. All we must do now is glaze'm up. Dip 'em in a clear glaze and whack 'em back on the shelvin. He was methodical. He always kept the glazin notes on his current series in the firing log. Give me one here. Let us see the new design.'

'Looks pretty much the same as the old. Though he has put the fane to one side, now. See?'

'Ah yes. How satisfactory. There's the fane and there's the persimmon tree, with the underglaze painted on as a clay slip, and . . . wait a bit, Shorn, what's this here? He stuck a tower at the back of the fane. But the fane doesn't have a tower! Go get that platter we looked at before, the one with the chip off the edge. We need to compare the old design with the new, there's somepin funny here.'

'He's written somepin on the back too, Adam. That's if you care to turn it over.'

'We could always sit the burger on the tower, if the worst come to the worst. What does it say? The tears were flowin to such extent I lost both contact lenses.'

'Only the one long word, which makes no sense at all.'

'But surely it must say "St Patrick's School Knocklofty, Class of Sixty-One Reunion"? Or perhaps it must say "To Them that Hath Shall be Given", which is the Pat's school motto?'

'Nup. Om. Omneinp. Omneinprick . . .'

'Latin. I'll have to show it to Carney. I've forgotten my Latin, haven't you? Frankly, after his performance this morning, I'd as soon never speak to him again. I wish there were some way I could have him removed as a member of the Steerin Committee, but it was me invited him on it in the first place. Did you ever hear a more vile valediction? I know Mike Hock was no saint. Still and all. I'll remove these platters and goblets now and stack them carefully on the bench. I'm sure you will find you can proceed, in confidence, with the meal arrangements. I mean, whatever he wrote on the back, it wouldn't matter, would it? The circumstance of the final firing being so poignant, and so touching, I'm sure it wouldn't matter if he put Homer Simpson on the front and "Up Yours" on the back. Every old boy will depart the Reunion satisfied with his memento, and I'll be surprised if Dud don't pledge his straight to the Guggenheim Museum. What a tale! Dying potter confers a last gift on mankind, repudiating his former work. Why that's almost Japanese.'

'I gotta go, Ad.'

'Don't forget them mags! We had a mighty outcome here today. Death and Transfiguration. I think I'll glaze these platters myself.'

'No, Ad. No! For Chrissake.'

'All right. You help me. We need a few cones for the glaze firing. You can find the appropriate cones while I find a clear glaze. In the meantime I'll take this plate to that bloody old priest, have him translate it, then I'll duck out to Crooked Corner, to see if the fane has a tower.'

'I'm pretty sure it doesn't.'

'Yes, I suspect you're right. The blood was going from his brain. But as I say, it doesn't matter. And I have another reason for my visit. I mean to make measurements on that fane, and here's something, between you and me. What say we do up that fane, on a working bee, and give it to Dud Leahey? If he spent just the one month a year here, think of the benefit to the district. Bob Hughes spends one month a year in Australia. Bob Hughes, Art critic for *Time*? Bob's a Living National Treasure. By Christ, we're a lucky country to have a hundred of 'em, ay. I dare say Indonesia, for all that population, would only have ten or twenty.'

'You can't give away the fane, Adam. They belong to the Catholic Church. And actually, see, we was burnin off up there the other night, and as it so happens . . .'

'No! Don't burden me with detail now. Please. Not now. Not today. I couldn't cope. I've been that moved by what we've seen here, I'm givin you forewarning. I'm tellin you straight, I'm doin up that fane and givin it to Dud Leahey. When all's said and done, it was him immortalised it. But that's between you and me. You didn't hear me say that. Now we've a meeting of our Steerin Committee at noon tomorrow, I'll see you then. Carney, of course, must know nothing. We'll put wall dividers in, Shorn. Build a loft.'

8

Next day, a Saturday, suggests early spring. The wind, a warm one, blows from the Simpson Desert. The window of opportunity for hazard reduction burning fast recedes. One of the problems a fire-fighter faces, in these years of recurrent El Ninyos, is that you can't get a burn going when it's safe to burn, and when you can burn you're not game, for fear the fire you light may crown. There is bush on Killaarney, down towards The Hole, Mount Nerong, hasn't been burnt in thirty years, and where the fuel load accumulating on the ground – sticks and bark – well exceeds the McArthur meter limit of twenty-five tonnes per hectare. It would take a brave man, or a foolish one, to attempt to translate that from the metric, and twice, in the memory of Patrick and Joseph, men died, fighting fires at The Hole. There is now, even on the part of MacEwes and MacHughs, a reluctance to burn it.

The Hole is so dangerous a place in time of drought, because fires tend to emerge from the bottom of The Hole, rather than off those moribund trees that stand under a ridge-cap, where lightning usually strikes. In drought, such trees, with their roots spread over bare rock, are always first to kark it, and there's always a number of them ready and waiting, below the top of The Hole. When lightning strikes such a tree, the bark tends to strip away, but may lie smouldering for weeks, until it kindles the sparse fuel on the bare rock surface. Even so, the resulting blaze would emerge from The Hole as no more than surface fire, and a hand-tool line can hold a surface fire, where the flame height is no greater than six foot. But a fire rising up a steep slope preheats the air above it and soon gets up into the tree crowns, to create an unmanageable holocaust. Bear in mind these tree crowns are 'blue' from a distance because they exude flammable oils. A dry sclerophyll forest, like that about the The Hole, Mount Nerong, is flammable most years, but the trees that form the dominant stratum are seldom bothered by firestorms. O'Mara, the last man to die here, ran from a truck on which the windscreen was melting, but the burning, blackened trees he ran through were sending out epicormic buds a week later.

Patrick MacPeatrick, all of six foot two, if he could be somehow straightened up, is slowly but surely prising the slabs off the hut which is, or was, the last of its kind in Yarrawongamullee. He has in part exposed the cubicle-like internal rooms of the slab hut, each of them individually accessed from the veranda he has already dismantled. A tall man like Pat could peep from one room to another over these internal walls which, like those in the houses of Chinese Malaysians, don't quite reach to the ceiling. The roof, originally a stringbark, more recently overlaid with iron, has joined a butcher's block of Queensland maple and a wash-stand of Huon pine, which smoulder, next to the beet, which has been well pruned by the geese. Old Joe emerges from the hut, with a washing basin and jug he found there, which, having flattened with a blockbuster, he pitches on top of the rubbish heap.

'Shorn can take this away with a Bobcat. What about them hooks 'n chains, Bubba?'

'Throw 'em out.'

Shorn, who is in fact standing on the brown carpet in the Ballymeaner Hotel lounge, staring at the Skychannel, watching Redcliff Race Eight and shouting 'Go, Rustic Prince!' has an hour to kill before the meeting of the Pat's School Reunion Steering Committee, which will occur in the Ballymeaner Hibernian Australian Catholic Benefit Society Hall.

'How much longer you think this'll take?'

'Hard to say, Bubba. Could take years. I found some newspapers in that room. 'Member how we lined the walls with newspaper?'

'Those were better days.'

'Oh yes, they were. It's hard to put a finger on what went wrong.'

'We did.'

Work then resumes, proceeding slowly, until a vehicle goes by.

'There goes Ad Hock in his Mercedes Benz, drivin like a devil as always.'

Adam, heading towards Knocklofty, belts by, gets as far as the tennis court, backs up. He can't believe his eyes. If his cousin just karked it from infarction, Ad Hock looks a candidate for stroke.

'What in the bloody hell's goin on here? What are you doin to that hut?'

'Pullin it down, eyesore of a thing, it is.'

'I don't believe what I am seein. I'll slap a preservation order on. Get your hands off that hut! You want to get rid of somethin round here, get rid of that fibro monstrosity. And for God's sake, put away them Ansett tickets, Joe. What's done is done. Be here now. Who burnt the Fane of St Fiacre?'

'We had a small problem Wednesdey night.'

'It's bad enough you puttin feed in there. You've damaged the fane now. You got a ladder? I said, could you lend me a ladder! I have to borrow a ladder a minute. Extension ladder, if possible.'

'One on the tanker.'

'All right. Give me the key to the fire shed. I mean what I say about that hut. That's a precious piece of local history there.'

'We want more sun on the garden.'

'Could you not more easily move your garden? Foolish old man. No one's gonna come drivin through here, in a coach, if there's nothin here to see. This could make a fine heritage museum, you could charge admission to this.'

'Here's the key to the fire shed, Adam. What do you want with the ladder?'

'I want to be sure there was no structural damage done to the fane in the fire. For that, I need to get on the roof.'

Paddy and Joseph watch as Ad Hock walks down to the

fire shed. They watch him emerge, struggling and cursing, under the weight of the great wooden ladder. They watch as Kerry Gurney, from Killaarney, in her purple Nissan people mover, flies by, with her long blonde hair and her dark glasses, and her two golden retrievers, one holding a pink frisbee. Ad Hock waves at her, dropping the ladder. He picks it up again and slogs up to the fane. He props the ladder against the front of the fane, footing it securely, but glancing around as if in hope some able-bodied person might materialise, to steady the ladder for him. It doesn't happen. He climbs up, step by step, till he gets as high as he dare climb, whereupon, after a furtive glance to each of the four quarters, he rips off the finial. It's a Celtic wooden cross, barely charred. He then descends the ladder, telescopes it and makes his way back to the shed, with the cross. He returns the ladder to its posse, atop the Ford Blitz, picks up the cross and hurls it, like a black throwing a boomerang, into the scrub at the rear of the shed. He then returns the key to Joe.

'I suppose you saw what I did down there,' says Adam. 'You'll see some changes here. Fortunately, not the ones you have in mind. I intend to restore that fane. Thanks for increasing my task. I could scarcely believe my eyes when I drove by and saw the fane all blackened.'

'You're wearing glasses, Adam.'

'Yes, I lost my contact lenses. As to the fane, well I've no choice now but to strip and completely rebuild.'

'We used to worship up there.'

'Did you. You're going to have to take all that hay and chaff out. What's wrong with this hut for a storeroom? It just needs straightenin up. My God, look at the time! I'm late for my meeting. You know that Kerry Gurney from Killaarney?'

'Yes.'

'Ever see her with Mike Hock?'

'No.'

'Well that's a relief. I heard they was an item and I mean to ask her to donate the stained-glass windows for the fane. See, the family give the commemorative windows to Saint Patrick's

Church in town. Listen, if you and Pat have time on your hands, you could take to that fane with a scrubbin brush and a piece of steel wool, and try to undo what you have done.'

9

'I think we have a forum, Shorn. You and me. All right. Is Feidhlim Foley comin?'

'I can't see why's he's on this committee, Adam. He never even went to Pat's.'

'He's Oirish. That's why he's on our committee. We mustn't forget our roots, Shorn.'

'Someone told me his brother just come out.'

'Yes, well, he was unemployed. The Deutscher does what he can for the Oirisher, to the tune of sixteen billion over the past ten years. That's what the Irish have managed to scrounge from the EU, would you believe. But unemployment remains high on the Emerald Isle.'

'Wasn't he drivin them horse-drawn carriages around Killarney National Park?'

'He was. One o'clock. Gone one. I think we can assume Carney won't be comin.'

'I hear him now.'

'Oh, bloody hell! Was it you torched that fane, Shorn?'

'I must accept responsibility.'

'I'll see you there first thing in the morning.'

'No, Ad! I got a big night tonight! Netball presentations. Then tomorrow, I have to get me float ready for registration.'

'And will the Haitch Ar pull that float?'

'No worries. Got overrider brakes.'

'I heard there was no springs on that float.'

'Can't have springs on a pacer float, Adam. It would interfere with their gait.'

'Well you're gonna have to give me half an hour. Let's make it early, say before you go to bed? I'll see you up that fane six a.m. I'll be workin all night. God, I am that far behind! Oh,

Father Carney. We was wonderin if you was goin to make it.'

'I saw Feidhlim Foley outside. He says he's coming to the meeting.'

'Good. I hear his younger brother's out, Father.'

'Yes, he has immigrated.'

'Things are changing in the Old Country.'

'Yes, changing for the worse, Adam.'

'I thought all change was for the worse. Let's make a start then, shall we? I have twenty-seven . . .'

The screen door to the kitchen opens. The door gets away in the wind and slams into the peeling weatherboards. The wind, a cool southerly wind now, has strengthened.

The Hibernian Australian Catholic Benefit Society Hall, known locally as the Camp of Beaten Fighters, is a former inn, a two-storey Georgian rubble-stone and sandstock-brick affair. You walk out the front door onto the street, Connaught style, while to the rear, the hall extends, downhill off the street, through outbuildings of ever-declining workmanship and ever-decreasing beauty. The Steering Committee actually meets in the kitchen, rather than the hall proper. The hall proper is now seldom used, except for Débutante Balls, at which music is provided by the Bush Band from Red Bullock. The Bush Band from Red Bullock, with Jimmy Field on windjammer and Simon Field on low whistle, is famous for its rendition of the old Mudgee waltz, 'You're Always in the Way'. It was with the Red Bullock Bush Band, at age ten, Dud Leahey began his illustrious career.

Built in eighteen thirty by Cheapjack Joseph Hock, the hall began life as a fellmongery, before becoming, in eighteen forty, the Travellers Rest Hotel. By eighteen fifty-seven it was the Crimean Inn. In eighteen seventy-three, now white-painted, it was bought, as a Camp for Beaten Fighters, by Tierney, Gillespie, Fitzpatrick, McConville, O'Sullivan and Elliott, beaten fighters all.

Two real Irishmen stand on the green linoleum by the door. They enjoy the deference they sense in the air, for these are real Irish, from the real Ireland. One is a pallid, bespectacled clerk, stocky, like Blue MacEwe, with the blue eyes and coal-black hair of World Wide's missus, Carol. This is Feidhlim (Fail 'em) Foley. Feidhlim has repeatedly declined to Anglicise his Christian name, although he does weary of repeatedly spelling it aloud, only to watch it being incorrectly written. Feidhlim has been in the New Country all of twelve years and no trace of his brogue remains.

Brother Jarvey, immigrant, is a darker man than Feidhlim Foley. Jarvey Foley has the skin of certain Aran Islanders, the dark, swarthy Mediterranean skin. Some do say these dark Western Irish are mixed-blood Spaniards from Armada stock, while others claim they are pre-Celts, the true men of the White Dreaming (and it would be fair to describe the Irish landscape as a Dreaming Landscape, in that each Hibernian geologic feature has one or more attached myths). There are quite a few dark Irish about the New South Wales New Country, and many rusty-headed, like Blue MacEwe, but the real redheads, those bright Viking redheads that enliven a stroll through squalid Dublin, have had to disappear, for the harsh Australian sun has said to them, marry out or die of melanoma. All MacEwes, like both Minogues, have freckles on their extremities, but the girls' breasts, like the bums on the boys, that don't see the sun, are alabaster.

'Feidhlim!' says Adam, genuinely pleased, for Feidhlim is Adam's little mate. 'How good it is to see you. And who's that you have there? Do I detect a certain family resemblance?'

'This is my brother Jarvey, Adam. Jarvey, this is Adam Hock, my good friend. Father Carney, Shorn MacEwe. Jarvey is after gettin off the plane.'

'You must be jetlagged, are you, Jarvey?'

'Naw, I'm grand.'

'So what do you think of Australia, mate?'

'Grand, though I haven't seen much of it.'

'You'll find this a very boring country . . . er . . . meeting. Feel free to walk out any time. We really must proceed. So far, in response to our forty-four invitations, we have twenty-seven acceptances.'

'That's not bad.'

'No, it's good, as we have two weeks yet to go, Father.

August thirty's our big night, Jarvey. I dare say you've heard of Dud Leahey, the country star? He's been declared a Living National Treasure by our National Trust and he was at school with us. And my cousin refurbished on his deathbed, as it were, the platters and goblets we shall need. Yes, we have all forty-four platters and forty-four goblets, close to ready. They just need glazin up.'

'What are the women going to eat off, 'n all?'

'What's that you say, Jarvey?'

'I say what are the women going to eat off 'n all. I take it the men is bringin wives?'

10

It's not yet light at six a.m., and it's six a.m. on a Sunday, so Ad Hock is concerned to find himself not the only vehicle on the roads. A Holden Statesman has followed him all the way to Crooked Corner from the Tubbercurry Road, but when it turns off at the golden elms that stand by Killaarney grid, Ad breathes easy. It has to be Harley Christian, so there's no cause for alarm. Not so long as he heads for the homestead and not the shearing shed.

Blue MacEwe is sitting in the Haitch Ar, parked outside the fane atop the hill. He moves to join Adam in the Mercedes Benz, which is the more comfortable of the two vehicles, and Adam notes him being blown backwards at one point and wonders if he's drunk, but he's not. It's just the gale is so fierce it is tossing Blue's ratty hair all over his bald patch.

'Mind if I smoke?' inquires Blue MacEwe, slamming the door.

'I'd rather you didn't. I haven't yet been to bed and me stomach don't feel good. Nerves. I would have called by at the Mackas but it doesn't open till six. I feel I need a moment of quiet time here. I want to watch the sun rise and think of Mike Hock. This is the best place in Yarrawongamullee to watch the sun rise. To think we'll all be dead, Shorn.'

Both men are snoring loudly by the time the sun does rise, in a clear sky. Adam wakes first and blinks to see the blackened fane before him, leaning now, at an angle.

'Shorn!'

'What ho.'

'That bloody fane is gonna go, in this wind! You foolish man. What in the name of heaven possessed you to light a fire up here? You have weakened the structure of the fane to the point it has become unstable. For God's sake, let us go round and see if the annexe is faring any better.'

But the annexe, if anything, has fared worse. A late addition, less soundly built, it is flapping and lurching and slouching like Blue MacEwe doing his famous 'Man from Crooked Corner' walk.

Adam sighs. 'This is all too much. We better get the hay out, 'fore the roof caves in. I was meaning to make some measurements here and discuss a renovation. There'll be nothing left to renovate, if this wind don't soon ease up.'

'Bit worried about me 'orses, Adam.'

'Then you go comfort your horses, go on. What am I supposed to do with this hay? It's only fit for mulchin strawberries.'

'You be careful. Don't get trapped there. I'll be back soon as ever I can. I'll bring up the float and we can load the hay in that.'

'Well thank you. I haven't the strength for this. I specifically ordered this hay be removed. To my way of thinkin, if they could load it in, they can bloody well get it out again.'

'I did most of it for 'em. Neither one of them can hardly lift a bale. If they was to try to lift out the hay in this wind, they'd do it biscuit by biscuit. Then it'd blow all down the hill to feed the steers on Killaarney.'

'I'm fast losin my temper, Shorn. This wind does somethin to me. I get as cranky as an old Jersey house cow. Soon as you settle them horses down, you bring your float back up and we'll load the hay. It's goin in the slab hut, and that's the end of the story.'

Ad wades fiercely into the hay bales, ducking beneath the flapping annexe roof. The hay bales comfortably fill the annexe, extending on down the fane proper. Adam works as he never now works, except when demonstrating how work should be done. Revealing surprising physical strength, he picks up the bales like biscuits, a finger under each loop of twine, and pitches them out the doorway.

'Woo!' He stubbed his foot on a trunk, a small metal trunk with a black lid. What's that doing here? He kicks it hard, with his stock boots. All the frustration mounting in him, he vents on the unfortunate trunk. Then his rage extends to the fane proper. He pummels it, knocks a hole through the plaster, knees a stud in half, then, observing the trunk is fitted with a lock, he kicks the lock to pieces. He opens the lid, to discern the trunk is filled with old papers and spiders' webs.

Half an hour later Blue returns to the fane, pulling the float behind the Haitch Ar. He sees the bales Adam has heaved out the door of the annexe scattered down the hill, but the wind has dropped to the point he can hear Adam rummaging through the trunk contents.

'Shorn,' says Adam, 'I found something of interest here. I found the parish records. I found your family tree.'

He also found the Kissanes', his mother's, family tree. He tucked that away, as he knows it by heart.

'Yeah? Un*real*!'

Shorn crawls into the annexe, which has settled at three feet off the ground. There's plenty of light to see by as half the roof has blown off. Adam is actually bearing the weight of the ridgepost on his shoulder. But he seems not to notice, so intent is he on the scroll he has before him. Being, as it is, the family history of the MacEwes, you might imagine he would pass it to Blue. Instead, he rolls it and holds it as far from Blue as he dare, behind his own back. And when he lifts up his countenance, blackened and bleeding, it bears a strange expression. Less one of delirious joy, more one of compassion and concern.

'Give us that here,' says Blue MacEwe. 'It's my family tree, not yours. So the long-lost history of our Clan MacEwe was in the fane, all this time. I bet it was up in some secret compartment, hidden in the ceiling of the annexe. Each man the maker of his own destiny, Adam. If I hadn't burnt the place half down, this trunk might never have come to light.'

'Just what do you know of your family, Shorn?'

'Only what I've told ya. I know I'm descended from Carmel O'Roy and MacEwe o' The Hole, Mount Nerong. All MacEwes is descended from Carmel O'Roy and MacEwe o' The Hole. What we would really like to know is how we lost

Killaarney! That piece of paper you're hiding there behind your back may yield a clue. That bloody Kerry Gurney, Adam, you never saw her at the funeral. She was the only person never sent me a card, when I had the win.'

'Well as you say, it's yours to peruse, but first, could I ask you this? What exactly do you know of Carmel O'Roy and MacEwe o' The Hole?'

'I know MacEwe was transported for life. He took great interest in other people's cattle. He always did his stockwork on foot, wearing only a shirt top.'

'And what about his good lady wife, Shorn? What about Carmel O'Roy?'

'Well no one knows much about Carmel O'Roy. She's a bit of a dark horse.'

'And what if I tell you she is described – are you sittin down there, Shorn?'

'I'm on me knees, Adam. No choice, ay. What, is she an heiress of some kind?'

'You could say that. You might say that. MacEwe's wife is described in this document here as "A Woman of the Kamilaroi". Are you with me, Shorn? It seems your great-grandmother was a full-blood aborigine.'

The colour drains from Blue MacEwe's face and he collapses, in a swoon.

11

Tuesday finds Joseph and Paddy MacPeatrick rigging up a tarpaulin, to act as a roof for the slab hut, into which, on Adam's insistence, every haybale not burnt in the fire or scattered downhill in the gale has been consigned. Blue was meant to have taken the float to the weighbridge at the quarry for rego, but the float, still straw-bestrewn, is sitting where he left it, across the beetroot patch. Joseph has been using the float as a ladder, to get a better purchase on the tarp, for the weather forecast predicted scattered showers and possible local thunderstorms. They don't eventuate. Paddy drags at the other end, doing the best he can, although he lacks the facility to secure it, on account of the arthritis in all his members. It's a bright-blue polythene tarpaulin, not quite big enough to cover the roof, and the nonagenarians have been at their task two days, while progress they have made is imperceptible.

'How you goin there, Bubba? You got that end tied down?'

'I have the rope across the slab, Joseph, but the fingers can't tie the knot.'

'Where's young Shorn? He might help us.'

'He's sittin in the umpire's chair. Never went to work all day yestey. I hear his phone ringin all mornin.'

'What's he doin in the umpire's chair?'

'Nothin, Joe. Nothin at all. He just sits there, starin at Killaarney.'

'Ask him to come here and help us. It's because he never mopped up that burn we had to remove the hay.'

'I went up to the tennis court to tell him his phone was ringin and touched him on the boot. He never moved.'

'I'll have a word. You hang onto that edge. When was the

last time he sat in the umpire's chair at the tennis court all day? Wasn't that when his father had to put a bib on him and feed him Farex from a spoon?'

'That would have been when he lost his mother. Woulda been thirty years back. Don't tread on the garden, as you get off the float. If Shorn decides to get down from the chair, he'll need the beet for the Reunion.'

'You know that ever since he had that win he expects to be treated like Lord Muck? I dare say Jack's as good as his master here. You hang in – Oh! Oh!'

'What's the matter, Joseph?'

'Fallen down. I think I may have hurt me leg. I shall have to lie here till I regain strength.'

'There's a car comin. Will I give'm a hail?'

'Who's in that car?'

'Adam Hock.'

'No, don't hail him. He's a fool and his father was a fool. I thought he was goin overseas today. Isn't today Wednesdey?'

'If it is, then someone should feed Shorn's horses. They're still locked in the stables.'

'Fancy you bein a builder,' says Adam to Jarvey, who sits behind Feidhlim Foley, as no one could sit behind Ad Hock. 'If you're a tradesman, why was you drivin jauntin cars around Muckross?'

'Oh, it wasn't just Muckross, Adam. Jarvey drove the jauntin cars all around Killarney, as far as the Gap of Dunloe, when not parked on the East Avenue Road.'

Jarvey is looking through the window at the country. It's not entirely unfamiliar to him. The Tasmanian heart-leafed silver gum grows thirty metres tall in the Muckross Arboretum.

'I love horses,' replies Jarvey. 'And besides, the money was better.'

'Better money than building! Go on. So much to be said for service industries. I should like to hear you repeatin that to Yarrawongamullee Shire Council.'

'Ah,' observes Feidhlim, 'but Killarney's the most beautiful

87

place in all this world, Adam. Admit it. To be sure, I'm an old Kerryman, but nothin out here compares with back home.'

'At least t'ey don't got t'e fookin Americans, pardon t'e French. Jaysus! T'ey reckon there's forty million o' dem, all descended from t'e Oirish. But t'at can't be right. There's only t'ree and a half million Oirish. T'ree and a half million Oirish, but we had two million visitors in the first half of t'e year.'

'Tourism on such a scale', concedes Adam, 'is a curse, Jarvey, but the people must eat. Now here's the fane. You know, Jarvey, when Feidhlim told me you was a chippie, it was only the thought I can't get back to the optometrist stopped me bawlin me eyes out? There it is. The Fane of St Fiacre. There's your world-famous fane. This little place is Crooked Corner. It's very scenic, very alluring. I don't want its charm destroyed. I favour a Bhutanese approach. Offer it, to the select few, at a highly exorbitant price. Nothin, I guess, here compared with Kerry, but not bad for New South Wales. There's a slab hut just needs straightenin here – that's it under the blue tarp – but the fane, well between you and me and the doorpost, that is a present for Dud Leahey. You didn't hear me say that. Regrettably, it burnt down and blew over, all in the last week. Can you fix it, Jarvey?'

'I should have to take a look, Adam.'

'Adam! Is that not Shorn MacEwe, sittin in the umpire's chair?'

'Yes, I believe so. Poor Shorn. I'm only a week away, Feidhlim. Somethin come up in regard of Shorn, I can't go into it now. There's such a mess in my office you'd think I'd left a window open all weekend.'

'I helped restore a church in Ballybunion.'

'Yes? How very interesting. Jarvey, what we have in mind here is not, strictly speaking, a restoration.'

'But, Adam!'

'Don't go on about it, Feidhlim! The church is deconsecrated and Carney never comes out. Anyway, I bought it, or the land on which it stands. Yes, I sent the bishop a fax of a photo

I took Sundey, and he accepted me bid. I own the Fane of St Fiacre.'

'Good God, if you're not a man with the best interests of Yarrawongamullee at heart.'

'You can blame my mother for that, Feidhlim. She was a Kissane. I was born in the Crooked Corner. Jarvey, could you do me an inspection? All may not be as bad as it appears. Feidhlim, while Jarvey is doin that, you and I better go for a stroll down the hill. I see the old boys are havin trouble fixin the tarp across the hayshed. It won't take us long. Water won't exactly be lyin there, will it, not on that skillion roof. God help us! Can you believe it? They pulled the shed over with the fire tanker.'

'Welcome to Crooked Corner, Adam.'

12

Wednesday morning, while Adam flies off to San Francisco via Narita, Jarvey Foley commences work on the fane restoration project. Biorhythmically confused, still keeping Kerry time, he is more weary when he wakes at three a.m. than when he lies down to sleep. Even so, he is glad of an opportunity to ease himself into the New Country by working, albeit unpaid, on a project of such topical significance. And Jarvey will need to work in the New Country as a builder, for as he has observed, there are no jaunting cars and no pony traps plying the streets of Ballymeaner, although he has detected in certain local eyes that hunger for a ride in a horse-drawn vehicle.

Feidhlim won't want him hanging round the house and he would anyway rather keep busy. And Feidhlim has lent him a few tools; a square, a plumbob, a hammer, a handsaw, a carpenter's pencil, a measuring tape. Nothing flash. It will be years before Jarvey can afford to purchase an air compressor. In the meantime, he will need to borrow money, or use hand tools, which slows you down fierce, and such lack of speed would appear a commercial disadvantage, but everything's in our best interests, whether we know it or not, according to both the Church and the Psychic Tele Talk Line. Feidhlim says a few local chippies, who never use hand tools, might sell them. It ought to be possible to scrounge tools together. And Adam has left Jarvey the key to Stillorgan. There may be tools in the pottery.

Riding a cycle, his gear in a sack, Jarvey arrives in the Crooked Corner. He couldn't sleep so thought he might as well rise up and get going to work. The cycle belongs to Feidhlim's daughter, the tall one who never now rides, as she works as a nurse at Ballymeaner base hospital and cannot find time for the cycling. The cycle, which has never been so far in its entire existence, except on the back of a vehicle, is missing a gear and squeaking by the time it approaches the fane, but functional enough. Jarvey believes that cycles, like horses, were meant to transport people, not vice versa, but though an accomplished cyclist, he has never before ridden one with brakes that work. So he stops the cycle by jumping from his seat and using his feet as brakepads, in the Irish mode. An astounded truck driver, seeing a helmetless cyclist on the road with no light at two a.m., reports it to the police. Jarvey will surely need to buy a light truck, or ute, or pick-up, but first he must have money, and it's been so long since he worked as a builder he does maybe need to ease himself back. The commission to restore this little fane will suit him fine for that purpose, although less than two weeks now remains till the Pat's School Reunion, and Adam has said he wants the fane restored by the night of the Reunion. Feidhlim feels this is ambitious, given Jarvey has only hand tools.

Leaping off his girl's cycle, leaving it to rove downhill as though it were a horse, to pick at the wisps of hay upon the blackened grass and the blackened tussock, Jarvey conducts an examination. He concludes, in the dawn light, the fane will need to be demolished. The tower, at the back, has disappeared and the fane itself is badly charred. Often, it is more expeditious, and less confusing, to start from scratch.

But can one man build a stone church, with a round tower, in a week, with a few hand tools? Jarvey reaches for the rosary he carries on him always.

Yes. It can be done. Relieved, he starts to pull at the walls, but he really needs a jemmy for this, and a ladder, for demolition is best conducted from the top of any structure, downwards. Feidhlim has informed him of an old pair of brothers, never married, who live in a nearby house, and it is with the customary spring in his stride, and singing, that Jarvey approaches them. The brothers apparently lived here with two sisters, also never married, but the sisters died. Jarvey has forgotten Blue MacEwe, sitting there in the umpire's chair, for the tennis court is a way from the fane and Jarvey arrived pre-dawn. Oh, there was a time when a man sitting in the umpire's chair would move at least his head, but there was a time, too, when the Fane of St Fiacre was filled, to overflowing, for reconciliation.

The old boys aren't yet out of their beds, as it's not yet gone eight.

'Anyone home?' Jarvey plays the door with his knuckles, like a bodhran to a reel.

'Who's that at this early hour? That you there, Shorn MacEwe?'

'It is not. It is Jarvey Foley, brother of Feidhlim and Conor. I am after comin out from Kerry a couple of days ago. I was wonderin had you a ladder perhaps and perhaps a jemmy. I'm restorin your old fane.'

Patrick, in his longjohns, peeks out a door.

'Wait a bit. Takes me a while to get movin. Have you had your breakfast?'

'Please don't think I am comin here askin for breakfast. Only a ladder.'

'There's a ladder in the fire shed. Only me brother has the key, apart from Shorn MacEwe, and I can't wake Joe. He had a bad night.'

'I'm sorry. I should return. Who owns the horses over the road, sir?'

'Those are Shorn MacEwe's.'

'Fine-lookin beasts. Mine were the Irish draught, you know, raised on the shamrock off the lime-rich soil, with the sturdy bones and the big feathered feet? Skewbalds. Quiet. They would stand, in the blinkers, all day long, with the nose pressed against a high stawn wall. Oh, they trot smooth and gallop nicely, but not a fast horse. Not a racing horse. Cross them with a thoroughbred, like Shorn's, and you have the Irish hunter. Now there's a steeplechaser for you. There's a hedge jumper for you.'

'Wait! Stay a while, Jarvey. I like the look of you. You're dark Irish, aren't you. My father was dark Irish. I do so love the sound of your voice.'

'Americans who come to Killarney, they love the sound of

92

my voice. They ask me to sing them "Danny Boy" as I show them the Gap of Dunloe.'

'Oh, you're from Killarney. We have a Killaarney here. That land you see, from Blanket Flat to The Hole, Mount Nerong, is all Killaarney. Can you pick the resemblance, Jarvey?'

Jarvey turns and looks about him.

'I can, sir. There are still a few trees hereabout, and a few trees growing in Killarney. And what's the name of that little bush?'

'Bottlebrush.'

'We have them in Killarney.'

You would need to venture down Kowmung river, beyond The Hole, to see the resemblance. There, the great casuarina trees that throw the shadows of their crowns on the river, still the most unspoilt in the whole state, as it runs over pink and cream river sandstones, under the figs on the quartzite gorges, were christened 'oak' by Irishmen, because of their resemblance to Irish sessile oak, in the shape of the crown, if not the form of the leaf.

And there were Irishmen here. Head off down the Oberon–Colong stock route and you come, eventually, to an abandoned silver-mining town, Yerranderie. From there, you could walk up Scott's Main Range, through Byrne's Gap in the Axeheads, dropping, at some convenient ridge, to the Kowmung river, thirteen hundred feet below. Ensign Barralier, guided by a self-confessed aboriginal cannibal, saw, from Gander Head in 1802, what he describes in his journal as a 'meadow' to the west.

Today, that range is heavily timbered, if back then it was a grassland, forever being put to the torch. The persistent burning of this countryside effectively ceased on British occupation, so that there are probably more trees now on the Blue Mountain Wilderness than before white settlement. A hunter would have a damnable task, to be sure, to survive off this country.

Hughes, Keefe, Pearce, O'Reilly, Dunn, Fitzpatrick, McMahon, Lannigan, Quig, Donohue – these are the names of cattlemen, who wintered stock on the Kowmung flats and drove their cattle through the Burragorang Valley. Always about, too, bushrangers, as well as miners and cedar cutters. Myles Dunphy of Katoomba, who mapped and named the Wilderness of the Kanangra-Boyd, beyond Mount Nerong, found, in country 'absolutely unknown to the masses' (as he puts it in his 1914 diary) cattlemen's huts, mullock heaps, even bags of potatoes.

Where the Kowmung enters the Cox's river, you can climb, via the Wild Dog Range, to Medlow Gap, and thence, up Taros Ladder, onto Narrow Neck and the tourist trap of Katoomba. And that's the town, as Ad Hock will tell you, gets all the Japanese coach tours, with floodlights trained on the Three Sisters and proper look-outs with telescopes.

An hour later, fortified with food and laden down with hand tools of every description, and every vintage, in possession of the ladder off the tanker, Jarvey returns to the fane. Both MacPeatricks insist he sleep in their hut, which is barn-warm and may be waterproof, and Jarvey admits it would save time, to sleep onsite, instead of commuting. The problem is, he has no money with which to repay the men for their generosity.

At half ten, World Wide drives by, in the battered Ford Cortina, the only vehicle to have come by all morning, apart from Kerry Gurney's purple Nissan people mover, which is always coming by. There has been a suggestion Jarvey might borrow MacPeatricks' Suzuki Sierra, more battered still than Webb's Cortina, but Jarvey doesn't like to impose further on these old men, and he has no driver's licence. Seeing Jarvey ripping the sheets of iron from the roof of the fane, World Wide stops, for a gander. He parks the car and strolls over.

'Nice day for it.'

'Grand weather! I am Jarvey Foley. Yourself?'

'Duncan Webb, but me mother was a Boyle. Whatcha doin up there? Looks like you're takin the roof off the fane. Shame about the fire, ay. What, ya been told to pull it down, have ya? Does look a bit unstable.'

'I have a commission to restore the fane, for its owner. Wait!

I could show you. Have you a moment?'

'I have indeed.'

Jarvey puts down the bar he is using on the roof and descends via the ladder. He goes straight to the hessian sack and removes a piece of blue plate from Stillorgan, wrapped in bubble plastic sealed with tape provided him by Feidhlim.

'Adam was in a great hurry to get off, so he left me the key to the cousin's pottery, and said I should find a piece of blue plate upon the floor, among the many pieces of blue plate there, and that I should find, on many of those broken pieces, a rendering of the fane, as it was once, as he has no photograph. Now here is the fragment I am after selecting. I asked Mary for guidance.'

Jarvey removes the bubble plastic and shows World Wide the piece of plate. It is blue, but, ominously, light blue; the fane upon it non-prototypical.

'See no!'

'Ah yes, I see. I dunno, Jarvey. I don't recall that tower. So who's payin for this? Ad Hock? That'll be the day.'

'I am volunteerin me labours. All the materials I need, Adam says I should find them in the Council Yard. Have they stawn, do you know?'

'Little stone, Jarvey. Gravel for the road.'

'I need large ones, Duncan. And you know? It seems there was a stawn fane on this site, a small stawn fane, with a round tower. You know what this reminds me of, this fane on this piece of plate? St Kevin's Kitchen. Have you been to Glendalough?'

'Never been to Europe, mate. What, is that in Ireland?'

'It is. County Wicklow.'

'We all know Ireland's a beautiful country which leaves Australia for dead.'

'Ah, it's ruined. The trees are gone. Most all the oak and birches. Only the rhododendrons and fuschias remain and they're not even Irish. And Ireland is all full of tourists, Duncan. Well, a few tourists is all right. But they are after takin over the whole country. We're all doin bed and breakfast for 'em.'

'Sounds awful. You a stone mason? No stone here in the Crooked Corner.'

'I love workin stawn. I built that sandstawn façade on the Torc Travel Agency, next to Scott's Gardens in College Street.'

'Well go for it, Buddy. Go for it. You certainly set yourself a task, but I'm unemployed, what would I know? Even if you just got the shell demolished, that'd be better than nothin. Might fall down and kill some cunt, the way it's leanin here.'

'I do think stawn suits a round tower. It was lovely talkin to you, Duncan.'

'Well I got nothin much on. Nothin important anyway. I might give you a hand on that roof. I was just goin out to see Breda Looney, back o' Tubbercurry. It has to do with the bloke who made that plate, as it so happens. Adam's cousin. As you may know, he died of infarction just before you got here, but I have the idea he was shacked up with Breda at the time of the City to Surf. I could fill you in on the details while I give you a hand on the roof. That's if you're interested.'

'I want to learn all I can about the New Country, but I don't like askin for help.'

'You're not askin. I'm volunteerin. Me missus is sick with the flu, see, but so long as I get home in time to cook dinner for the girls, no worries. Do you have househusbands in Ireland? I'm supposed to be at the fire shed by seven. I'm captain of Knocklofty Brigade, or at least, I am actin captain. It's all I got goin for me, Jarvey.'

World Wide feels a rapport with Jarvey, who is about his own age. As World Wide has no jemmy – he will bring one out for himself tomorrow – he throws down the sheets of iron. Every now and then, awaiting a sheet, he offers a commentary on what he sees. It's a mild day. No wind blowing and no rain. Quite a mild spring day.

'Geez, you get a great view from here. This'd be a good place for a fire tower. I can see all the way from Blanket Flat to The Hole, Mount Nerong. Actually, The Hole's a place we must visit, if you're so interested in trees. Heaps o' trees around The Hole. We gotta do a burn down there at some stage and char the fuckers. God only knows when. These are the worst forests in the whole bloody world for fires, they reckon. I think we may have already missed our window of opportunity. See, you want your 'azard reduction to burn quietly by day and go out at night, so you can't really burn unless your upper litter is dry and your lower litter is moist. I mean, what happened here indicates what happens when a burn goes wrong. They can be dangerous. Yes, a round tower here's a great idea. It'll have a staircase, I guess, and a window?'

'A little window. So Michael, Adam's cousin, the man who made the platter, he was a great runner?'

'Oh, a great long-distance runner, mate. Easily the best, for his age, in all the world, but the mean-spirited bastards round here, they wouldn't acknowledge his talents? I mean, if you can run fourteen klicks in forty-one minutes wearing a suit of synthetic hairs, how would you be in a pair o' shorts with a gold chain jumpin off your neck? Speakin of shorts, is that Blue MacEwe?'

'Sittin in the unpire's chair? Oh yes. That is Shorn.'

'God, he's sittin so still I wouldn't a picked him for a human bein. He'd have a few flies in his eyes, ay. He's not movin his hands.'

'Joseph and Patrick tell me he's sittin like that since early the Mondey, but I am feedin the horses. Well, Patrick has been doin it, but I am shall do it no.'

'You're stayin in the Crooked Corner? Wow. Rather you than me. He's a maniac, that Blue MacEwe. A pyromaniac. Bush Fire Brigades round here are filled with people who would rather light fires than put 'em out. I reckon I'd shift him with a fire under him. Might go down and torch his arse, ay.'

'Adam was sayin Shorn is after receivin a terrible shock.'

'Yes, well, he should be disgusted at what he's done here, burnin this poor old fane down. Still, he was runnin true to form. This was once a picturesque deserted village, Jarvey. All that's left now is the brick chimneys, thanks to Blue MacEwe. I wouldn't have thought, just from the way he's facin, he's lookin at the fane, though. I woulda thought, from the way he's facin, he's lookin at The Hole, Mount Nerong.'

'So we have both the fastest veteran runner and the quietest umpire in all Australia.'

'I suppose we have. Now what's gone wrong with Ireland, Jarvey?'

'Men need frontiers and Australia is the last, Duncan. Australia and the Wild West and the Amazon.'

'Speakin o' the Wild West, what did you think of the great Dud Leahey, the Wonder from Down Under? The Boy from Oz? The Livin National Treasure? That tape Adam's always playin in the Merc, "I Still Calls Knocklofty Home". He won a Grammy for that. Come from just down the road here.'

'Fookin shite. I'm sorry to say so, Duncan, but you did ask. Fookin shite.'

'Don't be sorry. I think that too. Everyone I talk to thinks that. Nothin but a heap o' fookin shite. What a poser. You know, I can clearly recall the last words Mike Hock ever said to me. We was after comin from the fire shed, Jarvey, when Mike Hock suddenly turned to me and said, "What do they see in this Dud Leahey business, World Wide? You know it's got me beat?" And that was the night before he got barred from the Bottom Pub and went grey. Toss us that jemmy bar here, mate. I'll have a go. You take a spell. Hot up here, ay. Gettin too hot too soon. Too fookin hot.'

Next day, Friday, another fine, warm day, World Wide brings out all his own power tools and runs a series of extension leads downhill, across the road, to the MacPeatrick residence. Were Blue MacEwe still in the umpire's chair, the leads would be going to Blue's place, but Blue, overnight, has taken off to create a ruckus in town.

'Yeah, they reckon he was in the Bottom Pub last night, Jarvey. Put on a real performance too. Started a fight. Smashed the window. Drinkin longnecks from the bottle. Funny that, I never seen Shorn drunk. Always thought he could handle his piss. Oh, Buzzacott's talkin o' sackin him at the Club, but I can't see how he could. Blenkinsop wouldn't wear it. All these chefs are temperamental types. Do you like chips and hamburgers, Jarvey? Do they have junk food in Ireland?'

'They have junk food in Sligo. Sligo at mass is the pigeons and gulls disputin the spew outside the Abrakebabra.'

'Yeah, well drunks come from miles round here when Blue puts on a prawn and chicken night, but his real strength is the burger. He makes the best burgers in the southern hemisphere. Shorn actually did his apprenticeship at some posh restaurant in London.'

'I do hear tell he is caterin for the Pat's School Reunion, Duncan. Feidhlim says he is goin to no end of trouble with his menu.'

'We just about got this roof off, ay. Look like a pair of chimney-sweeps now. I'll enjoy one last look round, 'fore I climb down the ladder. We're lucky with our weather, Jarvey. Be too hot to work on metal roofin, soon. Mate o' mine called Kakadu works as a tiler in Darwin. Fark that!'

'Do we need a saw, World Wide?'

'We do. We need a chainsaw. We'll use the old boys' chain-saw, in case we hit nails. They never use it. Can't get anythin goin that's got a pullstring. I think I drained the oil from it, this would have been May, just before the Meatworks closed. I did 'em a home kill and quartered a vealer usin the chainsaw with the oil drained. I bet we got no chain oil, ay.'

'I'll stack all this roofin iron here, then.'

'Nothin else worth salvagin. Adam's taken the pews. Oughta run a dozer through the rest of it. Wow! Look at that view! Hello. There's the suit. A suit without a suit is still a suit. I can see the Statesman. He's comin in from Tubbercurry. What would he want out here? He's a private eye, you know. Gimme a card with his number on, Jarvey. I knew I'd seen it before. Found it in me own itemised telephone account! Put it straight on the missus. Why'd you ring this number, I says. Got yourself a boyfriend in the city? Blame yourself, she bawls at me and digs out this sheet of newspaper, which proves to be the escort agency ads from the *St George Leader*. I was lookin for the garage sales, I says, but here's this Harley Christian advertisin, right in among all the beach babes, exotic Asians and Fortys but Naughtys, "Do You Know What Your Partner Is Up To?" with the number of the tell-tale mobile. What a fuckin mongrel, ay, but I got a clear conscience. Can't be you or me he's lookin for. Wouldn't be the MacPeatricks. Could be Blue? Hafta be Blue. Hello. He's turnin off towards Killaarney. What does he want up there? Spare me ten minutes, Jarvey.'

'Oh, you don't have to be workin, Duncan.'

'Well I am. We're workin as a team. Gets lonely, hangin round the house. What with the girls at school, there's only me and Carol there, durin the day. Billy says he's comin out tomorrow. Keyring. Willco maybe. It's really a Bush Fire Brigade responsibility, seein as how we cactused the joint in the first place. As to that stone, I got someone chasin that up. Says we might be in luck, too. They're demolishin an old sandstone residence where they're buildin the new K-Mart. Trouble is, it's sandstone, and it's green painted. But we can always blast the paint off.'

'Nothin wrong with sandstawn, Duncan. And nothin wrong with green-painted sandstawn.'

'Pink sandstone under the green paint. It's all we'll get free, at short notice. They reckon we can have it. No demand here. All bluestone here.'

'Killarney hills is pink sandstawn. I love to see the red deer on the pink sandstawn.'

'Well I'm glad I got somethin right, for a change. I shan't be long, my friend. Hey, what's this?'

World Wide stoops to examine a plant emerging from the blackened ground.

'Looks like a little cedar tree. And here's another one. And there's another one.'

Seeing World Wide ambling towards her, in his Versace glasses, clutching a chain-oil container and staring everywhere but where he is headed, Kerry Gurney excuses herself from Harley Christian and dashes off, through a door beyond a Gothic stone arch, into a mansion of the Queen Anne period style. You'd think she heard a phone ring. Harley smiles, though he is yet to receive eye contact from a single local. A single local man, that is. Kerry's been giving him heaps.

'Gettin a bit of a show here,' says World Wide, persuing his boots. 'Best pasture in the district, this. No burrs or capeweed or curse. Underground springs on Killaarney. Thought you mighta left town. Think it was Kerry runnin with Mike? I doubt that, as I don't think he started seein her till Breda Looney give him the arse.'

'You're Duncan from the Fire Brigade, right? Behold all ye that kindle a fire, that compass yourself about with sparks: walk in the light of your fire and in the sparks that ye have kindled. I'm here on police business, Duncan. Lady here has contacts.'

'You're tellin me. She's a pushy bitch. You wanta be careful o' her. The mouth of strange women is a deep pit, Harley. He that is abhorred of the Lord shall fall therein. Actually complained to my mother, when I had to cut her fencin to inspect a fire hazard. Well, I don't need her permission. It says that under Section Twenty-Two of the Bushfires Act, nineteen forty-nine.'

'Notice any cattle on the road, Dunc? We're lookin for a cattle rustler. Twenty head of stock disappeared from the station, some time over the weekend. I get a call on my mobile from the Commissioner, no less. How 'bout that. The poor is hated even by his own neighbour: but the rich hath many friends.'

'Thought you were seconded to the Ministry for Sport.'

'Yeah, reckon I still am. But no one wants to co-operate, Dunc. This, in a district where I'm greeted by every passing vehicle with an index finger lifted from the wheel. I can't make it out. I was real sorry to hear Mike Hock died.'

'Not as sorry as me. He was a great fire-fighter.'

'I figure the second gorilla had to be at his funeral. But no one wants to co-operate. It is the Glory of God to conceal a thing, Dunc: but the honour of kings is to search out a matter.'

'Nothin personal. This is bushranger country. We come out here against our will.'

'Better is the end of a thing than the beginning thereof. Time moves on.'

'It must do. I never saw a Tongan policeman. Well, not outside o' Tonga. So is Harley Christian a Tongan name?'

'I am a New Zealand-born Tongan.'

'Aha. You don't think you can close the case, Sarge? Seein as we both know it was Mike.'

'I don't believe it was Mike Hock. I need at least a shoe. If Gorilla Two can confirm that Mike Hock is Gorilla One, fair enough. But a statistician at the Institute of Sport in Canberra has done a convincing profile, from which it appears no man of fifty would be physically capable of winning a City to Surf.'

'Yeah? Well just because somethin has never been seen don't mean to say it can't happen. To them that hath faith and doubt not, a mountain can move into the sea. I took these dark glasses I'm wearin off a kangaroo.'

'I suspect Mike Hock was in the company of some younger man, non-drug-user, size twelve. Who could that have been, Dunc?'

'I can't or won't co-operate. See, it's like for me, Mike Hock isn't dead? I feel he is sleepin and I shall see him rise.'

'In your dreams. Where'd he keep his fireboots, Dunc? In the pottery? In the fire shed? They tell me he went barefoot, but I bet he wore his fireboots.'

'No flipflops on a fire ground, under the Bushfires Act. Oh, he had a locker at the Knocklofty shed. You're welcome to check it out, Mr Private Eye.'

'It's true. I sometimes do private work for the Lord God. I need a second earn, to preserve me from corruption. I did search that locker, Dunc. All I found was a studded penis belt.'

'Ah well. This is the nineteen nineties, ay.'

13

One week before Reunion, a Saturday, the day on which Jarvey hopes to complete demolition, World Wide appears at the site driving a red Council Acco tipper, laden with green-painted sandstone blocks. Billy Minogue rides shotgun. They find Jarvey taking down what's left of the annexe, using the MacPeatrick blockbuster and a Stihl saw.

Leaving Billy in the truck cabin, World Wide leaps out with a concerned expression.

'Carol's recovered from her influenza! I shall have to get a lift out Mondey. Where do you want these blocks, Jarvey? I'll fetch you another load when these are off. I'll fetch as many loads today as I can. Not too big, I hope? If so, we could cut 'em in half with an angle grinder. Seen a gang saw somewhere about.'

'T'at's grand, Duncan. T'at's loovely. Just put t'em down dere.'

'Sorry, mate. I've left you short-handed. Me and my big mouth! I didn't really think Willco would front, he always commits himself to everything. But Keyring has let us down badly, I feel. Billy! Come here and meet Jarvey.'

Billy seems shy today and a bit moody. He is prone to having moods. He ignores Jarvey and World Wide, and picks up a block of sandstone. World Wide lets it pass.

As the three unload the blocks, a familiar vehicle pulls up. At the wheel is Blue MacEwe, with five or six other MacEwes or MacHughs. All are swigging at longnecks, which are going round the Haitch Ar like joints.

'Where you doin there, Gub?' Blue doesn't step from his vehicle. He doesn't even turn off the engine. 'This hill here's our country, and all Crooked Corner, includin that tennis court, and all Killaarney, from Blanket Flat to The Hole, Mount Nerong, is all our country.'

'In your dreams! It belongs to quite a few other people as well. Drunk as you be, get outta that car and I'll introduce you to Jarvey Foley.'

'Don't wanta meet no priest. Dey bin teachin a mob o' gammon.'

'Jarvey's no priest, he's a builder, Blue. So how are things at work?'

'Shorn and me already me,' confirms Jarvey, 'at the Hibernian Hall.'

'I ain't got no work, Brudder. They just give me the sack.'

'Well join the club and meet Jarvey Foley, for the first or second time. I think Blue lost his memory, Jarvey. Self-abuse has done it. Jarvey's been feedin your horses for you. Don't feel you'd like to thank him?'

'Get off my case. I better be goin. Got a big party tonight.'

'Party on then. We invited?'

'Only MacEwes and MacHughs.'

'Then git fucked!'

Blue drives off, without a further word. He heads downhill to Killaarney. He parks by the golden elms at the grid and his kinsmen emerge, but they don't cross the grid. World Wide frowns, as he tosses the last block of green-painted sandstone at Billy Minogue.

'Keyring just smashed a longneck, mate, and dropped it down the cattle grid. How would ya be? OK, that's it, first load off. Wanta stay here with Jarvey, Billy? I can manage. You stay here and help Jarvey.'

Billy's wearing the yellow overalls his mother Molly made for him, on the Singer sewing machine at the Top Pub, Minogue's.

'Don't think I introduced yez. I'll have another go. Jarvey, this is Billy Minogue. He's a strong boy, a good worker.'

Jarvey smiles and extends his hand, having first wiped it clean of soot. Billy's freckled face blushes deeply as he takes the dark Irish hand in his own freckled one.

'Billy. How you keepin, are you well? 'Tis not every young

boy I know would sacrifice Saturday to build a fane. Now what would you be doin at home, Billy? Playin football? Doin homework?'

'Try swabbin out a bar, Jarvey. Billy's the useful at the pub. Need a haircut, Billy's the man. Dab hand with the scissors. Been here only three years. Billy's off to Holland, for his holiday soon. Ain't that so then, Billy?'

World Wide pauses, as he stands on the tips of his boots, to see over the roof of the Acco.

'Here they come again. Comin back to town now, all pissed as newts. If they give you trouble, call Joe. I'll give'm a little touch-up.'

Stealthily, World Wide moves out the tipper, as Blue comes racing uphill in the Haitch Ar. Blue is obliged to swerve, then brake and fishtail, to avoid collision, and World Wide gives him the finger. First up, he lasciviously tickles the air, then he stabs the finger at Killaarney.

'There's one for you and one for you 'orse. Christ, you're a fuckin wanker! First up, ya burn down a perfectly good fane, with a little help from Keyring, then you get yourself the sack. What, have ya lost your sense of responsibility?'

Eager to get on with his party, motivated by Great Expectations of Native Title, Blue slams the Haitch Ar into reverse. He wheelspins past the green-painted stone, almost clipping Billy's leg. Jarvey instinctively puts an arm round the boy, to ensure he is unharmed, as World Wide, in stunned disbelief now, watches Blue's treatment of the antique Haitch Ar. It is driven, fast, through the barbed-wire fence delimiting the cemetery from Blue's property, then plunged and bucketed and bottomed out cross-country to the orchard, with much hilarity. At least one death bag, the silver content of the cardboard wine cask, is tossed out a window.

'Look at that,' says World Wide. 'That's the sort of thing could choke a horse to death. How would we be if fire broke out? Every one o' them boys got a pager. Pissed as newts at ten a.m., ah well. They're goin into the house. Must be gettin old. Was a time I'd a bin down there, invited or not. Today, I just wanta get this church built. Call Joe, if they give trouble.'

And he's off, although he pauses outside Blue's residence, to give Blue the finger again, this time from the shoulder.

'Are you married, Jarvey?' inquires Billy of Jarvey, as they work quietly away.

'I am not,' replies Jarvey emphatically. 'I don't think marriage works, Billy. When Christ, Matthew twelve, thirty-nine, insults the Pharisees, He calls them "an evil and adulterous generation, that seeketh after a sign, and shall be no sign given to it". He don't call them "an evil and murderous generation", or an "evil and greedy generation", or "an evil and drunken generation" or even "an evil and quarrelsome generation". Oh no, Billy, adultery's the worst crime, the very worst crime Christ can think of. Well, that's all right, except He already told us, in His Sermon on the Mount, Billy, "That whosoever looketh on a woman to lust after her hath committed adultery with her already in his heart". And He goes on to say, you'd be better off cuttin off your member, than let that happen. Now I've talked to a lot o' married men in my time and you know what I found, Billy? Not one of them could honestly confess he never lusted after other women. They was all sinners.'

'Webbie don't lust after other women. He don't even lust after Carol.'

'Well that would be my problem too, I suspect. A virtuous man, like Duncan, has difficulties in the married state. It seems to me no, the natural state of man is adultery or celibacy, Billy. This makes marriage problematical. Have you read James Joyce? Beasts that we are! Married men lose sight and favour o' the Virgin Mary, so they do. Mary and Christ is within us all, Billy. Within you and within me. That said, I prefer to remain a virgin, which is not to say I shan't ever marry. I should need to know it was God's will for me, though. I should need some sign to be given me. Oh, I fell in love with a nun once, Billy. Never touched her, but she come into my bed! These young Irish girls today, well they have no idea what a nun is. In the meantime, the best life for me is workin, with a young virgin boy like yourself, to the greater glory of God, as we are here. It's what the Irishman wants, you know. We hanker for the Dark Ages, so we do.'

'Have you heard o' the Three Tenors, Jarvey?'

'Have I heard o' the Three Tenors! I have indeed, and I liked what I heard.'

Sunday, Patrick is disturbed by World Wide Webb, with Billy in tow, seeking Jarvey.

'That you, Shorn MacEwe?' says Paddy. 'If so, I got a shotgun here. Be warned!'

World Wide gives Billy the meaningful eye. 'It's me, Paddy. It's only me, Duncan Webb. I'm lookin for Jarvey. Seen him? He's not up at the fane.'

'He's in his hut nights. Sleeps in the hut nights.'

'Has he had breakfast, would you know?'

'I wouldn't, as he washes the dishes and puts them away.'

'Wonder where he could be? We've a load of sandstone for him. Looks like they had a bit of fun over the road.'

'Oh, you've no idea what it was like, Duncan. You never heard nothin like it. Brawlin and shoutin and drinkin and yellin, but it stopped round dawn. It always does. See where they pulled out a door and bargeboard off the house? They dropped 'em in the blue pacific, and that was then best blue pacific this side of Grabben Gullen. They then built a fire and roasted a beast. Still eatin a bit o' that beast, when I took me hot coals up the fane.'

'Hot coals up the fane?'

'I forgot you pulled it down. I pray up there every Sundey, with a bit o' fire, now don't I.'

'I getcha. What kind of beast, Paddy? Friesian steer?'

'No, I think it was a wombat.'

'Meals from under wheels. Where they gettin the money? Must be drinkin Blue's severance pay.'

'They had a fight round three a.m. Sounded like MacEwes versus MacHughs. But they settled down when the sun come up. Been quiet ever since. Too quiet. I had no sleep. I think Joe wet his bed.'

'This can't go on, Paddy. We'll have to do something here,

without, of course, involving the police. I'll give it some thought. In the meantime, I'll check the hut. Got a team comin out today, managed to round a few up. Well, I see Jarvey has the first course laid.'

'Oh, he's a good worker. He's Irish, you see. They're a hard-workin race. They'll work away from dawn to dark, and if you provide them with artificial light, they'll work on into the darkness.'

'Just like chickens on a battery farm. OK! Catch you later. Come on, Billy, we'll check that hut.'

Jarvey is not in the hut. They can make out the fresh indentation in the straw where he slept, but he has gone missing.

'Wonder where he went?' Puzzled, World Wide sits on a bale to light a joint. As he does he looks over the road towards the MacEwe residence. In a city, this might be considered a slum, *a fortiori* with the door missing, but here, surrounded by lush acres, it constitutes a property. Just a shame it abuts on the road. Adjoining the orchard, the trees of which all but two are dead and hanging with grey lichen, the house has indeed had the front door ripped off, for there it is, burning by the gate. About the ash, beneath what's left of the door, passed out and dew dampened, lie men – long grassers, as they're described in the Top End of the Northern Territory. The morning light glints off a dozen drained and discarded longnecks, the sort of thing could start a grass fire, were the grass fully cured.

'Jarvey say anything yesdey, Billy, to imply he wouldn't be workin today? Here, have a toke and don't Bogart the joint.'

'Nup.'

'Wonder if he's over the road. I might go check. You stay here.'

'Careful!'

'What of? I'd say the danger is past. But supposin we had a fire break out. Would we want that team turnin up?'

Full of sudden purpose, World Wide stubs out his roach, swallows it, and strides over the road. The Acco's up the fane, but the Haitch Ar, the worse for wear, is in the derelict orchard.

The float is still parked over the beetroot patch. Billy watches as World Wide walks into the silent wooden home, which boasts, in the shape of an isosceles triangle, a hole in the woodwork next to where the door was.

Billy, if he knew how to pray, might pray no harm come to Jarvey Foley, for if Mike Hock was hot-blooded and hard-natured, then Jarvey is tender and compassionate.

Five minutes later World Wide is back.

'Couldn't get any sense from any of 'em. Someone has thrown up all over the bath. There's a couple crashed out in the kitchen. Shorn's in the chill-out lounge, that's the backyard. Couldn't wake him to save me soul. Can't see Jarvey. Don't think he's there. Ah well. Come on. Let's unload and hope he turns up.'

Without enthusiasm, in Jarvey's absence, World Wide and Billy unload the stone blocks. It seems, in Jarvey's absence, a stupid and ridiculous project on which they work. When they have finished, World Wide heads off to Ballymeaner for more of the same, while over the next half-hour some half-dozen unemployed Knocklofty meatworkers front. They are sitting on stones, deploring, with envy, the squalid scene they see below them downhill, when World Wide returns, with Jarvey riding shotgun, the cycle in the back of the tipper.

'Found him!' World Wide grins. 'Went to mass, expectin to see us there. Cycled his arse off all the way to Knocklofty and half-way back, ridin a girl's bike. And this without a helmet! After gettin no sleep!'

'Oh, they had a great time down there last night,' affirms Jarvey, 'but they couldn't wake for mass. You must always stay awake to go to mass. We like to drink and fight in Ireland, but we need to be forgiven, so we go to mass. And they wasn't singin, and we don't wear helmets in the Old Country. I wouldn't normally work on a sabbath but we are buildin a church. Old Father Carney! Did he give us some crack this mornin! A priest is comin to visit the Father what makes his water in a fog pattern, because he had his penis cut up as a boy, and Father Carney says, in the pub, when he's had a few jars in, he can ventilate the bar!'

14

If hope is gone from these young Knocklofty meatworkers, who live in poverty and despair, hire-purchase commitments unmet, ignored and spurned by Big Syd, too low in their self-esteem to comb their hair, disgraced by the fact of their unemployment, a disgrace akin to the disgrace of being raped, spending their days in front of the plug-in drug, drifting down, on skateboards, to one of their watering holes, there to sip one beer, all they can afford, tequila a thing of the past, moaning of their fate to the barmaids, cursing the Meatworks, cursing the Ovine Johnes Disease, cursing politicians, unable to sleep nights through thoughts of lenient sentences handed down by judges to child molesters, watching Stephen King movies from the Video Parlour, listening to Smashing Pumpkins while smoking dope and contemplating suicide – they have now before them, in the Crooked Corner, an exemplar, a man with a vision: Jarvey Foley – and in the deteriorating scene at Blue MacEwe's, insouciance beyond their comprehension. Tearing down your own home is like walking out of an examination. There are five vehicles in Blue's orchard now, the fence of which has been torn down to accommodate them, and the long grassers, when not slumbering, fly-blown, in the long grass, settle themselves on the veranda, there to swig at long-necks and death bags, and glare uphill at the fane and, beyond the fane, The Hole, Mount Nerong. Every night they light a fire and Blue bakes damper, a primitive bushman's bread, in the ash.

Aidan MacHugh had a wife in town and a good job on the road gang, so two vacancies exist now to be filled: chef at Ballymeaner Sportsman's Club and flagman on Knocklofty gang. The unemployed have a diary they must complete, to receive a benefit, in which they list jobs applied for since their last counselling session. They are aware that should one of their number break rank to rush to Council to apply for Aidan's job – and Aidan will tell you he has the intention of never working again, although Shorn's job may take longer to fill as he was an artist on the griddle – then the last Knocklofty vacancy liable to arise in a lifetime will be lost. But no one has broken rank and no one will. Indeed, all have put the sordid circumstance of their unemployment from mind, temporarily, now they have someone to feel inferior, and someone to feel superior, towards.

The fane goes up with amazing grace and astonishing celerity. By Wednesday, a tiny, random-rubble-stone fane, with an iron roof, is close to completion, and work has commenced on the round tower. Jarvey has a good eye. Rosary in hand, he surveys the piles of sandstones, to indicate the precise stone he needs. He never selects a wrong one. As most of the work in building random-rubble structures consists of endless measurement and the lifting up of successive stones only to set them down again, the work proceeds apace. Eager hands seize every stone selected by Jarvey, to convey it whither he wants. The mud is being mixed up by Billy, who has taken the week off school – Billy pronounces the fane looks 'heaps good' and finds the work 'so fun' – while someone else hands Jarvey the tool he is using to tuckpoint the stone, an art lost here since the nineteen twenties. The speed at which Jarvey works, his cheerful disposition as he works, the songs he sings, so Irish in their innocence, so distinct from the carnal Americana on local radio, the hours he puts in, his unerring eye – these factors, but most of all the fact he works gratis, are a tonic to his team. Their numbers vary, day to day, but Wednesday they constitute a baker's dozen, all performing the simple, but essential, building tasks, under Jarvey's supervision. They are handymen, these Knocklofty men, which is a consolation to their womenfolk.

The fane resulting is smaller than the fane it replaced. So much smaller indeed, that Adam, who means to install a kitchen, and bedroom, and bathroom, must meet frustration.

Nothing like the size of St Kevin's Kitchen, itself a diminuitive structure, the Fane of St Fiacre now resembles a movie-set mock-up of the shell of the Dark Age cell, the seventh-century Cill Chearnnannach by the dock on Inishmaan, south of the pier. You have to bend your head low to enter the fane which, while no doubt pious, precludes wearing a Stetson. And some do say Dud Leahey is bald. Still, it will be a durable structure, and fireproof, being stone. Those who saw Dud Leahey's photo in *Time* magazine will confirm he's lost weight. He'll have no trouble, Stetsonless, getting in the door, and he can only get thinner. Moreover, he is not a man would need or want to cook for himself. His millions permit him an Eagle Boy pizza sent out from Ballymeaner. He could afford to have a fresh rock lobster flown in, daily, from WA. This will be more of a bedsit for him, a base from which to rove his beloved New Country. It's all wired up for electrics (keyboard, dialyser, water bed, coffee machine), with cyprus flooring and white plastic elbows emerging from the stone for the plumbing. Jarvey has left, for the windows, apertures in the shape of the round tower to come, and it shouldn't set Kerry Gurney back a motza to cough up the cost for these two. It's not asking much, only insisting she do what her family did for St Pat's, given the Queen Anne-style she inhabits abounds in armorial windows. Kerry drives by, almost hourly, in the purple Nissan people mover, ferrying kids to and fro, but she never looks out to see what's going on. She takes no interest in the village. When she passes Blue's house, the long grassers stir, to shake unsteady fists at her disappearing vehicle.

Jarvey assures World Wide there will be stone sufficient to complete the job, and the reason he has built the fane small is because so much of it was smashed by the labourers building the K-Mart. As Jarvey superintends the site, he keeps glancing at the piece of platter, selected by the Virgin, to ensure the final structure accords completely with what Dud will see upon his platter, beside his burger.

After returning the tipper, once for all, to the Yard, World Wide absents himself from the site, to eyeball Blue MacEwe concerning the missing steers, in the fear Blue may have requisitioned them, for his Hamburger from Hell. Paddy has confirmed to him it is a regular occurence, this stock going missing off Killaarney, and the reason the Gurneys switched to wool, despite the hazard of the dingo.

'Blue,' yells World Wide, 'you in there, mate? It's Wednesdey. You goin up the shed?'

'What you want, Gub?' Blue rises in the long grass, too drunk to stand precipitously.

'Look at you. Where's your self-respect, Shorn? Where's your Motorola? Where ya gettin the money?'

Blue can't find his self-respect but his pager's in the pocket of his putrid shorts. He digs it out and holds it before his eyes, mesmerising himself.

'I recommend you hand in that pager. You can't drive a vehicle, striker, tanker or troopie, in that condition. I haven't seen you sober in a week. But that is not what I'm here for. What is that bone you have been chewin? Where is that beast, whose guts you've strewn? I know it wouldn't be one of your horses, as Jarvey removed them for their own welfare.'

'Get off my case.'

'I'm not on it. There's coppers snoopin on Killaarney, Shorn. Twenty head of stock gone missin.'

'Check it out.'

'What?'

Blue kicks awake some comatose cronies. They have fiscal interest in Killaarney now, so that two MacEwes, with three MacHughs, stumble up the hill, Blue some distance ahead. Periodically, a memory comes to mind to torment and incense the poor man, whereupon he turns and, slowly extending his right blue arm, berates a kinsman, with intermittent abuse, repetitious if incoherent. The butt of the abuse, in no position to respond as being fully occupied remaining standing, reels under the force of the admonition, before resuming the lateral staggers. This goes on maybe half an hour, till Blue contrives to drop one leg down the cattle grid on Killaarney and his team can't get him up, whereupon World Wide, wheezing with laughter, runs down to lend the assist.

Town girls resolve to marry farmers here, while town boys

resolve to buy a farm for themselves. It was the ambition, unspoken, of every town-dwelling boy who passed through St Patrick's School, Knocklofty, in the nineteen sixties, to some day have the means to buy a property. To become, thereby, a somebody. It was to this end they left, in droves, for the legal and medical professions, and many of them, now, do possess financial clout sufficient to buy themselves a rural holding, but by now they also enjoy the status conferred by their profession, and the arse has meantime fallen from family farming, which is all life-style and no money. They never really wanted to be farmers; graziers, maybe. So their homesteads have become weekenders. They thought they wanted status, a resolve that began on the school bus, but what they wanted was *lebensraum*. *Lebensraum* for alpaca and ostrich. *Lebensraum* for olives and vineyards. A real farmer hates nothing worse than living among such hobby farmers and this can cloud judgement. So the townies end up with the homesteads, while the farmers end up in the 'burbs.

Even a slum looks good, be it set back off the road among trees. Or that has been Ad Hock's experience in his stock and station agency. Even in its present condition, Blue's home could attract a buyer, were it set back off the road. He owns – or, more strictly, leases, his land being pastoral leasehold of late – a hundred and twenty acres here, but his house, regrettably, is right upon the road, this being thought the best place to build a house, in Crooked Corner's heyday.

Become a plumber or marry an heiress. Then you will see that mystery world that is set back off the road.

Kerry Gurney is an heiress. Her husband works in Hong Kong. She is flirting with Harley Christian, but runs off, as though she heard a phone ring, when she sees World Wide Webb leading a posse of drunks up her driveway, under the oaks.

'Duncan!'

'Harley, allow me to introduce to you Shorn MacEwe known as Blue. When I mentioned the missin cattle, he would insist on comin up. He's aboriginal. Drunk, as you see, but I wouldn't let him drive. No way. He lives in the Crooked Corner. We walked.'

'What's your story, Blue? Did you hear or see anything here? It's not the value of the cattle so much as the cowardly nature of the offence. You've no idea how Kerry suffers, because of the OJD, but as a sheep before her shearers is dumb, she openeth not her mouth to complain. Destocked for two clips.'

'Yards,' suggests Blue. 'Baths. Gates. Sinks. Dams. Soaks. Tracks.'

'What?'

'He means to investigate, for tracks, Sarge, the ground where no grass can grow. So in all thy ways acknowledge him and let him direct thy paths.'

'OK. Let's do this thing.'

Pursued by kinsmen, who stare at the oak with perplexed acrimony, Blue, sobering by the minute, strides to the cattle-yard. An affair of grey hardwood with a metal crush, it has a ramp ascent to the height of the truck tray. Blue scrutinises the superficial corrugations on the hardened surface of the yard, which verge on those of an arid pig wallow, at one point cocking an ear towards the shearing shed, as though he heard something there.

'I got a result on the DNA match on the hair I found on the size twelve, outside the Hakoah Club, and the hair I found on the pottery sink, Dunc. I was a bit confused at first, as the one was black and the other white.'

'And?'

'No match.'

'I thought there was some doubt about the DNA technique. And a negative result proves only the fact you got the wrong hair, Sarge.'

'Keep on truckin. Where they goin now?'

'Headin towards the top gate.'

'Those boys know what they're doin?'

'Blue comes up here once in a while. He's captain of the local fire brigade. They hold a bonfire every year and I think Killaarney contributes sparklers.'

'What a day! Look at those beasts of the earth and fowls of the air. I wish I could bring up my cycle, and would, but for the belt drive on the dirt.'

'Dunno why they stick with a belt drive. I like somepin leaves 'em at the lights. Gimme a chain and a sprocket.'

'I'm a big man, Duncan, so I need a big bike. Got me a Heritage Springer.'

'Yeah, well they're not a bad bike. Last bike I rode was a Trumpey. Missus made me sell it.'

'Friend of mine rode a Bonneville. You ever hear of the Mongrel Mob? 'Fore the Lord Jesus came into my life, Duncan, I rode with the Mongrel Mob, for there is a way that seemeth right unto a man, but the end thereof are the ways of death. I reckon those Mongrel boys are lookin for me. Oh well, I'm ready to go. Always ready to go, Duncan. Are you ready too, Duncan? Ready to go when the Lord calls? Let's you and me now call upon the Lord.'

'Ya never had a record, ay, or ya wouldn't be a Fed. Sorry, mate. 'Scuse me. I gotta move. Renovatin a church.'

'Guess I tag along with Blue?'

'He's headin off for Blanket Flat. That's rough winter pasture, only tussock on Killaarney. Take your blanket. Horrible swamp, all covered in ti tree. Cross the grid and over the road.'

15

First thing Adam does, when he returns from his world tour, is sleep for seventeen hours. When he wakes, at one p.m. Wednesday, he straightway rings the Sportsman's Club, Father Carney and Feidhlim Foley, in that order, but only at the last number – Council Accounts – does he obtain satisfaction.

'Feidhlim. Howdy. This is Adam. Could we convene an extraordinary meeting of the Pat's Steerin Committee? Ta. Seems Shorn's in a spot of bother, he lost his job at the club, did you hear? Dunno why they had to sack him. He doesn't really need to stand, as he does, in his chef's hat behind the warming trays. They could have hidden him in the kitchen. I did ask Carney, he says he can't make it. Can't make it ever again. Lost his licence while I was away. No, he just forgot to renew it. Pulled up, in the Simca, by the Breathalyser Unit and they asked to see the licence. Well, it expired twenty years ago. Render unto Caesar. Actually, I'd as soon he weren't there. You and I will do fine. So much to report. How's Jarvey going on the fane? Serious? Oh, that's grand. Serious? That's excellent. OK. Catch you in the kitchen of the hall, Buddy, shall we say, two a.m.? Three a.m.? You prefer six p.m. I could make that if I hightail it.'

When Feidhlim arrives at the Hibernian Hall, for the extraordinary meeting of the Steering Committee, he finds Adam in the white-painted kitchen, wearing a Greg Norman Akubra.

'I never saw you in a black fur hat.'

'Well I bought this in Sheridan, Wyoming. He's the man said "the only good Indian is a dead Indian". Sheridan? It's a long story. Want to hear it? I must first report my visit to Tokyo proved a disappointment. As you may know, forty-seven per cent of Japanese tourists visiting Australia nominate the longing to hold, in their arms, a koala bear as the main reason for their visit, while eighty-three per cent of that forty-seven per cent wish to be photographed so doing. Now we have koalas aplenty in Yarrawongamullee. They reckon they're endangered on the mainland, too. It's vital we get the money in now, if you see what I'm tryin to say. There's that colony on the manna gum above Blanket Flat, which reminds me, I enjoyed, was it only yesterday? a meal at the Roadkill Café, Montana, "from your grille to mine", which has given me a few ideas. We need a few o' them yellow signs by the road, with a black koala bear on, but to get back to the Japanese, Feidhlim, their main complaints – and bear in mind, these are honeymooning couples – are the silly ban on smoking in our airport lounges, and the poor quality of the digeridoo lessons, opals and toy koala bears on offer. Futhermore, they claim our cuisine lacks spark. They're fast losing interest in the Gold Coast, which they perceive as more expensive than Hawaii, and are off to Las Vegas and Milan in droves. And what is more, because o' the failin yen, the forward estimate shows 'em down by 2.4 per cent, this comin year, to 3.17 million.'

'We can't compete with Milan, Adam.'

'No. Tuscany perhaps. But conjure up a vision of Knocklofty, Feidhlim, as a kind of bluestone Vegas with koalas. I think we'll keep Crooked Corner pristine, bearing in mind the need of the tours. Welcome to Knocklofty. Starlight's Casino, where smokers are made welcome, fine Japanese food to go from the many sushi bars – we'll put those unemployed meatworkers back in a job – real aborigines – I'll get back to that – posing for photos and teaching didge, bushranger re-enactments on Ballymeaner Road, Rodeo all day every day, with none o' them newfangled crash hats, a free trip out to the Wilderness, for such as are game, and a bungy-jumping tower, Feidhlim, and fine koala bears, made by local women in our factories, from superfine wool, all but as cuddly as your actual marsupial, and don't piss. The Top and Bottom Pubs' five-star accommodations, and lots of drive-up photo-processing facilities. I don't think I've seen one in all Australia. Christ, we're behind the times.'

'That would cost a motza, Adam.'

'It would. And who are the neighbours with the money? Oh, I'm aware of the pitfalls. You have to think these things through. The Moran Group built a two-hundred-million-dollar private hospital and five-star hotel complex at Tugun, on the Gold Coast. This was back in ninety-one. Today, that hotel stands empty. Wealthy Japanese are meant to be getting implants and transplants while their families romp on beaches, but immune response intensifies when you're stressing, and people on beaches are soft targets for theft. We have no soft targets in Knocklofty. No, I was lookin for investment in Knocklofty, now Dud Leahey has put us on the map, and what with Sydney Two Thousand comin up, I had a portfolio prepared. But I had only the one day in Tokyo and that, in hindsight, was insufficient. I have a few contacts there, of course, through my wool-processing facility, but they let me down. It may have been partly me own fault, Feidhlim, partly the fault of the downturn. My Japanese is none too flash, and perhaps I should have taken with me a toy bear, to get the point across. I was afraid it might have been perceived as substandard. No form better than dead form. As I understand it, they'd never even heard of Dud Leahey, which I find hard to comprehend. Don't they read *Time* magazine?'

'Maybe they don't like Country music, Adam. So you flew on to the States?'

'I flew on to the States, and I wasn't that crestfallen, tell you the truth. Oh no, not with these Olympics comin up. They're a licence to print money. I went to New York. Pushin me way through the panhandlers, I made me way to Dud Leahey's loft, but he'd left a note to say he'd gone to his ranch in Wyoming and could I join him.'

'He has a ranch?'

'He has a ranch. He misses the homeland to such an extent, he bought himself a ranch in Wyoming. That's the Wild West. Lots of Aussie shearers in Wyoming, Feidhlim. They went there when the Maoris come here, sorry, the Heartier Rowans.

Mike Hock would have done well in Wyoming. By the way, Feidhlim, how are the acceptances? RSVP was Tuesday, was it not?'

'Thirty-eight, Adam, with six apologies.'

'That's it, then. They're all in. We have them in. Six empty platters. I'm goin to ask you to the Reunion, Feidhlim, to eat off one of them platters. Speakin of which, I better get glazin. Can't really see it, as Jarvey sees it, an oversight the women eatin off conventional plates. Surely one commemorative platter and goblet per household is heaps.'

'Thanks, Adam, for the invitation.'

'You bet. Dud Leahey's coming.'

'Great news, Adam!'

'Yes, but he's not well. He has the skin condition, these blue welts, and he's lost weight and has a terrible cough. And oh, the pressure on the poor man. He tells me, these days they want to hear somepin from the CD after the next.'

'Did you mention the fane to him?'

'Only in the context of the Grammy win. I didn't reveal our little scam. He couldn't keep tears from his eyes, mate, as I sang him my rendition of "The Fane of St Fiacre". This was in the Mint Bar at Sheridan, where they have all those trophy heads on the walls there. Ha! We used to call Dudley "Trophy Head" at school, because of his big ears. He hadn't forgotten. Pronghorn goats, bighorn sheep, mule deer, elk, moose – that kind of thing. Six-point bucks, their antlers fatally locked in a mortal combat. Sausage-makers do well in the West. Taxidermists too. We was drinkin Wild Turkeys, because there's turkeys on the six lazy nine, dozens of turkeys. Dud and his pardner own six thousand acres of sagebrush, in the foothills of the Rockies.'

'Dud has a pardner?'

'He has a pardner on the range. Billy Bob. I didn't get to meet Billy Bob. He's a younger man, apparently, and Dud wants to bring him to the Reunion. I said we'd be delighted. We'd be honoured and thrilled. So everything's looking good, Feidhlim. Our guest of honour will be here. He's flyin in Satdey, it seems, and comin straight up. Just keep that to yourself. You know, he said to me a funny thing? I flew out of Billings, Montana, where we stayed overnight at the Dude Rancher Lodge, and as I was breakfasting on pancakes and syrup, buffalo sausages and eggs and coffee, Dud turned – he didn't feel like eating – he turned to me and said . . . you know what he said?'

'What did he say?'

'He said a funny thing. He said, there is one part of the New Country, Adam, one part I miss more than any other, can you guess which it is? Well I said, I guess it would have to be Knocklofty? He says, no. Guess again. Then it must be the Crooked Corner, I says, where stands your famous Fane of St Fiacre. No, he says, and it's not Tubbercurry, despite my song "The Tubbercurry Farrier" as covered by Travis Tritt. It's not Ballymeaner, it's not Bannaby. It's not Golspie, it's not Black Springs. It's not Rockley, it's not Trunkey Creek. I'll tell you where it is. It's Rugby.'

'Rugby?'

'Rugby. He says he dreams of Rugby. Can't get Rugby out of his head. He dreams of the little Fane of St Aidan, on the hill there, which he says is more picturesque than the Fane of St Fiacre and the fane at Georges Plains combined. He says he dreams of a boy called Croker he met there, playing rugby once at Rugby. He sees, in his mind's eye – and God, he must be taking fifty kinds of pills and vitamins, Feidhlim – he sees, in his mind's eye, the granite boulders, and the grey shearing sheds and the silver yellowbox leaves. He sees, in his mind's eye, the grey road to Wheeo, with its white surface of aggregate stones. He sees grey lichens on the hawthorn trees. And he sees grey clouds scudding overhead, and the grass is green, for it's always spring, in Dud Leahey's vision of the New Country. There are freshly shorn sheep on emerald-green oats. An echidna crosses the Boorowa Road. There's a dead crow hanging off a fenceline.'

'Sounds to me like another Grammy-winnin effort incubating in Dud's head, Adam.'

'Precisely. That's what I said. Oh, I'm not too worried. Does Jarvey understand Latin, Feidhlim?'

'Anyone who spent three years in a seminary would understand the Latin.'

'Then I must get him to translate for me what's written on the back o' them platters. I meant to show Carney, but I cannot stand the man. And now he has no licence, we can avoid him.'

'I think you better go out and talk to Shorn.'

'Yes, I was gonna suggest the same thing. In a sense, that Shorn is now out of work could prove in our favour, Feidhlim. He is free to pay his full attention to the victuals for the Reunion.'

'I hear he's gettin in grogstrife, with a bunch of MacEwes and MacHughs.'

'Alas, poor souls, are they to blame? Hmm? We took their country from them, Feidhlim. We dispossessed them and, frankly, I think we owe them an apology, don't you? Well, that's Dud Leahey's view. It's the same with the Red Indians, sorry, the Native Americans, in Wyoming and Montana, the Crow and the Sioux, sorry, the Crow and the Lakota.'

'What in God's Name are you talkin about?'

'You haven't heard? No, you wouldn't have. They're abos, mate. All MacEwes is blackfellas, which accounts for their low self-esteem. But we're not prejudiced, as we'll prove, by havin Shorn doin our caterin.'

'Blackfellas?'

'Yes, and I shouldn't have said that, for "Koori" is the preferred word. They're all Kooris, but they didn't even know that until a week ago. We robbed them of their birthright. It's not enough we stole the country, under the bogus premise of "Terra Nullius". It's one long story of conquest and deceit, and what can a Gub do to make amends? All I can think of is to somehow raise their self-esteem, in acknowledging their true identity. I'd like to see them givin didge lessons to Japs, I think that's what's needed here.'

'You better get Shorn onto the caterin, Adam. There's only days left to the Reunion.'

'Is it me or is it warm? Christ, it's hot today. I intend to do just that. Here, Feidhlim, here's a present I bought you in Sheridan. It's a display, as you see, of various types of barbed wire, all in the one box. See, they get no rain out there, so nothin rusts.'

'Thanks, Adam.'

'You bet.'

16

Crooked Corner was never the most vibrant village in Yarra-wongamullee, but Adam, three a.m. Thursday, finds it a hive of activity. Work proceeds on the fane round the clock, in an effort to have it completed on time, with illumination provided by the headlights of Crooked Corner One, the Ford Blitz, which is idling as though it were drilling a bore hole off a power take-off. Concerned to see what could be a hillfort taking shape upon the hill, Adam drives by, without a glance, the MacEwe residence and the MacPeatrick residence. Had he looked sideways, he would have seen both Blue and the MacPeatrick boys up and about. Blue confers, in the long grass, with an envoy from the Koori Legal Service in Sydney, while Pat pokes about at the beet, and Joe swings round his head, in the manner of a Marlboro Man a lariat, what could be a rattling soccer fan clacker. Consisting of a wet and dry bulb thermometer, it is, in fact, a whirling sling psychrometer, as used, by group captains, to ascertain relative humidity (RH) in the field. After slinging the psychrometer, which must be slung in the shade at least three minutes, Joe takes a reading, the wet before the dry bulb. Water, wherewith to moisten the wet bulb, which must be distilled, he took from a cell on the battery, which World Wide brought out, at eight p.m., as he was tiring of roll-starting the Blitz. World Wide is driving the old boys' Suzuki.

Like Adam, unwilling to believe his eyes, Joe repeats the procedure again, for the reading that he keeps coming up with is scarcely credible to him. At an RH like that, fuel moisture levels at, say, The Hole, Mount Nerong, will be down to five per cent, and potential exists for ready ignition, high combustion rates and erratic fire behaviour. Not since the dreadful year of nineteen thirty-nine, when fires in the Brindabella Range, south of Canberra, were spotting on the city, twenty-five kilometres north, has Joe recorded such a reading so early in the season. Bushfires, in New South Wales, invariably start to the north of the state and work south. Except in nineteen thirty-nine, that is, when they started in the south of the state and worked north.

Noting Adam but ignoring him, as he never did like the Kissanes, Joe takes a reading, then, shaking his head, replaces the muslin wick. With the Dwyer wind meter he has measured the wind speed at eight on the Beaufort Scale, and the milking bucket, hanging off the clothes prop, serves him as the Crooked Corner pluviometer. If Joe could recall the number of days since rain, and the rainfall at that time, he could estimate, using the McArthur meter, without reading instructions, the Fire Danger. But though the bucket on the clothes prop is dry, and has been for months, the registration book is gone, perhaps buried under all the hay in the slab hut. Conditions certainly point toward Extreme Fire Danger and a Total Fire Ban.

Ad Hock drives slowly, carefully studying the scene on the hill before him. While waiting for his breakfast to settle, before he caught his flight to Denver from the Dude Rancher Lodge, he took advantage of a free psychic reading, on the Psychic Tele Talk Line. And as well he did, for the psychic assured him that, though due for imminent disappointment, everything would, in fact, turn out for the best, and on no account must he manifest concern, of the kind he feels welling within him.

Billy and Jarvey are up the round tower, which is now taller than the fane. It must be twenty foot tall and, from the angle of inclination, looks as though it's meant to rise another twenty. World Wide, who has a bruised nose, has rigged up a long-throw bucket hoist, to get the stones to the top, and is busy mixing mud in the mud-mixer, when Adam quietly taps him on the shoulder.

'Yo.'

'Christ! Ya gimme a start, Ad. I wouldn't expect to see you up at this hour.'

'That's an aspersion. I often work nights. I'm runnin on US Mountain Time. What's this s'posed to be, this thing?'

'Ask Jarvey. I'm just a labourer. Bet you wouldn'ta thought it possible, for us to have done all we done here, in one week. It's a miracle! Speakin o' miracles, how's the Boy from Oz, the Wonder from Down Under? The Livin National Treasure?'

'He's all right. You'll be seein him shortly. I don't know what he's going to think of this.'

'We can blast off the green paint. Jarvey says to wait till we finish and the wind has dropped. Wouldn't want to enter a public bar with your eyes full o' green sparkle.'

'I wasn't alludin to the green paint. Could you ask Jarvey to come down here, please? And would you mind turnin off the tanker engine, so I can hear meself talk? It's bad enough, bellowin into this wind.'

'What's that you got stickin outta the Merc boot.'

'That is an advanced persimmon. I had to drive all the way to Burrawang to get it. You got a shovel handy?'

'One on the tanker. Careful o' them cedars, Ad! Whole lot o' little cedar trees sprung up. See? Seems there was a bit o' cedar seed in the hay.'

'Jarvey! Could I please have a word with you down here?'

Billy and Jarvey are so excited Adam must wonder at their intelligence. Billy has a big scratch upon his arm and Jarvey a scratch upon his cheek-bone.

'What's this you've built here, Jarvey?'

'I am after buildin you a stawn fane, Adam.'

'Yes, I see that. That much is clear. Jarvey, we all know a fane can't be cobalt blue, whether it be stone or wood, but the thing is, Dudley's fane was wooden. Why would you let him do this, Duncan? You knew bloody well it was a wooden fane!'

'This is better than the old one, Adam. Fireproof. Anyway, I'm not in charge.'

'Adam,' says Jarvey, 'did you not instruct me to follow the design on a platter?'

'I did, but that is not what you have done. You have let your imagination run riot. That you did all this in under a week is, I suppose, to your credit, but this is, well I don't know what to call it. I know it's not the Grammy-winnin fane.'

'Adam, you was in a hurry to get off, so you left me the key to Stillorgan, and you said I should find a piece of blue plate on the floor, among the many pieces of blue plate there, and that I should find, on many of those broken pieces of plate, a rendering of the fane, as it was once, because you had no photograph. Now here is the fragment I am after selectin, with the guidance of the Virgin. See no.'

Adam accepts the proffered piece of blue-glazed shard and examines it coolly, in the headlights. He must concede Jarvey has constructed an adequate depiction of the clay simulacrum.

'How many shards of plate did you observe? What was your sample size, Jarvey?'

'I asked the Virgin to guide my hand, Adam, so I scrutinised only the one plate.'

'How unscientific. Had you bothered to peruse more than one plate, you would have seen this one was unrepresentative. This would appear to be a platter from the final firing. I thought they was all in the kiln. True, the fane you realised, as a thing of stone and plastic, is the one depicted here, and the one off which we shall dine at the Reunion. But Jarvey, the purpose of the exercise was to strike a chord with Dud Leahey! Far as I'm concerned, you may's well tear it down, for it serves no purpose now, no purpose at all. This is no fantasy of Dud Leahey's here. This is a fantasy of Mike Hock's!'

Jarvey's head sinks at the admonition and he walks off, a study in dejection.

'How could you say that,' says Billy, 'you fat, bloated cunt. You've no idea what this meant to him.'

'It isn't what the shire needs, Billy. I realise I'm partly to blame, in not taking Jarvey into my confidence, but what cruel fate caused him to select a specimen from the final version? This was to be a gift, from the Class of Sixty-One, to Crooked Corner's greatest son.'

'What? You're gonna give this fane to the Wonder from Down Under? No fuckin way! We haven't broken our backs on this to see it go to that prick!'

'I own the fane, Duncan. May I remind you? I'll do with it as I choose.'

'Bullshit, you own the fane!'

'I own the land on which it stands. I could show you the fax from the bishop. Look, there's been a misunderstandin. All right? I know everything works out for the best. I just can't quite see how.'

'That's your problem. Don't you go criticisin Jarvey, not after all he's done for you. If you only knew the work he's put in.'

Adam shrugs. 'I'm not concerned. It may well prove to Dud's taste. Who knows? It don't shake my tree, but may represent a more close approximation to the quintessential fane. It may resemble the Fane of St Aidan at Rugby, which I have not yet seen. I sure hope so. Does Molly know you're out here, Billy?'

Billy replies by poking out his tongue at Adam, then rushing off to comfort Jarvey. When he is out of earshot, World Wide gives Adam the come-hither nod, like a tout at a two-up game.

'Adam. Wantcha to look at somepin, mate. Take a squiz at this 'ere.'

World Wide withdraws, from his pocket, a piece of paper, but the wind snatches it from his grasp. It's gone. Meantime, Adam is looking at the fane. Pacing about it. Scrutinising it. Looking into it. Appraising it.

'You know, if I were a Japanese girl, I wouldn't really mind gettin married here. They're a diminutive race.'

'I wanted to show you a love letter, Adam, written from Billy to Jarvey. It fell out of his pocket. I don't think he knows it's gone.'

'I wouldn't be too concerned. It's common for young boys to have these crushes. I had a crush on Carney.'

'It is not common. It is most uncommon. I can't feel the same about Billy now.'

'He never intended to send it, I'm sure. Forget the whole thing, Duncan. It's more a reaction to Jarvey being Irish, cultural deprivation confused with carnal desire. Reckon there's room here for a tripod? Where would you throw your rice?'

'Nothin carnal about it. That, I could understand, but this was full of soppy talk about "Love Between Men". Think I should say somethin to Molly?'

'Are you mad? These things pass, if all concerned have the wisdom not to make a fuss. The worst thing you could do, Duncan, is humiliate Billy over this. Bear in mind he was most upset when Mike left Molly for Breda, and it may well be he sees in Jarvey a sort of stepfather substitute.'

'Put this in your pipe. Jarvey wants to go back to the seminary and become a priest! He's that impressed by what he's built here, he wants to be the priest o' Crooked Corner.'

'Well that's not a bad idea, but I'd take it with a grain of salt. There were no Christian Brothers professed in this whole country last year. Not a one. And you know how many Jesuit priests were ordained? Only the one. They'll be closin down these seminaries soon. God knows what goes on in 'em now. Only priests we can get is darkies; but listen, we've none of us had much sleep. I'm jetlagged, and so is Jarvey. You're destitute. Billy's adolescent. I caution calm and forbearance. I could have been more upset than I was, but I must keep me head, to glaze them platters and goblets. Is there water in the tanker, son?'

'Eight hundred and fifty gallons, Ad. I filled it at the hydrant.'

'Well done. I want to plant the persimmon. It's our sole link, now, between the old and the new. It may be our only hope, Duncan. But first, I better talk with Shorn. How is the poor black bastard?'

'Took the driptorches off this tanker, and the driptorch fuel, while me back was turned.'

'Why?'

'Because he is a pyromaniac. You should see the fires he's settin down there. Bigger every night. Bonfires. I reckon, with this weather, it won't be long before Joe slaps a fire ban on. Then we'll see some fun.'

'That Harley Christian still about? He find them cattle

rustlers? I want him out of here before any fire ban. They snoop round fires like kookaburras.'

'Gone back to Sydney to fetch him his Heritage Springer. Seems he's a born-again Mongrel, Adam.'

'Nothin could surprise me any more. I've just returned from the USA, where I met people with spendin money. You have a nice day now, Duncan, and put from your mind that business 'twixt Billy and Jarvey. It's a load of hot air.'

On his way to Blue MacEwe's, Ad sees Patrick nursing a lacerated wrist and struggling with a garden fork.

'Why you up at this hour, Pat? Funny time to be diggin your garden, and everyone here's nursin fresh injury. What the hell's goin on? Billy got a big scratch on his arm. Jarvey got a scratch on his face.'

'Wind suddenly dropped a bit there and all of us fell over. No one can sleep, with the noise in this village.'

'Won't be for much longer, mate. What's that you're harvestin there?'

'Beet for the Reunion, but I'm crippled with arthritis.'

'Stick with it. I'm on me way to Shorn's now. What's that car outside Shorn's house? Who's that visitin Shorn?'

'Looks like one o' them very dark Irish.'

'Very dark Irish you say?'

'Know how Jarvey's dark Irish? There's Irish darker than him. I recall twice seein some very dark Irish at The Hole, Mount Nerong.'

'I'll take that on board. What's old Joe doin there?'

'Slingin the sling psychrometer.'

'Very dark Irish, you say. Would they come to town, do you know?'

'Was a bit shy. One might turn up with a mob to sell, at the Camden Sales, from time to time. Wild men, Adam, the very dark Irish. Cattle thieves, whiskey makers, always harbouring a sense of grievance. And there was very dark Irish indeed here once, but I suspect they're gone. They was as black as the ground where a non-crownin firestorm has come through, but we knew they was Irish 'cause they drank like Irishmen. Blacks, as you know, don't drink.'

'I wonder, could they have pilfered the cattle from here, them very dark Irish? What do you reckon?'

'Would have been them, a hundred years back. MacEwe o' The Hole, when he stole cattle, t'was said he took 'em through the Burragorang.'

'Well that can't happen any more, as the Burragorang is flooded.'

'Oh? I never knew that.'

'Sydney Water, Paddy. Warragamba Dam. They flooded that valley in the sixties. Think it was him took them Friesian steers? Was he a very dark Irishman?'

'No darker than you. He come from somewhere in Connaught. He had the three sons, MacEwe, MacHugh and MacYew. Now MacEwe was a redhead. Shorn's a MacEwe. And MacHugh was darker and MacYew was very dark. So MacHugh went up to Blanket Flat, MacEwe come here, while MacYew remained at The Hole, and that way they had a corridor of theft, for movin stolen stock, which is now Killaarney. Once they had 'em at The Hole, then they would drive'm through the Wilderness o' the Blue Mountains. No one ever knew which way they went, through 'tis certain they went through the Burragorang.'

'I'm gonna get this on tape. This makes fascinatin oral history. Dud Leahey says they lynched a man, in Johnson Country, for rustling cattle recently. If you refrain from rustlin cattle and spotlightin elk, you can do as you like in Wyoming.'

'It was like that here at one time, too. Now we get these wombat-headed politicians.'

'You didn't mention what you just said to that Black and Tan, I hope, Paddy? That policeman who stood at the cemetery gate, grinnin, in the gorilla mask?'

'I don't talk to policemen. Because none of my cattle was ever taken.'

'I wonder is it possible there may persist a pocket of the very dark Irish at The Hole?'

'MacEwe would still be there. He can never die. I heard, as a boy, he's fallen in the Kowmung River Gorge time without number.'

'I shall have to keep an eye on the Camden Sales, but right now, I've more important fish to fry. I need to talk to Shorn MacEwe about that School Reunion.'

'Tell him the beetroot's ready.'

'I will. Better yet, I'll load 'em in the barrow and take'm over to him now. Motivation's a problem here, Paddy. We all know he's a fine chef. Did his time in Wandsworth and he's all full o' surprises. What about the time he served up the same meal at the club three weeks in a row?'

' 'Tis the Irish comin out, Adam. They was huntin and gatherin, in Ireland, as recently as eighteen forty-six, and when hunters aren't huntin, they're drinkin. They won't work a regular job. Jarvey took the horses and put 'em on my place, to keep 'em out of harm's way. Drunks was lobbin bottles at 'em.'

'And were they horsemen, these very dark Irish?'

'Well there's one over there now. Ask him. MacEwe o' The Hole did his stockwork on foot, always usin, to draft 'em, a hazel cane singed in a Midsummer's Eve fire. Too sheer for horses, down there. Dad said he always went barefoot, and often stark naked, in winter.'

'Good God!'

'He was from Connaught.'

'I forget.'

'Adam!'

'Yes, Joe?'

'You goin over the road?'

'Soon's I get this beetroot in this barrow.'

'Tell Shorn to extinguish that cigarette and have him move the indicator needle on the fire danger board outside the fire shed from "Moderate" to "Extreme".'

Billy sits next to Jarvey, who is leaning against the headstone of McGlynn, Cavan County.

'Don't let them get to you, Jarvey,' says Billy. 'They'll break your heart if you let them. We know what you've achieved here, for you never picked up one wrong stone. Anyone holy or lovely or lucky or clever or rich, they destroy them, and

God help you, if you're holy and clever as well, or lovely and wealthy. Mean, bitter little people here, with mean, bitter little natures. Don't let them get to you, Jarvey. I won't have them destroyin you. I won't have them destroyin you, as they destroyed my poor stepfather. What you thinkin, Jarvey?'

'I'm thinkin I'm in Fairyland,' says Jarvey. 'I'm thinkin I'm in the Land of the Ever Young. For when it is winter here, Billy, it is summer in the land where I come from. And when it is night here, it is day there. And when it is day there, it is night here. And when it is summer here, it is winter there.'

'You won't go back to Killarney? You won't leave me here all alone?'

'I can't go back to Killarney, Billy. I'm gettin too old for the buildin work and I lost me jauntin-car licence. I had horse-drawn hackney-carriage licence t'irty-one from Killarney National Park, but old man Doyle, who owns the four jauntin cars, he took it from me, Billy. Because an American said I was rude, and reported me to the Bord Failte. But all I said was I don't see how Americans can be Irish, when there's t'ree hundred million Americans and only t'ree million Irish. Oh, I miss the sound o' the craws and the smell o' the horseshite on the rawds, but I'm glad I come to the New Country, Billy. It's a fairyland to me. And Mary's with me here. You saw Her guidin my hand. Oh yes, I feel a vocation here. And I don't want to pull down the fane, though Shorn and Adam say I must.'

'Shorn too?'

'Oh yes. Shorn come to me in the slab hut and said this hill is a sacred place to him, and that all we shall build is to come down in the cause of reconciliation. But I think I am meant to be priest of Crooked Corner. There's room for a good five or six in that fane.'

'Jarvey! No! It's a dead-end job!'

'Did you see what your father wrote? On the plate? *Omne in praecipiti vitium stetit*, you can't have your wife and your inside woman too. I mean to go talkin with Father Carney, soon's we get the tower up. He's lost his driver's licence, so we have that in common. He'll know what to do, I'm sure. Has World Wide said any more to you about the bluestone for the tower roof, Billy? We're all but out of sandstones.'

'He means to demolish Knocklofty lock-up.'

'Why you cryin, Billy? Rejoice!'

'How can I rejoice, Jarvey? I was hopin we might listen, some day, to the Three Tenors live in concert.'

'Don't feel sad, Billy. Here's an idea may cheer you. What say we snatch, from our labours, a moment of silence to honour the Virgin? You fetch the others while I think of somethin to say. Is that not a brilliant idea?'

Well Billy thinks not, but he slouches off to do as he has been bidden. He rounds up World Wide, Paddy, Joe, Shorn, Keyring and Adam, but the others won't come, and the very dark Irish lawyer, who's been talking with Shorn, has driven all the way back to his small terracehouse in south Sydney. He has been here to tell Shorn there's a Gundangara Native Title claim on Shorn's own place which, like Killaarney, being pastoral leasehold, is subject to such a claim.

'Why the driptorch?' inquires World Wide of his errant deputy, Keyring. Shorn and Keyring carry a driptorch in one hand, a longneck in the other. 'Should any fire break out now you'd be fightin defensively. Eh, Joe?'

'We'd need to wait for night to fall before we'd burn a break. We'd confine ourselves, as you say, during daylight hours, to observation. But if the wind drops, Duncan, we could mount an indirect attack on any fire. So leave the boys holdin their torches.'

'They're drunk, Joe. Can't you smell it? Can't you smell their breath?'

'We get our biggest fires Midsummer's Day, and we always fight those fires dehydrated.'

'Yes, but that's different. That can't be helped. You can't relax, on Christmas Day, unless you've had five inches. Why must we have our Festive Season in the middle of the bloody summer? Why can't we have Christmas in winter? Just jokin. I don't trust this pair, Joe. Shorn's been ravin on to me about the damage that cloven hooves inflict upon our soils. He wants to go back to firestick farmin! Wants to hunt 'roos and sell 'em to Sainsbury's.'

'Pray for rain. Bubba! You go first, go on. You got your rosary out. That's unless our Mister Deputy Mayor wants to go first.'

'Age before Beauty. I've no more chance of gettin in there than a camel through the eye of a needle, Joe. I own a structure I cannot enter. That's a Japanese-sized door. We need a PA.'

'Duncan! Give us a hand with Paddy.'

Patrick lays down his horn-handled stick and submits, with a sigh, to indignities. The way his back is Y-chromosome bent, he has to be twisted to enter, but his broad old shoulders won't fit. With Adam shoving, World Wide twisting and Billy pulling from within, they contrive to jam his body in the door, and part strangle him with his own rosary.

All watch as, wincing, he grasps the green-painted stone in his crippled old hands, then slowly, koala-bear-like, releases himself, falling heavily down.

All watch, unbelieving, as he stands upright, to his full and former height of six foot two. And all watch as he kneads his hands, and wiggles and straightens his old, bent fingers.

'Joe,' he says, 'look here, Joseph. I'm cured of me arthritis. It's a miracle.'

17

Miracles, regrettably, invariably pass, the more rapidly the newer the country, and life is always permitted to revert, in the saintless lands, to its normal dreary muddle. Having restored Patrick to his former height, the fane, it seems, has served its purpose.

'Well,' says Joseph, as dawn breaks in the form of a dust storm and a fiery sky, 'this is the first time we ever saw extreme fire danger in the month of August. It's enough to make me doubt that when it is summer there, it is winter here. Shorn!'

'What ho.'

'Get the binoculars out of the tanker and hop up on that half-built round tower and take a look at the lie of the land. Check for smoke.'

'Shorn will be busy today,' explains Adam, who just put old Patrick to bed with the aid of some German Valium syrup, given him by Dud Leahey at the Dude Rancher Lodge. With luck, Paddy will sleep the weekend through, not wander round extolling the miracle, so upsetting the Reunion.

'Shorn has a job tomorrow, Joe. He needs to think. He wants to collect his resources.'

'Who says I want to be involved?' says Blue. 'Who says I wanta cook for Gubs?'

'I do,' says Adam, 'for it's plain to me, you've a spiritual connection with this land goes beyond what I could hope to comprehend. True, you may not look that black and you may not always act that black, but it's my guess you've a black heart, Shorn. Would I be right? Yes, I thought as much. You will enjoy Council backing for any land claim you wish to pose, but posit the effect of a word in the ear of a well-regaled Dicky Shillinsworth, mate.'

'Dicky comin?'

'Royal Commissioner Shillinsworth has accepted our invitation. So you'd be caterin to two Old Boy signatories to that letter, callin on our Governor-General, that Livin National Treasure of a Moss Vale horse-breeder, not to extinguish Native Title, Dicky and Dud. The decision, of course, is yours, but I know what I'd do in your position. I'd honour my commitment.'

'Fire-fightin comes first.'

'Shut it, Joe, you has-been! I suppose you're about to tell Shorn and me that Rupert owns the paper in which the letter was printed? Save your breath. I know, had you your way, you'd put a stop to the spiritual advancement of this multicultural nation, but you've been outvoted on the seaboards.'

'Yes and aren't I always.'

'Not to worry, Joe. Your interests will be attended to, soon as we've attended to Shorn's, which will be some time after Sydney Two Thousand.'

'I'll just get up there for a quick look, Adam.'

'Christ Almighty, can't Duncan do it? He's actin captain of a big brigade where yours is a laughin stock. I don't want you tumblin down and breakin your crown, Shorn.'

'What do you mean, "laughin stock"?'

'Never mind. You will do the caterin, won't ya, Shorn?'

'Appears I 'ave no choice.'

'Thanks, mate. On ya, Cobber. Oh, you're all-important to us. We can't manage without ya. We want to avoid, at all costs, those apricot and lemon thyme glazes with the champagne and raspberry veloutés. That's just what they're expectin.'

In the end, it is Jarvey climbs the incompleted tower, and he's there to hand the binoculars to Billy, who would, it is reasoned, have the sharpest eyes about and Billy's already up there.

'Look west, Billy,' shouts Joe, from ground level. 'Tell us what you can see.'

'Fog hangin over Blanket Flat. Or it looks like a fog.'

'That's normal. What about Mount Nerong, boy? Take a particular note of The Hole, for the fuel loadin there is very heavy. I was hopin to get a burn in.'

'Can't . . . no, wait a bit, Joe. I do see movement there. Or thereabouts.'

'Smoke?'

'No.'

'Fire?'

'Don't think so. Could be dust.'

'Hmm.'

'Wait a bit. Somethin movin. Bit of movement on the ground. Not so far as The Hole, though. Goin towards The Hole, though. Looks like somethin black with a lot of white, or white with a bit of black.'

'Christ, it's them Friesian steers,' says Adam.

'Why is my brigade a laughin stock?' inquires Shorn.

'Oh, because, for example, when you went to the Wolga Hill fire, Shorn, you was told, by Forward Command, to switch from channel forty-one to channel forty-two. Which you never done.'

'Bullshit!'

By nine a.m. Crooked Corner One, under the command of World Wide Webb, with a crew, none wearing yellow overalls, of Billy Minogue, Keyring MacHugh and Tampon MacHugh, crosses the grid, heading off towards The Hole, Mount Nerong, with Keyring driving, Tampon, Red Bullock deputy, one of those wiry, olive-skinned men, with long brown hair and a long brown beard and thick lenses in his spectacles, poring over the appropriate one in twenty-five thousand topographic map. Tampon has on his knee the Fullerton map, the Arkstone map, the Shooters Hill map, the Burraga map, the Bindook map and the Gurnang map, none laminated. All are greasy, dog-eared, torn, tea-stained, covered in holes and arcs, but the red contour lines across the parish where lies The Hole resemble a thumb print. No way would you drive a vehicle down The Hole, not even the redoubtable Studebaker six-wheel drive from neighbouring Wingecarribee Shire, which lives the other end of Limeburners Lane, a fire trail frequented by hoons on trail bikes, all of them made in Japan.

Once the Killaarney oak grove is cleared, and having passed the cattleyard, the crew strikes a paddock ploughed up for oats, but never actually sown down, whereon the topsoil is blowing off like sand from a sand-dune in the Simpson Desert.

'Can't see a thing now,' reports Keyring. 'Where's that gate gone, Cuz?'

'Never mind yer gate,' replies World Wide. 'I got a compass here and a pair o' bolt cutters.'

'Why are we out here at all,' says Billy, 'when Jarvey needs our assistance?'

'I wanta check out The Hole,' says World Wide. 'Can't get out there any more. Gurney's went and put locked gates all across the access roads. And o' course, we have the Mystery of the Missin Friesian Steers. Shorn reckons they're out this way.'

'If we get a lightning strike,' adds Keyring, 'this is where they always hit us. Dry storms like dry forests.'

'We fear the wet kisses of Jupiter. If them steers is on Killaarney,' says Tampon, 'they wasn't even stolen. They're ours.'

'No road where they're goin. Anyway, they wouldn't go there of their own accord. Look at the feed around that mansion! You saw the clover flowerin. If you had a choice between clover and hop bitter pea, what would you eat? How far you reckon they went here, Billy? Could you give an estimate of the distance?'

But it's hard to estimate distance here and Billy knows better than to guess, so they drive along, bouncing down a compass setting, losing a McLeod tool here, a foam branch there, with World Wide tearing down fences they encounter, until they're descending the rugged terrain so slow they'd be better off walking.

'Leave her here, Keyring. Just turn her round. Remember O'Mara, for Chrissake. Gotta be somewhere about here. Mike Hock used to come out here, Billy. This is before your time. Cut all his big strainer posts here. Red ironbark down here. Only grows on shit-poor soils. Well, I reckon our black boys wanta check out the land of their Spirit Ancestor, while I'd quite like to see The Hole again. Used to be some interestin trees there. Bark like cocopops. You wanta check for signs o' Mike Hock? Or would you rather moon over Jarvey Foley?'

'We should be helping him. You know that.'

'We will. We will be helpin him. We'll finish that fane, weather permittin, if I have to demolish me own home. We won't be long here. Got the map there, Tamps?'

'Hey!' Keyring found a fresh meadow muffin. It would normally be covered in flies, but the flies, today, are gathered in cool, dark premises, houses and churches. If fire breaks out they sip, in their thirst, the sweat from fire-fighters' faces. By the end of the day, hands black as coal, fire-fighters cease to brush them off.

'Well done, mate! Fresh steershit. Gissa look at that map. Is there a dam? Adam put half a tank on the persimmon tree. We need to fill up. Look for a square blue dot on the map. I know it ain't easy. Whoever is usin a protractor here oughta use a pencil not a blue pen.'

'That'd be Blue.'

'Wanta know somepin? I reckon he's leadin you darkies astray, turnin yez into stereotypes. Can't yez see it? And Jarvey reckons he wants our fane demolished. Next thing you know, he'll want an apology! Well, he's not gettin one.'

'We're gonna lose Joe on the mobile, when we down The Hole.'

'We won't be goin down The Hole, mate. Too steep.'

'There's yer dam,' says Tampon, indicating a square blue dot with an oil-dark nail.

'Jeez, you got good eyes, Tampon, and filthy fingernails. So this must be that hill. So this is where we are now. I reckon if they're goin down that way, they're gotta be drinkin at this tank. I make this creek here three hundred metres down the hill and it's probly dry. He won't be takin 'em down there. Only movin 'em a bit each day, if he's been on the track a week. I reckon they're somewhere about.'

'Who is he?'

'Dunno, Billy. That's what we must ascertain. See, no white

man ever come out this way.'

'Except Mike Hock.'

'Except Mike Hock.'

'Except Mike Hock and MacEwe o' The Hole.'

'That's it,' says Adam to Joe. 'I'm off. Gotta get glazin me platters. Soon as Jarvey takes delivery of the bluestone, which should be here any moment, I want an assurance you will ring me on my mobile, so's I can get straight back out here, to pick up Shorn and take him in. I expect most of the lads will be arrivin today. Shorn!'

'What ho.'

'Hear what I just said? I need to visit Kerry, to get an undertaking regardin the stained-glass windows for the fane, and then we're goin in to Ballymeaner, just you and me. You order them sesame seed buns?'

'Adam, tell Joe I see smoke.'

'What? Oh Christ, that's all we needed. Where?'

'Blanket Flat.'

'That can't be right. We never have fire on Blanket Flat. But if it's true, bloody hell. That's koala habitat! Joe! Where are ya?'

'Seein if a leaf from the bottom of this litter can be angled upward and still burn from the tip.'

'Shorn got a fire. Put out an alert. Get onto Fire Control. Above Blanket Flat is a forest with a whole bunch of long-term strategic significance to our shire. I want Headquarters Brigade out there and Ballymeaner Townies. Copy that?'

'Looks like a number of fires on that Flat. They're by the esses on Tubbercurry Road.'

'This could be serious. Sweep your binoculars three sixty, Shorn,' says Joe. 'Any sign o' Crooked Corner One? I can't raise 'm on the mobile. Blanket Flat is all ti tree. It'll burn like a kerosene wick.'

'I do see a truck, creatin a dust storm, headin out from Knocklofty, Joe.'

'That'll be Jarvey's bluestone,' says Adam. 'Not a moment too soon. Jarvey! We've a crisis on our hands here. This'll be a learnin experience for you. Study us, how we deal with it.'

'I'm gettin Duncan on the mobile,' says Joe. 'I can't make out what he's sayin, but I'll get him to move to the Blanket Flat, offloadin Billy on the way. Grid reference? Wait a bit. He's comin through! What's that you say, Dunc? Tell Adam you found the cattle, unattended but yarded? Roger Willco.'

'Here come that truck Shorn just seen. What's that truck got on? Don't look to me like bluestone. Yes, I heard ya, Joe, but cattle may have to stay on hold. We gotta think wildlife.'

'Duncan wants a word, Adam. He sounds a bit upset.'

'Go to your house, Shorn. See what the truckdriver wants. He's parked outside your place. Duncan? What's your problem. Serious? Wow. Good God. You don't say. Yes, well I understand how you must feel, but . . . No, I don't think it was an honest thing to have . . . Duncan, can you get it in your thick head there's a fire on Blanket Flat? First one in memory. Get out there. Save the wet forest, please. Them gums is fire sensitive. So you're makin for Tubbercurry Road. That's the *old* Tubbercurry Road. The dirt road. Yes, I'll tell Kerry you've torn down her fences and emptied her dams and tanks. Please make haste.'

'Roger Willco is drivin the truck, Adam.'

'Yes, I believe you're right, Joe. That's his Hino. What's goin on down there? Shorn is signin up for somepin.'

'Shorn don't like Roger. Reckons when he had the win, Roger sent him a card of con-gratulation, with nothin but the printed message, signed "Roger Willco". Too tired to write a few words of praise. I need Shorn up the tower, Adam.'

'Jarvey, could you climb the tower for us, please?'

'Might wait for me stawn, Adam. What's upset World Wide? He's me foreman on site.'

'I guess I shall have to climb up, Deputy Mayor though I may be. Thanks. They should have taken the ladder on the tanker, in case they need to rescue bears. I guess Headquarters tanker has one. Jaysus! I see smoke, from the second rung! Thick, black pulsin smoke, and the flames on top of the smoke! God help our poor wildlife. Oh, there's been a contretemps, Jarvey. Turns out Billy's gender confused. We can all feel betrayed, but Duncan, as you may imagine, is distraught. They staked out the bush yards where them Friesian steers is apparently bailed up, and Billy had to go relieve himself, and turns out he's a drip dry not a flip dry. He's a she. What's that comin off that truck, Joe? What's that bottle they're swiggin at, Jarvey? You make it out?'

'Tell 'em not to throw bottles in the grass, Adam, for that's what starts these roadside fires.'

'Puligny-Montrachet.'

'Come again, Jarvey?'

'Puligny-Montrachet. T'at's what's written on t'e sides of t'e crates comin off t'e truck, Adam. Puligny-Montrachet.'

World Wide has taken over driving the Blitz, in order to occupy his hands. In irate silence, the set of his moustaches implying he's bent on revenge for the serve he is sure to receive from Carol when she learns his mate was a teenage girl, World Wide thrashes the Blitz through the bushes, taking out iron-barks the thickness of his thighs. Old Tubbercurry Road, with stone lips might test out Dud's new Hummer (a prestige vehicle, albeit one Blue could leave at the lights in his Haitch Ar), ends in the Wilderness on what is described on the map as a helicopter pad. You wouldn't land a helicopter there, even the tiny Forestry Squirrel. Last slashed before gazetting and declaration of the National Park, it commands, or did, a look-down on The Hole, which nowdays intruders are discouraged from viewing by means of 'Private Property' signs and locked gates on Killaarney. The old road joins the new just before the Crooked Corner turn-off, where World Wide intends leaving Billy, committing the gender-confused youth to finding his own way home. Billy is sobbing and asking himself why he chose this moment to expose the blunder, since at Support Group meetings he always claimed he would rather burst his bladder. It was, as he is bound to report to the Support Group, with a sense of inevitability, he watched the twitching of World Wide's ziff as World Wide, puzzled by the sound he'd heard, entered the scrub to find a mate using a wrong nozzle setting on the hose branch.

143

Both MacHughs stare impassively forward, in the manner of men who don't wish to be involved.

'Effin *c* of a thing!' The Blitz has no synchro and World Wide is often obliged to engage reverse before it will go into first gear. He ploughs, at max revs, backwards through the wattles, his head and right elbow out the non-fireproof window, as he feels the grip of Keyring's hand upon his non-sword arm.

A large, riderless motor cycle, canary yellow and grey, with chrome furbelow and hand-tooled leather saddlebags, hurtles through the scrub towards them. At the last moment, it veers aside as if to avert collision, and the crew observe it cruising towards The Hole, till it is lost to their view.

'Now there's a well-balanced motor cycle.'

'Oh, they'll go for miles like that. Strong-willed. Heritage Springer. Where are we on this map? Where's this road from here, Tamps? Gotta be up that hill ahead.'

'Think someone's fallen off it?'

'I think that very likely.'

'Better tell Joe.'

'No, don't bother, mate. I know who owns that bike.'

'Madness! Should never take a belt drive on the dirt. I might see if I could track it. Let me out!'

'No! Stay where you are, Keyring. There's a fire on Blanket Flat and we may need to render assistance to the rider. Let's go, boys! Sorry. Shouldn't be sexist. Boys and girls.'

'I *am* a boy! It's just I was born within this girl's body!'

'Ah! *Now* we understand.'

'Puligny-Montrachet,' says Adam, cradling a bottle with affection. Residual long grassers have decimated one crate by the time he arrives on the scene. He is, however, delighted to find Blue MacEwe quite sober and discussing finer aspects of the onion price with Willco.

'No card or nothin here, Rodge? No transcript? No matter. I recognise the label. Billy Bob's favourite tipple. Dud must have taken it on himself to provide refreshment for our function. How sweet. One, two . . . Good

God, there's three bottles here for each guest.'

'Hope this don't mean Dud's not comin.'

'What makes you say that, Shorn? He'll be here. Follow me, Rodge. This lot's goin back to town. We'll stash it in Stillorgan. Shorn!'

'What ho.'

'You happy for me to do the glazin? Readin the glazin/firin notes Mike made in his logbook, we only need a couple of hours at thirteen hundred degrees. Take about ten hours to heat the kiln, if we want 'em oxidised all the way up, so we don't have to do nothin fancy with the burners. I found a bucket of clear glaze, next to the *kaki* and *tenmoku* glazes, and cobalt carbonate comes up a treat, under a clear glaze. Once I locate the appropriate cones, it's . . . Hell, what's up now?'

'Joe's on the mobile, Adam.'

'Bloody old pest. Wonder what happened to that bluestone? Council tipper should be here by this. I must ask Molly to this function, Shorn. What a strain to produce a weirdo don't know whether he's Arthur or Martha. Oh *no*! The *gas*, Shorn! Christ, I just remembered. We're out of gas at the pottery. I forgot to order it in. Who's got me mobile?'

'Settle down, Adam. You're gettin flustered. More haste less speed.'

'Yes, you're right. I'm very tired. I need some disco biscuits. I think I'm losin it, Shorn. I just had a terrible feeling then. I felt I was over Australia. "Dim Dim" Dud Leahey calls our New Country. I'll get straight onto that gas.'

'Let me do it for ya, Ad. I gotta go in anyway.'

18

Adam receives the call, via Joe, to come inspect two bodies, lying, not so far apart, on the old Tubbercurry Road. One proves to be that of Harley Christian, who wasn't wearing a helmet, the other that of the Gucci 'roo, struck by the cycle and transfixed by a spear. When Adam turns up in the Sierra, World Wide is still pacing about. He thinks he knows what happened.

'I couldn't say why he was out here, Ad. But his motor cycle went down The Hole. He hit the 'roo, cause there's where they collided. See? Right there.'

'Why'd you remove the jacket and the spear?'

'I thought I might wear the jacket to the function, seein as I did all the work on yer fane. Give Carol a night out.'

'Oh, all right. But the jacket has a hole in it, Duncan, where the spear went through the lapel.'

'I'll have Carol mend it.'

'Please do. You're not to lower the tone of my Reunion. So they actually carry spears on these motor cycles. Good God. What next. He speared the 'roo from this cycle, losin control of the cycle as he did. Is that what happened?'

'No. I think the 'roo was already wearin the spear when first they met. I'd say they found 'emselves goin the opposite way down the same track. Someone else speared that 'roo.'

'And who could that have been? Do we have the spear?'

'Got the MacHugh boys checkin it out.'

'They'd know about as much about spears as you or I would, Duncan.'

'They have an incentive to learn, now they got the Native Title claim on Killaarney. 'Cordin to Shorn, they're gonna go back to huntin 'roos, for the export trade. Well I'd say the bloke who stole them cattle speared the 'roo as well, but whether he fancied the meat or the coat or both, I couldn't tell ya.'

'Had to be one o' them very dark Irish. Can't we nab him, Duncan?'

'Who's gonna stake out his yards, Ad, if we're occupied with the fane and the Reunion? Cattle be gone by Mondey. I emptied that dam. Give the bitter pea a drink.'

'I see. I take your point. Can't get them dark MacHughs to do it?'

'They're as white as ghosts. Reckon as only a spirit 'roo'd wear a man's coat. Tampon says the spear belongs to old man MacEwe, the Spirit o' the Hole.'

'God, I hate superstition with a passion, but Pat mentioned him. Who *is* this Old Man MacEwe? I sedated Paddy and I want the situation here put on hold. Just till Mondey. I can't cope with another crisis now. Gotta get glazin. Where's the nearest bathtub, Duncan?'

'In that paddock over there.'

'And where's the nearest ice machine?'

'Ar come on, Adam. Ya can't do that!'

'Knocklofty Shell. No, I'm sorry. This situation is goin on hold. I accept full responsibility. You fetch that bathtub, put the body in, while I find a plug and some ice. Fact is, you better get two bathtubs, Duncan. One for the kangaroo. Billy, you want a lift back to town? Save you walkin.'

'I'm helpin Jarvey on the fane.'

'No, you're not. I won't have a woman upset him. You're goin home to your pub. You could get a few in the bar, this arvo. Tonic drinkers. Big spenders. Duncan, when you got them bathtubs off, I want you fightin that fire. I have platters I must glaze, and rolls I need to order in, and stained-glass windows I must see about. God, it's a bummer, this multi-taskin. I swear to Christ I shall never convene another Pat's School Reunion. Get in, Billy. What's your real name then?'

'Billy.'

'I wish I could give ya some counsellin, son, but I've too much on me platter.'

19

Dropping Billy in Knocklofty, where the Union Jack flies high on the flagpole at the Bowling Club and the house opposite, Ad heads back out with plugs and ice. Metal-roofed bluestone cottages, built in the nineteen twenties, line Ballymeaner Road, but craftshops often stand empty for months, awaiting a propitious astrological moment. There are homes that belong to old ladies here, scrupulously clean but dangerously unsound, and the newer homes are fibro-tile constructions, all from the nineteen fifties, most boasting a loading ramp and at least one shed of earlier vintage. No money hereabouts, but sure is wood aplenty and a man with nothing else to do can always be ordered to cut some.

Mud-spattered utes, pick-ups, Holden and Ford, stand, nose to kerb, outside Minogue's. All have collie dogs on the tray and Billy, though he knows they use their tongues for toilet paper, fondles every one. There has been no decent rain here in years, no water to wash a vehicle, but see the gleaming Range Rover, parked beside the utilities. Drought, interest rates and the mortgage make hard work for Molly Minogue, but thank Christ for the licence to vend fermented and spirituous liquors.

Billy finds the cellar trapdoor open and Mum struggling with a keg.

'That you, Billy? Oh, I'm tired of you I am. Where the hell have you been up to?'

'Told ya, Mum. I bin helpin a friend build a church in the countryside.'

'Helpin build a church. You haven't taken your 'ormones in a week. God, they cost enough. Now when you've taken your 'ormones, Boy, I want you to wash them glasses and clean the men's loo, please. It's gettin dirty.'

'But, Mum, if I can't be sure any more if I . . .'

'That's enough! That's enough o' that. Have a thought o' poor Mike Hock. One of your friends was here, earlier in the day, lookin for you, Billy.'

'Who, Mum?'

'Don't recall the name, although it sounded most unlikely. And for all his efforts, you could see he was born a woman. He had a bald head and ear-rings, like them Newtown girls.'

Molly Minogue is a plump, short woman with grey hair and a fierce temper, a deep voice and a smoker's laugh that ends in a raucous cough. Not greedy, for when she thinks a punter has had a skinful she orders him out. Hardly more than forty, she wears a pair of gold-rimmed glasses with a pair of Nike joggers, size twelve, and a blue jumpsuit, and smells of cognac. Card machines ('cardies') and poker machines ('pokies') and Skychannel have all been recently installed here, and the surreptitious tones of male badinage have yielded, as they needs must, to the glockenspiel peel. A dental ceramicist from Picnic Point with a public servant from Swinger Hill drink, to the soundtrack of a Disney animation, a can each of draught Guinness, laughing uproariously over a copy of the *Tubbercurry Examiner*. Here is the first of the urban influx of Pat's Old Boys, Class of Sixty-One, though the Range Rover, from which they have descended, looks oddly out of place in the New Country.

Billy collects ashtrays. The police turn a blind eye to the fact he's too young to work here, by law. Adam wouldn't stop in Crooked Corner, but sped straight through to Knocklofty, compelling Billy to stare out the window at Jarvey, who struggles manfully on to complete the tower. To Billy's concern, Jarvey, up the ladder, descends with a piece of bluestone on his arm, as though he had tried to slot it in and found it wouldn't fit.

The letter! Billy reaches in his pocket, but the letter he wrote Jarvey has gone. Billy rushes to his room and plays his favourite compact disc of the Three Tenors. He doesn't take his hormones. The logic of taking hormones is to prevent onset of puberty, pending the forthcoming hysterectomy and dual masectomy in Utrecht. But Billy doesn't know whether Jarvey would like him taking the hormones. Perhaps he had better let Jarvey decide, should he persist with the hormones. He won't be quite so strong a lad, if he doesn't take the hormones.

In the meantime, Jarvey needs Billy's help. And Billy loves Jarvey, so he does. So Billy descends the fire escape adjoining the old stone pub and walks out of town towards the House of Prayer, his right arm extended like Christ's on the Cross. As he reasons, with all that traffic about, he has the chance of a lift.

Adam heads back with plugs and ice, obliged to pass through Crooked Corner, and scarcely glancing at the Fane of St Fiacre, Version for the Twenty-First Century. He also avoids old Joe, who's out on the blacktop, waving him down, but notes, approvingly, the Haitch Ar missing. Swinging right at the golden elms, he heads up the drive to Killaarney.

Kerry's not there, so he leaves a note, asking her to ring him on his mobile. On the way out Ad's egress is blocked at the grid by Jarvey Foley.

'This better be urgent, Jarvey, because if it's about that fane . . .'

'It's about that fire, Adam.'

'The fire! But I thought the bloody fire would be out!'

'I see it burnin from where I work.'

'Good God Almighty, can't anyone do anything right around here? Is it like this in Ireland? Thank Christ for the USA. Who's monitorin that fire?'

'Joe is half-way up the ladder, observin.'

'I better speak with him. Blast!'

'Joseph,' says Adam, thinking of the bodies in the heat, 'is that fire not under control yet?'

'Ballymeaner pagers never went off and I don't blame the FCO. Tubbercurry pagers went off instead, but no one home in Tubbercurry. Only crew out there's Duncan Webb. Check how he's doin, would you mind, Ad? Fierce little fire, but I think he pinched it out, before it made much of an inroad. Nowhere much it could go, once it burnt out all the ti tree and the gum. All that white smoke, I'd say that's the tussock on Killaarney. They can douse that with the wheel wetters.'

'Aren't you in radio contact?'

'They turned off the radio.'

'And you want me to go out there, trudgin over the blackened ground in me good moleskins.'

'Just see if they need help blackin out. If they do, ring the FCO.'

'I can't and I won't, Joe. I haven't the time. Get them long grassers downhill to do it. They're all deputies.'

'I did suggest that to Duncan, Adam, and that's when he turned off his radio. I was flankin with him, through Fire Control, but I can't converse with him now. He don't answer his mobile.'

'That fire has nowhere to go in my view. I wouldn't waste further time on it. Frankly, I think it's gonna rain, Joe. See the sky to the west?'

'If it don't, we could be in trouble, Adam. 'Cause a dry storm over a dry forest is just what we don't need.'

'If I made a list of all that I have that I don't need I'd be here all bloody day. Jarvey!'

'Yes, Adam.'

'How's it goin, mate?'

'Can't understand it, Adam. Seem to be losin me touch.'

'Stick with it. Your touch may return. Anyone seen Kerry Gurney?'

'Drove off towards Blanket Flat.'

'In the people mover?'

'On a tractor. Pullin a water tank in a cart.'

'Well there you go, Joe. Reinforcement. We'll have to hope for the best. I'm off. Our native animals are wonderfully intuitive. There's probably nothin to worry over.'

'I won't have a woman on my fire ground.'

'Joe, are we livin in the twentieth century here? I think you better come to this Reunion, just to see what this century's about before it's gone.'

* ★ ★

Having secured, in the tubs, which needed a scrub they never did get, the bodies, and having concealed them in crushed ice and camouflaged them best he could, Adam, painfully conscious he is starting to act irrationally, removes his fencing gloves and heads off towards Stillorgan. It's quickest via Crooked Corner, where he notes, despondently, Billy back on site and talking animatedly with Jarvey while measuring up stones, at the tower base. No sign of action on Shorn's, though, and Joe must have gone to bed.

In time, but only just, for a McBreakfast, and stimulated by the bottomless cup, Adam, mentally confecting excuses he may need to offer police if taken to task, delights to see the rain spitting on the Golden Arches he was instrumental in attracting.

May the heavens open! May the Old Boys review their New Country in all its verdant glory, with soft rain falling on green fields, as stipulated in the Irish blessing. In wet conditions a white Australian rejoices in this hinterland, and the sense it was all some dreadful mistake to have come here and remained here is dispelled.

In cooler weather MacEwe o' The Hole, a noted Biblical scholar, dons trousers, and sits to read his Good Book on a comfortable rock shelf.

Rain. You beauty. Adam puts down his coffee cup and returns the *Time* magazine to the rack, repudiating, with a glare, the *Tubbercurry Examiner*. *En route* to Stillorgan he rings his wife to authorise purchase of a new gown and when, finally, suitably besmocked, he takes up his first platter to immerse it in clear glaze, he notes that Shorn has done the right thing, seen to the gas, for the gauge on the large tank is reading close to ninety-five per cent full. Adam double-checks to make sure the burner valves are all closed.

Midday. A slight mist and a clear glaze dip on every platter, every goblet. All Adam has now to do is find a few pyrometric cones, which are bound to be hidden, pressed in their fire-clay wad, behind one of the crates of Puligny-Montrachet.

It passes over Ad's mind, as he stacks the stoneware in the kiln, he may well keep this pottery, as executor of Mike's estate. It is a soothing pastime and certainly calms the nerves. Adam smiles as he contemplates the prospect of Mister Justice Shillinsworth partaking of imported wines from a gorgeous hand-made goblet. Why, he'll think he's still at home.

The last item is in the kiln, the kiln door all but closed, when a woebegone, blackened figure appears, to the whiff of marihuana, by the annexe.

'Thought I'd find ya back here. How's it goin?'

'Fine. Good. Under control, I think. Mind where you're sittin.'

'I gotta sit down, mate. I'm exhausted!'

'We're all pretty tired, but it's gonna be worth it. They'll speak of this function for years to come. You didn't fight that fire in a Gucci coat? I'll shout yer dry-cleanin bill.'

'Thanks, mate. And thanks, too, for yer invitation to the dinner. Carol's wrapt.'

'She's a beautiful girl, that wife o' yours, Duncan. You wanta take better care of her. No, I do appreciate your assistance. I only hope Shorn is on top of our victuals. Seen him about?'

'He was at home, musterin the troops, when I went by just now. Ar Christ, what a schmoozle, that fire on Blanket Flat, Adam. We never get forest fires in August, this far south o' Sydney! What's goin on?'

'I just read in a magazine we're comin into a new Ice Age. They reckon the hottest summer we get is the one before the new Ice Age. Contemplate that Old Country without the Gulf Stream, Duncan. It's the same latitude as Newfoundland. You're cryin, boy. I see tears, under your Versace glasses. What's up?'

'Adam, you never seen more burnt koala bears in all yer days.'

Adam says nothing to this. Words would have insufficient legs. He walks towards the light, stares at the mist, then gives a New Country smile.

'Why? Can you tell me? I thought the tide was turnin for

this shire. Without bears, we have no future, Duncan. No bears, no Japanese.'

'Joe thought you might be concerned, so I brought 'em in.'

'What? In the Cortina?'

'No! To the Fane of St Fiacre. In the Blitz. It's cool and they're dehydrated.'

'But they don't drink water. They only eat gum leaves. How many burnt bears ya got?'

'Seventeen, with a couple of orphans. God, you wouldn't credit it, Ad. We found 'em curled up like wombats, in the hollows of the burnt-out trees. Bloody Ballymeaner Brigade never fronted. Waste o' resources, givin 'em that Cat One. We should have it in Knocklofty. Don't you remember O'Mara's funeral, when we was supposed to lead the parade, and bloody Ballymeaner Brigade pushed ahead of us? They wasn't even there!'

'I'm afraid that's beyond my control, Duncan. Speak to the man with the braid in the car with the driver. You know, I sniff a bob in this. There's Japanese'd give their eye-teeth, surely, for a chance of a holiday nursin burnt bears. I wonder is it not too late to have Beverley lookin into it?'

'Ar, they won't last the weekend. They wanta go on a drip. You oughta see their ears, poor bastards. They're all got burnt ears and paws.'

'Many dead?'

'Only two. Plus me 'roo and that Fed.'

'Well that's not so bad. Way I see it, that colony's the future of Yarrawongamullee. It's *vital* it survive! Make'm comfortable, Duncan. That hay, down in the slab hut. Put it back in the fane.'

'Yeah, Jarvey and Billy are on the job now, as regards the hay and chaff. But Joe thought you might have some lambs-wool fleeces, and we want a couple of teddy bears, too. You know. For the orphans to sit on?'

'Duncan, I never saw you more upset.'

'Oh, fire can be so *cruel*, Adam. I mean, O'Mara's sufferin was bad enough, but poor little bears don't understand *why*.'

'Think the press should be informed?'

'No. People'd want to see the bears pullin through. Right now, I'd say they're on the way out. I done all I could, but you're Deputy Mayor.'

'Thanks. I'll get straight onto it. Think you could mind this kiln for us? I just lit the four burners. You can watch the pyrometric cones through this spyhole. Don't let the temperature climb more than one twenty-five degrees an hour. When the last cone has drooped over, keep the temp steady on the pyrometer. Hold it steady a couple of hours. When you turn the gas off, the burners should go "plop plop plop". Mind you cover the burner ports with these scraps of fibro when you're finished. That will stop cold air rushin in.'

'Adam, I have a confession to make. The night Mike Hock died, I was in here.'

'Yes, I know you was. I figured that, from the way your vehicle was pointin next morning. You was comin back out. But he was already dead, Duncan, and the thing is, since he was already dead, what stopped you admittin you were here? Thanks for your candour, though, and thanks for sharing your feelins with me. We'll discuss it some other time. Right now, I'm going back to the agency, see what I have in the way of saline drips. Now be sure to let that kiln cool. We're cuttin it a bit fine. Don't ruin me firin, will ya. Your life won't be worth livin if you do.'

'As if it's worth livin now.'

'Well I am tryin to get you a job. That's what I'm about. All heart. Here's your instructions. The whole purpose of my Reunion is to get boys like you in a job. You have to accept you may have to change, but I'd say you was already changin, Duncan. I didn't think you had it in you, to show compassion for animals.'

'I know I could never work as a slaughterman again. But I wouldn't mind bein a zookeeper.'

'I'll bear that in mind.'

20

Contrary to Adam's expectations few Old Boys have, in fact, decided to make a weekend of it, but those who have will stay in one or another Ballymeaner motel. Even Old Boys with ageing parents, or parent, or locally living rels, will, understandably, opt for paid accommodation, because it is cheap. There is not one three-star, leave alone five-star, accommodation in Yarrawongamullee, for all Adam's agitations and exhortations to the likes of Best Western. The three Ballymeaner motels are family-operated, two-and-a-half-star affairs, with shower curtains that have seen brighter days, no room service, no telephone in the rooms, diminutive thread-bare pastel towels and a fridge, containing nothing but two sealed thimblefuls of longlife milk. Just to rough it again like this will prove an adventure in itself, but the lads won't be spending time in their rooms as once they would have done. The concave beds, chenille bedspreads, board-thin walls and incandescent bulbs will act as an anaphrodisiac on even those Old Boys blessed with young companions, for the squalid impulse that delights in being heard having sex belongs to some later generation that has grown up in an atmosphere of sexual licence inconceivable to the Generation of Sixty-One.

Ursula Mulcahy would do anything to increase her under-standing of the criminal law. A criminal lawyer, given to tossing her lank blonde hair over her judicious face, she stands, long legs apart, in a doorway, hands on the cheeks of her bejeaned bum. Young enough to have witnessed the rise of the supermodel as superstar, she had a portfolio herself, while doing Arts/Law, and modelled for an agent – no catwalk, catalogues only.

'I ought to ring the 'orspital, Dick. She ought to be in recovery by now.'

Ursula, British, older than she had seemed to the proprietress, though twenty years younger than Dick, is more concerned than Shillinsworth himself with Dick's mother's post-operative progress. Shillinsworth, Ursula's common-law companion, with whom she's been living in sin six months, is slouched on the bed near the window, curbing an impulse towards nostalgia. Though he specifically booked a double he's been given a room with twin beds, but then, tradition dictates that bride and groom should sleep separate the night before the wedding.

Dick opens the more opaque of two wall-length curtains before him and surveys, with professional dispassion, what at Paul's would be a quad. Beyond the snout of Ursula's yellow Subaru Impreza WRX are a scattering of bland commercial vehicles, all boasting possession of the Gold Card. Dick, a slight, trim-bodied man, who wears a red bib in the City to Surf, can feel the weight of Ursula's languid fingers, caressing his knotty neck. He raises, perfunctorily, a hand to join hers. It's worse here than he recalled.

'You're tired, Dicky. Want to sleep?'

'I can't sleep here, I shouldn't think.'

'Then I might ring the 'orspital. Can you see a phone?'

'There isn't one. You'll have to ask the lady. I'm sorry, Ursula. I've said my goodbyes more times than I care to count. I can't do it again.'

'You're sure you won't kip?'

'I might take a shower, although to get in the spirit of things, I ought to give each armpit a hit of deodorant, from a pressure-pak. They call that the truckies' shower.'

'Is this all we could get?'

'It's all there is. Ballymeaner hasn't changed. Care for some take-away? Could you go a battered saveloy, with potato scallops, in tomato sauce, washed down with lime cordial? Or would you prefer a cuppa? I see we've Lanchoo tea.'

'In tea-bags! No thank you! I've dandelion coffee. Someone should go and ring.'

'I thought I put the phone in your car. Sorry, darling.'

'It'll be fun to use a public phone. Do they still have buttons, I wonder?'

'I recall a phone inside a crêpe house here, and that phone certainly had buttons. And the crêpe house was downstairs, Ursula, with sandstock bricks, and exposed beams, and colonial chairs, and red serviettes.'

'Dicky, given what's on tomorrow, can you make the effort not to be so down?'

'If I am, it's not because of you, She-bear. It's coming to this place. You see, I avoid the New Country.'

'I didn't want to come here.'

'Ah yes, but you wanted privacy and this is one place we're assured of it. I was born here, and the fact I took silk and assumed horsehair means nothing to these people.'

'Then I'll close my eyes and think of Perpignon.'

'Yes, do, please.'

'Have you fucked anyone here, Richard?'

'I beg your pardon! What a thing to suggest.'

'Have you? You have, haven't you. Probably *her*.'

Through fear of disturbing the bears, Jarvey has ceased to work on the tower and Adam glumly notes the pile of bluestone by the base.

The miracle, which saw this fane, as it were, half build itself, would seem to have ceased the moment Jarvey heard the truth about Billy Minogue. From that point on he couldn't find the stone for which he sought. In future years, cedar trees, which sucker up a treat, will overshadow the unbuilt tower, concealing the particoloured folly below. For the moment, the transplant persimmon, all leafless in the mist, defies a Celtic graveyard for dominion over the fane. Adam, his arms laden with lambswool fleeces, stoops to inspect it.

Jarvey appears in the Romanesque porch, pushing open an extemporaneous curtain. From the curtain, a trail of hay leads downhill, over the road, to MacPeatricks'.

'Adam! How you keepin, are you well?'

'I'm fine, thank you, Jarvey. Just checkin me persimmon. It

seems to be doin all right here. They're Japanese, you know. On the platter, Mike Hock, for reasons we shall never understand, depicts it in the fall, but I don't suppose that would worry anyone, least of all Dud Leahey.'

'Have you coats for the bears then, Adam? Oh, it's a bad scene here.'

'I take your word on that. Your design excludes me.'

'It's not my design, Adam. I was ever usin the scene on the platter to guide me as I built.'

'How many bears you got? I got only seventeen fleeces.'

'Fifteen, but two have died. Is it only the two, Billy, have died? Adam's here, Billy.'

'I found ten saline drips. I need more. Billy! Billy Minogue!'

'She's afraid of you, Adam. So she is.'

'But why, when I'm a stranger to prejudice. Is Keyring MacHugh downhill there, do you know? Him or Webbie'd be the man to find the vein in a bear's arm. Do they bite? Are they sleepin?'

'Oh, they prefer darkness. We had to block off the windows and darken the fane to settle them. The fuss they make in the light, Adam. Listen to this!'

Jarvey opens the curtain and switches on a torch.

'Christ, is that them little *bears* makin that noise?'

'You wouldn't credit so small a creature could make so harsh a roar, Adam.'

'All males. Ooo, that's unsettled me. I gotta sit here a spell. Sound like the spirits of the damned in there. Have we done a wrong thing with this fane?'

'Once we had in the hay, we collected leaves off manna gums, Billy and me, in the Suzuki, for Joseph says the manna gums is what they like to eat. Only could find one or two unburnt boughs, in that whole forest. The manna gums is burnt. See, they don't drink, they just eat manna gums. But there's only unburnt orphans is eatin, Adam. Burnt adult bears is too distressed to eat. Could you not call a veterinary surgeon?'

'Well now, you're gonna find this hard to believe, but the last vet here, a Dutchman, just shut up shop. There's not the money for treatin pets, as what there is in Sydney, and farm animals are not worth gettin the vet to, Jarvey. We shoot 'em or fix 'em ourselves. I do quite a line in shotgun cartridges and veterinary pharmaceuticals.'

'Can I take the fleeces?'

'Go for it. I'll sit here a spell. Phew. The noise o' them burnt bears. Wow. I never heard nothin like it. Resonatin off them stones. Man ought to make a tape recordin and sell it to a DJ, for a sample.'

'It's a terrible noise, Adam. And the smell of the burnt fur.'

'Shockin. Dreadful. Yet here I am, enjoyin the best sunset in all Yarrawongamullee.'

'I'll just take them fleeces.'

'Make the bears more comfortable, Jarvey. Do. Saline packs in the Merc. Haven't stands, though. Have to improvise there. There you go, mate. T'ere's the key to me car. Greater love hath no man. Somepin comin to an end here, don't know what. Me, probly. Yet this gentle mist continues, like it did when O'Mara died. After the hottest winter's day anyone recalls. It's as well we're not superstitious. Billy!'

'Piss off! Fuck ya! Get some travel and sex inta ya! I'm not goin back to town with ya!'

'Don't you dare speak to me like that! Poor Molly. I blame Mike Hock for this.'

'Jarvey and me's to be married, Adam.'

'I wish I could give you some counsellin, son, but I've too much on me platter. Someone comin up the hill now. World Wide in that wreck of a Cortina. If he's here to tell us he's ruined that firin.'

Tada! World Wide holds out the window of his vehicle a platter and a goblet, both completed, grasping them with the rag he uses to check the oil in the engine.

'There you go, Adam! Glazed up and warm. Hey there, Billy Boy. How's it goin, Babe?'

'You mean to say', says Adam, 'you took them vessels from that kiln, pipin hot? You fired up the oven too fast, you fuckwit! And what did I say to you about duntin? Even so, look at that blue there, Jarvey. Thank heaven for the power of beauty, it's all that's keepin me goin. I feel refreshed. Duncan, would you go and see if you could find Shorn, please? Billy, we're gotta rig them drips above the bears somehow. The bleatin o' them bears had me snookered for a bit, but I'm over it. Now I gotta find Shorn. I'll ignore what Duncan's done. I just hope you shut that kiln door again!'

'Well o' course I did. Don't stress. Hey, we come close to gettin that tower up, ay! Well near enough was always good enough in the New Country.'

As Webbsta speaks, the platter in his hand dunts up, sundering the fane blueprint.

Blue's not home, so World Wide makes an inspection of the premises, noting mainly the blue videos, while Jarvey and Billy make some trips to and from MacPeatricks' to inspect junk for height. Adam, who hasn't yet visited Kerry, makes haste at once to do and he comes running up, waving his arms like a scarecrow in a cyclone, about the time that World Wide recalls he was meant to pick up from Preschool his youngest daughter, Iona, spelt, on her birth certificate, 'I own "er" '.

'Duncan, thank Christ I caught ya in time! Can't start me bloody Merc. Dead as a dodo.'

'Get in. Where are ya?'

'Parked under the trees on Killaarney. I wanted to speak to Kerry about that fire, but she wasn't home.'

'She's never 'ome. I pity her poor children.'

'Think someone lit that fire, Duncan?'

'Thought had crossed me mind. Get in.'

'Abos?'

'Could be.'

'Can't have these nomads in our brigades, lightin all these fires.'

'What's wrong with your Merc?'

'No idea. It's never given me trouble. Me Merc was the one thing in life I thought I could rely on. German built.'

'OK. Open the bonnet. Give it a crank. Hmm.'

'Shorn home?'

'Nup. They was headin off towards The Hole, the pyromaniacs. Wearin their shearin clobber. Give it a hit now.'

'Take the driptorches?'

'Nup. Wouldn't get a fire goin in this drizzle. Ya got no fuel here, Adam. Could be your injectors.'

'You're sure you understand diesel engines? That was your plate got broke, by the way. You'll be eatin off a white plate.'

'I don't care. Want a lift?'

'I'm not leavin 'er here! Not with these very dark Irish about. Give us a tow back to town.'

'Ah, fair crack o' the whip, Adam. It's twice the weight o' mine!'

'I'll pay ya petrol. Take me home. I'll pick up me wife's Bambino. We're not leavin 'er here.'

'I'll see what I got in the way o' chain. There's this. Not very long.'

'I don't like bein on Killaarney when Kerry's not about. She'll think I'm snoopin. Keep on the right side of her, she'd offer us money for the windows for the fane. There's a family history of philanthropy.'

'Can't you get that bloody fane outta your stupid head? It's over, mate. And what's yer Boy from Oz gonna think when he sees the place full o' burnt offerins?'

'He's a compassionate man, Dudley. Haven't you listened to his lyrics? He's a soft touch for any woman with a broken heart, I know that for a fact. You can't imagine he'd look on a burnt koala bear with indifference. Fact is, he's not too good himself. I think it's big of him to come.'

'Oh, he's big all right. Big bank balance. Big ego. Pity about the talent. There's bound to be a better chain than this at Shorn's. This has got a split link. Look.'

'Duncan, my time is at a premium. I gotta talk to Blenkinsop and Buzzacott.'

'All right. It's your funeral. You wanta keep an eye on that chain. Don't let it slacken, for Chrissake. Take yer corners wide. When we're goin down a hill I'll accelerate and don't you touch that brake, whatever you do.'

'You've done a bit of towin, have ya?'

'Always towin, Adam. Mate'll ring in at three a.m. sayin, Pick us up in Adelong. Drop it in fourth, once in a while, too, put some oil on the gears.'

'Sounds good. Should I put on me hazard lights?'

'No one'll see'm in the dust, but suit yourself.'

'What if a car comes the other way?'

'You will just have to deal with it, Adam. But if it's a copper, hit the anchors while I put pedal to the metal. That should snap the chain. S'posed to use an A bar to tow.'

'I'll give the Club a ring as we drive. Shorn leave a note sayin when he'd be back?'

'You're jokin.'

Joe can't wake Paddy. The sight of Patrick stretched to the full provokes some reminiscences of childhood. Scratching about the slab hut, Joe finds the bottle of port he was meaning to give to his auntie in Melbourne, and drinks it himself. Drains it down. As he drinks, he thinks of Fire as a Woman, and of all the fires he has fought, and of how they used fire to clear the land, in the days when blacks and the very-dark-indeed Irish were still about. At length he falls down dead drunk, more drunk than he's been since he come home from the war.

Through positioning devices from MacPeatricks' junkheap, sufficient to elevate the drips – a birdcage, a hat stand, a lowboy, a stove flue, a roll of deer netting and the like – Billy and Jarvey liberate themselves for the business of hydrating the bears. The bears have been tranquillised, using Blue MacEwe's air rifle fitted with pre-dipped darts, but Blue's long gone by the time World Wide drives by with Adam in tow, so Billy and Jarvey have to find the veins and fit the drips to the bears themselves. At least they can work in the light, as the tranquil bears no longer roar. Artificial torchlight. It's gone six p.m.

'I only seen this done once on TV,' says Billy, struggling with a needle. 'We should have asked Adam.'

'Do your best, Lad, for it's all you can do.'

'I'm wearing a dress to this dinner, Jarvey. Then you'll

please stop calling me "Lad". If you don't want to live with me as a man, have the decency to live with me as a woman. I won't let you go.'

'And did I hear you tellin Adam that we are to be married, Billy?'

'Well you said you want me to remain a girl!'

'I do, as you were born a girl and it seems to me we ought to respect the hand that we were dealt. Even so.'

'I won't stay one if you don't marry me. Be it on your conscience if I have a penis built.'

'I wouldn't have a penis built. They're more trouble than they're worth. And yours won't work properly, anyway. Have you thought this thing through, Billy?'

'Well of course I have. I'll have to be a "bottom", that's all that means, Jarvey. I want you to be my "top".'

'Well I don't want to be your top, whatever that may mean. I want to be a priest, Billy, or rather, it's not so much that I want to be a priest as that I am a priest, and must remain what I am.'

'Be an Anglican priest!'

'I beg your pardon. I'll pretend I didn't hear you say that. But you say it was here then, workin on the fane, you fell in love with me, Billy?'

'Yes.'

'Are you sure?'

'Yes. I fell in love with you, Jarvey, the moment the stone wouldn't fit upon the fane. See, I did so want to comfort you. That's when I fell in love with you. But already, I'd decided that you would be my top.'

'Oh, I wonder what that can mean. I must pray to St Fiacre. Good, you got the needle in. There's blood. Look! Well done.'

'Say you won't leave me, Jarvey. Say you won't break my heart.'

'I should need time to think it over. I'll discuss the matter with Father Carney.'

'You have till tomorrow night, midnight. Then I'll announce our engagement. Now where's the blanket for this bear?'

'Here's your lambswool blanket, Bear, and you know, it smells to me as though it is fresh off a sheep, Billy, and fine wool too.'

'There's no wool growin hereabout, with the OJD, Jarvey. These bears need medicines.'

'Adam's bringin 'em. He says he'll go round tonight with their pain-killers and antibiotics, if we hydrate'm. He'll get in through the tower. We shall have to restrain 'em, too, while they're tranquil, else they'll pull out these drips. I've soft-fencin tie wire here, Billy. Let's put this bear on his haybale no, tucked in his lambswool blanket, then I'll tie him with the wires. Oh, I wish he could see we're only tryin to help.'

'He's dyin, Jarvey.'

'Don't say it! Don't say these bears is dyin! I didn't build this fane, with the Virgin's help, to be a bear's place of resurrection!'

'Adam thinks that fire was deliberately lit.'

'Then I'd like to catch the man who lit it, Billy.'

'What would you do if you did?'

'I would first show him the consequence of his act, with a visit here, then I'd ask him to pray to the Blessed Virgin for reconciliation. We've a great many fire-setters where I'm from. They find it hard to get accommodation, so they sleep rough in the fields, Billy. I do hear tell they're always very well-behaved in gaols.'

'And why do they do it?'

' 'Tis the way they get their sexual pleasures. Here's a sturdy bear! He got a nose, look, pink as a horse.'

'Mary built the fane for the bears, Jarvey, to save this district. She don't want you as a priest.'

'I wouldn't mind trainin horses to pull fiacres, I suppose. I could always, if I must, train a horse to pull a fiacre.'

'You see? We could be happy, Jarvey! Did you ever kiss a girl?'

'I did! If you cannot kiss a girl then you should never be a priest, for it wouldn't mean a thing to the Virgin.'

'Kiss me.'

'All right.'

Ursula's late-model WRX has a factory-fitted immobiliser. An earlier model, lacking the device, is widely known as the 'stolen generation', following admission from State Police their V8 pursuit cars cannot catch it. A fraction of the price, but almost as quick off the mark as a Porsche 911, the Subaru Impreza WRX has quickly become the very dark Irish ram-raiders' vehicle of choice. It is fast, inconspicuous and has a snout well-suited to smashing plate glass. Contracted to remove, from a menswear store, some quantity of specified designer labels, the Sydney ram-raider commences his task by stealing a Turbo Impreza. More rally-bred than thoroughbred, laborious in traffic, she comes into her own when fleeing police, or fanging, as now, down a country road unencumbered by traffic.

Shillinsworth winces as Ursula enters a corner with all four wheels in a drift. He is obliged to raise his voice, too, as the radio, blasting forth the dubby triphop, is a four- if not a six-blocker, and the fine art of cabin noise isolation has yet to be mastered in the Orient. Dicky's fingers, where they grip the seats, are as white as the hair on his well-groomed head, and he cannot but lie, to his svelte companion, how he wishes he could enjoy the views. The tinted windows with which the car is fitted obscure his lateral vision, even in daylight, and how Ursula, who wears a pair of dark Versace glasses, can see at all he cannot tell, in this mist. But of course, if he could see the view it would sadden him, as it saddened him, always, on the school bus.

Ursula ignores him, as so often she does, when she feels his comments merit no response. Dicky is destined to lose his own mansion, as Ursula will certainly dispute the value, causing it to be disposed of by auction in the certain event of divorce.

'Carney,' says Shillinsworth, 'the priest in question, he doesn't answer the phone. Oh God, he was the terror of my life at school, though never so bad as Sister Patrick. This is the New Country I referred to. They've been hard hit by El Ninyos of late, and in the grip of some vile, tubercular sheep disease.

I think it's called "scrumpy" or is it "scrapie".'

'Speaking of scrumpy, why do New Zealand horses run so fast, Dick? Because they've seen what happened to the sheep.'

'Aha. Yes, very droll. Ursula, this is Tubbercurry Road, you've taken the wrong turning. You need to go back to where you turned and turn right, then right again. Might I suggest you slow down? This is not the Northern Territory.'

'Dicky, I'm a fast woman! Remember? Why can't you ring your mother?'

'She was thought to have been dying two years back. I can't keep saying goodbye.'

'Naughty Dicky forgot to pack a mobile.'

'I wonder if Mike Hock will come? I shouldn't think so. He was the great bully of the year. Tremendous bushman. We all so admired him.'

'I thought you were all lawyers?'

'There were some doctors among us. All those with any ambition left, with the sole exception of Mike Hock, and yet the soil here is arable. There ought to be a living to be made, but that, of course, would require initiative. Ursula, please slow down! If we should meet a wombat. They graze nocturnally, by the roads. I do so wish they wouldn't slash these roadsides.'

'Don't be such an old poofta.'

'Has there been a fire through here? It looks as though there has. You can't properly tell, despite these headlights, and foglights, and spotlights, with these tinted windows. They're illegal, you know, Ursula.'

'Good.'

All goes well, if hardly smoothly, on the tow back to town, till the 'Give Way' sign at the intersection with the old Red Bullock Road. Here World Wide, as he looks neither right nor left, should have gone straight through, but his nerve fails. Adam, owing to the inclination, has failed to keep the chain properly taut, and when World Wide, looking neither to left nor right, accelerates off, he jerks the Merc, snapping the chain at the split pin and leaving Adam to roll, slowly, into the path of an oncoming truck, on which nothing projects or reflects light.

Too stunned to put his stockboot to the pedal, Adam is hit towards the rear of the vehicle and spun completely arse about, before collecting a snowgum. The cattle truck – for such it proves to be – knowing better than to deviate off course, comes shuddering to a screeching, bellowing halt, whereupon the door flies open.

'Adam,' says the driver. 'You all right there, mate?'

'Shaken,' says Adam. 'Get goin. Go on! Clear out. Off you go now.'

'Sure you're OK?'

'Bit shaken. Who wouldn't be? Just as well I got a safe car here. No damage to your 'roo bar, I see. Someone pullin me. They'll be back, soon as even they notice I'm gone. You takin them Friesians to Cooma?'

'Well those were your instructions. As it happens, I was callin by at your place shortly, pick up some tailtags.'

'Been a late change in plans, James. Take'm to Killaarney.'

'Yeah? Quite sure you're OK now?'

'How many more bloody times? Go on, James, get out of here. Go on. Go to Killaarney. I'm tryin to protect you from the implication of the speed that you was doin, plus the fact you have no lights.'

'Fair go! You're the one in the wrong, Adam. You were s'posed to give way!'

'Put 'em up in the yard up by the house. I'll be there tonight. Were you aware you have no lights?'

'You asked me to protect meself. Adam. I'm just tryin to protect meself.'

The truck has gone by the time World Wide takes a look in his rear-vision mirror and hastens back to find Adam sitting beside the wreck of the Merc.

'Fark! What happened here?'

'Chain broke while you was crossin the road. Something must have collected me in the dark. I don't recall.'

'Thought I heard somepin. Bloody Cortina's got that many rattles! Shoulda looked back.'

'Perhaps it's just as well you didn't. We'll leave 'er here for the time bein. It's all for the best. I dare say who did this had a 'roo bar. It wouldn't damage a 'roo bar.'

'What about insurance, Adam? They'll want a police report.'

'We can fudge a day or two. We're got bodies on hold, ay. No, let's get goin to town.'

'Sure you're not hurt?'

'Me heart's broken. That was me all-time favourite car, C 200 Classic, one o' the few Mercedes manuals. I had a premonition somepin was coming to an end today. Now I know what. Oh well. Just take me home. I'm goin straight to bed.'

'Can't it wait till tomorrow? What about yer meetin with Buzzacott and Blenkinsop?'

'They'll have to wait. No show without Punch. I'm pooped, mate. I'm shakin. They could take advantage of me. We can't agree on a price for tomorrow night. Let's put a few branches over this Merc and camouflage it from the road.'

'You look very pale, Adam. I hope you're not bleedin internally. I might take you up to the hospital, and let 'em check you out.'

'What? And let my insurance company off the hook? No. Just take me home.'

When he gets there, he tells his wife how lovely she is looking, congratulates himself again on having met her in the first place, inquires over his daughter's new boyfriend and pours a whiskey for himself. While thinking seriously of a second he rings Feidhlim Foley.

'Feidhlim? Yo. This is Adam. You right for tomorrow night? I decided to invite Jarvey but I've a bone to pick there. Why couldn't you have told me that brother o' yours is simple, mate? It would have saved misunderstandin. Yesterday he's gonna be a priest, which I thought not a bad idea, given his lovely brogue, and Carney's past it, and we need a younger man to look to the future, but today he's gonna marry Billy Minogue! Oh, I hate to think what Dud Leahey will think of that Fane of St Fiacre. It's a joke. I was hopin to get it fitted out, so's Dud could sleep there tomorrow night. No way would you get a bed in. As things now stand, it's full o' burnt bears. No, koala bears. Bears on hay. I can't go into it, Feidhlim, I gotta grab me some shuteye. I'm pooped. Gotta get out there later and give'm their shots. I'm gonna grab me some zees.

'What's that you say? The *venue* has been changed? To Bobby McGees at the Racetrack? We'll see about that.'

Ad hangs up, turns on the tele and watches *The Simpsons* while drinking a third whiskey. Today was his alcohol-free day, too, but he couldn't find the time. His wife comes in to find him passed out, boots on the antimacassar.

21

In contrast with the Hibernian Australian Catholic Benefit Society Hall, which was the only other possible venue when Buzzacott at the Sportsman's Club refused Blue access to the kitchens, Bobby McGees, in the new Ballymeaner Race-track pavilion, is as modern as. Feidhlim Foley, whose notion it was to shift the Reunion to the Track, is at a loss to understand his buddy's reservations, *a fortiori*, when, standing in the parking lot outside and directing guests to the lift well, assuming, for the purpose, a sound Oirish brogue and passing on his benison in Gaelic, Feidhlim is struck by the marvellous mood the guests appear to be in, a mood Adam, were he half serious about tourism, would be advised to dissect. But Adam is preoccupied, getting the crockery from the van, and he may well be over tourism: he may well be into the manufacture of 'roo bars for the Wild West, a market in which, despite the number of deer on the roads of Wyoming, there exists no competition, using for the purpose a factory in downtown Gillette, on which he has already paid a lease.

'Thanks, matey,' says Adam, accepting the genial offer of assistance from Dick, the use of the epithet 'matey' showin he don't know Dick from a bar o' soap. 'Already broke one. That'd be mine. Bloke I entrusted to glaze these up fired too fast and opened the kiln door prematurely, so I hope we don't see'm all duntin up, before the night is out.'

'Adam,' says Feidhlim, 'how you keepin, are you well?'

'I'll be right with the help o' me mate here, and his charmin associate. Where to, Sport? Can't rush this. I'da bin here sooner, but I been all day out Crooked Corner tendin burnt bears. We lost a few and I don't know what happened to the bodies. We can't find them anywhere.'

'Lift well's over there, Adam. Through that little door. Take the lift to the second storey.'

'Isn't this where Shorn had his win?'

'He's been dashin in and out, with the Haitch Ar loaded like a car bomb.'

'Good. I knew he wouldn't let us down. I got the wine coolin at home. Soon's I get these seen to, I'll duck back out and get it. This van belongs to me daughter's new boyfriend and I really liked the old boyfriend, too. I doubt I'm over him yet. They expect a lot, these girls.'

'We drinkin *wine*?' inquires Dicky with a grin. 'I should have thought beer, in the New Country.'

'Oh, there's porters on tap,' says Feidhlim. 'We have a wide range of whiskeys and sambucas. Wine's a foreign wine.'

'Sounds promising. Ursula! Open the door! My God, this stoneware's heavy.'

'Made by Mike Hock for the occasion,' says Adam, staggering under the weight of a carton. Dick's coping well. He's used to sitting on a case, it won't hurt him to pick one up.

'Mike Hock? Mike made these pots? Good Lord. Now there's a man for all seasons.'

'Whatever he was, he's passed away. Passed away, the night he bisque-fired these.'

'No!'

'Infarction. I'll, ah . . . put me carton down on the floor of the lift. Phoor! Me back's crook. In a car accident recently.'

'This lift *moving*?' inquires Ursula, after about fifteen minutes.

'There's only the fire stairs or this lift. Imagine being trapped on the fire stairs!'

Bobby McGees is a long, low room, with a bar down one side and along the other a platform, on which is a table intended for the bridal party at wedding receptions. It commands a view of the track, if the groom wants to stand and turn his head. Imagine the ambulance racing along on the inside of the rails, and now imagine what looks to be a bed of coal glowing there, with someone raking it.

The kitchen is behind the bar. Feidhlim, considering he never went to Pat's, did a great job distributing name tags, and early arrivals, who include World Wide, his wife Carol, Jarvey Foley, Billy Minogue, Billy's mother Molly, are ordering drinks and downing them fast while admiring the views. These, according to Oblong Donlan, who just came back from the Old Country, resemble those of the track at Listowel, from the dining-room in the pub on the square. Unfortunately, no one can find a balcony overlooking the track, but there is a room, with a pool table, *en route* to the men's loo. It is here those who regret coming already are bound to be gathering. The most punctual, of course, are those from Dick Shillinsworth's swat-group, all of them now Queen's Counsel and multimillionaires. By seven forty the mood in the room is more polite than roisterous and the room is seeming a trifle claustrophobic.

Father Carney, as President of the Steering Committee, takes pride of place at High Table and Adam wonders how he got in, since he has no driver's licence. He's probably staying at the Josephite Convent, a two-storey brick building downtown, with Celtic crosses in lieu of finials and garden consisting of a lone hydrangea, which stands next to the Ballymeaner Sacred Heart Primary School ('*semper fidelis*') and which, so far as anyone locally can tell, is uninhabited.

People belting drinks in are starting now to relax. Classroom dynamics are re-emerging. Doblander, from the Equity Court, still has his unforgettable laugh and what a blow-out, hearing Doblander laugh again. That brings it back. Adam, who can't recall a soul, greets everyone most affably, while replacing every second item of crenate Chinese porcelainware with a sturdy platter on which gleams Mike Hock's vision of the Fane of St Fiacre. And Father Carney won't be getting one and where the hell is Dud Leahey?

By eight, the guests, Dud excepted, are seated, the platters and goblets *in situ* – if there were a menu, it would be a New Age menu, with just the one word, 'Acceptance', on a blackboard – and the wine, the labels soaked off, in the barman's custody. Oblong Donlan MD, whose father was a buyer for Smiths Crisps, President of the Pat's Old Boys' Committee, bashes, loudly, his fork on the champagne tulip that stands beside his goblet. He rises to his feet and holds up his hands, to applause, like a pope blessing a bus-tour.

'Ladies and gentlemen,' he says, 'could I have your attention, please? It is my pleasure to welcome you here this evening, at this marvellous facility, at our new racetrack – it appears a certain government has money for some things – where we shall celebrate the Feast of St Fiacre, that notable Irish expat, renewing old acquaintance, as classmates at St Patrick's School, Knocklofty, eating what I've no doubt will be a first-class banquet, prepared specially for us by one of our own classmates, Shorn MacEwe, and who could forget Shorn's famous "Man from Crooked Corner" walk at the bus-stop? I can't. I hope he'll do it for us later.

'To compare notes. To reminisce. To take time out, to be with old friends. I see photos coming out. A certain person tells me he actually kept that coffin – that shoebox – in which we flung items on our last day in school. It will be interesting to see what those were.'

Laughter, for the items were French letters.

'It will shortly be my pleasure to introduce Declan Carney, Father Carney, our unforgettable mentor – but first let me share a few of my own more vivid memories of St Pat's. St Patrick, that famous Pommy expat.

'May I have my reading glasses, please.

'Now the German philosopher Arthur Schopenhauer, in his essay "On the Sufferings of the World" makes the following observation: "If two men who were friends in their youth meet again when they are old, after being separated for a lifetime, the chief feeling they will have at the sight of each other will be one of complete disappointment in life as a whole; because their thoughts will be carried back to that earlier time when life seemed so fair as it lay spread out before them in the rosy light of dawn, promised so much, and then performed so little. This feeling will so completely predominate over every other feeling, that they will not even consider it necessary to give it words; but on either side it will be silently assumed, and form the ground-work of all they have to talk about." '

Well that went over like a bomb. Up with the ezy-out.

'I certainly hope we have no gloomy Arthur Schopenhauers here tonight.'

A mobile phone is heard to ring and an Old Boy scurries out to make love to it.

'Could all mobile phones and pagers please be switched off? Those who interrupt me again will have their teeth bashed against the bubbler, the water fountain. I recall having my teeth bashed against the bubbler, by Mike Hock, every time I was thirsty. He was the bubbler monitor. I recall the district nurse treatin the whole class for dehydration, with lime cordial. Yet it's my duty to report to you that Mike died earlier this month. Before he died he made these beautiful platters and goblets on the tables, and we'd like you to take one of each home, when you leave here, in memory of the occasion, and the times we all shared together, at St Patrick's School, Knocklofty. Never a leader, Mike, because where Mike Hock led, who could follow, and I recall having my port – there's a distinctive New Country word, I never heard that word said in Sydney – I recall having my "port" kicked from my hand, many a time, with a well-placed axe-kick on the stairs, by Mike, who was always looking for a fight and who embodied, I suppose, the best and the worst characteristics of our New Country. Poor Mike. He could have done so much better for himself, I'm sure, but he wouldn't leave the district. I understand he died penniless. He was a great man, perhaps. He could have gone far as a footballer. But he wouldn't leave the district.'

Molly Minogue is in tears. She blows her nose loudly, and when Oblong glances at Adam, for guidance at this juncture, he gets a frown and a nod of the head.

'Indeed, friends, before we proceed, we might take a glance at Mike's stoneware and study the design, before it's taken from our view. And we might, as we look, observe a moment's silence for Mike Hock, the first among us to die. I believe that's correct, is it Declan?'

'You'll be followin!' Carney's cheeks are bright red with the single malt. 'Everyone in this room will soon be dead and there's a fact.'

The kind of thing he was always saying at Pat's, when he wasn't thrashing them blue. Yet something in Mike's platters, too – whether it be the blue of them, or the cobalt fane, with its penile round tower at so impressive an inclination, or the fruit on the leafless persimmon – subdues the murmuring gathering. Doblander's good lady wife, who owns a gallery in Paddington, grabs a platter and turns it about, brusquely, prompting Adam to rise from his seat, for fear it dunt up, but it don't.

Smack! The swinging doors to the kitchen are brusquely kicked apart with a workman's boot and Blue MacEwe, un-shaven, in a grubby, tall chef's hat, blue singlet and boxer shorts, fag dripping from his mouth, stinking of lanolin, bearing a huge, stainless-steel saucepan with a stainless-steel lid, enters the room, followed by kinsmen from the Kamilaroi, likewise attired in shearer's clobber and bearing stainless-steel saucepans.

A fragrant aroma fills McGees, prompting salivations. Blue nods curtly at the young barman, who starts to whip the corks from the Puligny-Montrachet, handing the bottles to Billy Minogue, who, wearing a pink off-the-shoulder cocktail frock, swaggers about the room, unfemininely dispensing the pre-cious fluid and allowing the blue goblets to overflow onto the tables, following Blue's strict instructions.

'A word about yer fare,' bawls Blue. 'I aim, as an ex-shearer's cook, to leave a single flavour in the gob, so you're only gettin one wine, although you'll find it a bit of a larrikin. I won't trouble you with vintage or vineyard. Real drinkers don't care about such things. They just belt it into 'em, ay.

'For entrée, you're gettin a mess of freshwater yabbi, taken live, an hour ago, from dams out Crooked Corner. I hope they're dead. If one starts crawling off, just belt it about the ears with your fork. The almond butter glaze is not almond butter, it's witchety grub, and she comes on a warm green salad of oakleaf lettuce and coriander. Sweeter than what you'll find in the fourteeth *arrondissement*, because all picked and killed within the hour, in the New Country, my country. Sugars are not yet starches. Organic, locally grown, pesticide free. Enjoy yer tucker, Gubs, but first, our Irish convict grace. We eat and drink to please us, We piss and shit to ease us, And that's the truth, by Jesus.'

The food, and plenty of it, is piled in the champagne tulips till, once more, on Blue's instructions, the tulips overflow. Those who knew the local yabbi, an indigenous crustacean, as at best tasteless, are in for a surprise. Thousands of yabbi here.

'*Ummm!*' says Ursula. 'Good God, Dick, what has this man done? I'm reminded, slightly, of the entrée we had in that villa hotel in L'Albereta. You know, where the walls were covered in the frescoes and they had the sculpture on the tables? We had prawn for entrée, I recall, with sliced pickled ginger and red peppercorns, but this is better. This is exquisite. Oh Dick, the flavour in this yabbi! I can't place it. So *fresh* on my palate, and you know, I'd always longed to eat witchety grub. Dicky, you'd better be careful not to drink too much. You're on a promise tonight.'

World Wide, who's sitting opposite, laughs a trifle too loudly at this, and sustains the first of many conspiratorial smiles and vicious nudges. For his part, Dick savours the wine, its anonymity serving as a challenge to him. He swills it over his palate, neglecting only to spit it out.

'This is not local,' he pronounces eventually. 'I doubt this was foot crushed, unfiltered and unfined. Perhaps too strong for yabbi.'

'But you haven't *tasted* the yabbi. Taste the yabbi, Richard!'

'All right. Hmm. Quite astringent. Beats the sox off a battered sav.'

'Gum leaf,' says World Wide. 'Gotta gum-leaf flavour.'

'That's it! He's right! Oh, Richard. This is a culinary moment.'

'Waiter! Could we please have another drop of this wine, do you think?'

While the Old Boys and partners hoe into the entrée, Adam, who can't quite come at it himself, moves in behind World Wide and, fingering the shoulders of the Gucci coat, with approbation, grins at Shillinsworth.

'Glad you find it to your likin,' he says. 'Good vintage, is it? That's the ticket. Duncan, care for a game of pool?'

Duncan can wink too.

'What, can't you go to the toilet by yourself?'

'I need to make a call on me mobile and want to do somepin with me hands as I speak. That's the advantage of havin three chins, you can speak on a phone as you play a game o' pool. Come on, Boy.'

'What's your problem?'

'I gotta ring the airport, Duncan, see why Dud's not here yet. I didn't want 'em knowin he was comin, he hasn't even got a nametag. What's keepin him?'

'Who cares. Whattaya want me to do?'

'If anyone should happen by here, I want you to engage'm in small talk. Maintain the surprise of our guest's appearance. Talk about the bushfires, if you like. How you fought 'em, that kind o' thing. Damn! The line's busy.'

'May's well play a game o' pool while I'm here. Isn't that Blue's photo on the wall?'

'That's him. He had a win here, remember? I won a few bob on that. Go on then, set up the table. Is there a jigger? There had better be.'

'I'll go grab a beer.'

'Don't fancy your Puligny-Montrachet?'

'Can't drink it, mate. Cat's piss.'

'You ate the entrée. I'll break, while you're away.'

'I ate the entrée because Carol wouldn't give me any lunch. She detests me now, on account o' Billy Minogue. What does he look like in that dress?'

'What did you make o' the taste o' that yabbi? Leavin aside the coriander.'

'Eucalyptus.'

'You're right. I'm a bit concerned about that. Go on then, grab your beer. Wait – get one for me. Pity they got no Pabst or Bud. No decent beers.'

'Nice shot! Side pocket. Every time I do that, I go in off.'

'Why you stressin about that yabbi for? You know the man went off to London when he stopped cookin for shearers. Ain't much he can't do with a sauce.'

'That weren't no sauce. No such thing as a gum-leaf sauce. Even a shearer's billy tea gets only the one leaf added. I haven't played pool in years, Duncan. You wanta give me a chance? Always a better game, I think, when it's down to the black ball. As I understand it, yabbis don't eat gum leaves. They're scavengers, like the prawns that fatten off the dogshit that washes into Sydney Harbour.'

'So?'

'Well to get a flavour like that in yabbi, you would have to finish it on gum-leaf-flavoured meat. Catch me drift? Oh, hello? Yes, I'm inquirin about a flight arrival. Thank you. No, I'll hold. As I say, he'd have had to have fed 'em gum-leaf-flavoured meat, which is where I'm a bit nonplussed. Ain't too many gum-leaf-flavoured meats. Shot, Duncan! That Gucci coat brings you luck. Think they're enjoyin 'emselves in there?'

'I'd say they're 'avin a fabulous time. I know I am. Ursula drives a WRX! What a woman. Too good for that old goat. So you think he dumped the bears in his dam, is that what you're tryin to say?'

'Well I'd be surprised if he didn't. All his dead horses go in and he culls them hard, as you know. Two o' them bears, that died o' burns, had gone missin 'fore I got there, but I accidentally knocked a couple meself, though I hate to admit it.'

'*Wot?*'

'*Don't* knock the balls off the table, if you don't mind. It won't bring back the bears. Oh, I know how you must – just a minute, Duncan – thank you! Yes! I'm inquirin about a United Airline flight out of San Francisco, that's UA 863,

179

shoulda got into Kingsford Smith at 8.40 a.m. this mornin. Was it late, do you know? It was on time. It landed. Thank you. It landed, Duncan. He's probably meetin some local A and R man – he hasn't been back since he left. He may want to go out and see Darling Harbour. Media must be chasin him.'

'So you murdered me poor little bears?'

'Only the three! It was accidental. I'd arranged with Jarvey to give'm their shots, but I can't quite fit through the door o' me own fane, so I had to climb up the ladder to the top of the tower, well, not quite to the top, to where yez got – and let meself down with a rope, and as I did, me veterinary medicines got mixed up, because I took a bit of a tumble. Just a few foot, but it shook me, and the medicines in me veterinary vademecum got thrown outta their slots, see, so I s'pose in the dark, though I had a torch, I went to pick up the wrong ampoule. See, I knew where I had me penicillin, and what I picked up was the same size, though viscous, like the stuff you give cows 'fore they calve, stop 'em gettin milk fever. What's that called again? Had a hard time pullin it into the barrel, though I used the thickest needle I could find. Used the big horse syringe.'

'You couldn't have looked at the label, idiot?'

'I did, but these new contacts, I dunno what it is with them, but when you get hit with a truck, or fall down a round tower, you can't see straight for an hour. I thought I had the penicillin. Whatever I give'm, they went toes up frothin at the mouth within seconds. Never suffered. Three times. Then I twigged. Slowin down, ay. Oh, I got it here somewhere, it was this . . . just a bit, got it in me . . . bumbag here. Fuckin back! Oh, you've euchred me back somepin fierce, with your towin. Yes, here you go, Duncan.'

'And is that the syringe you used?'

'This one? Oh yes. I used this big horse syringe.'

'Give us a closer look.'

'What, you've seen one o' these before?'

'Mighta done.'

'Gotcha! So you've seen one o' these before! But there's

180

only one way you coulda seen one o' these before. You can't get them in this country. They're Dutch. We'll talk about that later. You bloody rogue, you coulda saved both of us a great deal of . . . Here's your ampoule. Can you read what's written on it, Duncan? My arms aren't quite long enough. Think it's written in Dutch. I bought a swag of superseded stock, from the last vet we had here. He was a dodgy type of man, too. Wouldn't, perchance, be that horse-dopin stuff, would it? God, I hope not.'

' "Sap van Olifant". Wasn't he governor of South Australia?'

'My worst fears are realised. Fark! You think I should say somethin? Will it rise up the food chain, like DDT?'

'You're not even sure o' your facts. Settle down.'

'I can't ask Shorn. No chef will divulge culinary secrets to a man with a bit o' meat. Now you tell me if you don't feel well. I best get out to Crooked Corner, see if Dud's out there. Who's tendin them bears?'

'Well, Joe, I imagine! Someone better be! You feel like another game?'

'No, thanks. I hate gettin beat. We better go back in. You know, I can't understand what's keepin Dud.'

As Adam resumes his seat Oblong gets up to introduce Carney, only Carney's dozed off. A great man for the dozin, he thereby provides a bit of unexpected sport for the Reunion, as a favourite game at Pat's consists in guessing what Carney dreams of, when he falls asleep. As Carney dozes he always mutters and moves his hands in weird patterns.

'Come on!' says Oblong. 'Uneaten entrées to the man who can tell us what he's dreamin of!'

While many of the more traditional suggestions here would be out of order in mixed company, others are put forward in an atmosphere to suggest the floor of a stock exchange. It's a contest of wit among barristers. Adam moves over to Jarvey, who is sitting next to Feidhlim at the one table that can take no part in the contest, being too intent upon the crack; for the one place each and every Australian feels at home is the Republic of Ireland.

'Shame – us had not got but one fare for his bawt the day before,' explains Jarvey, 'so the tourists was all but gone. It was early November, I recall, a Sundey mornin. Ragers was in bed still, the pious in the churches. So quiet, up there, in the Gap of Dunloe, not one soul did I see, the whole hour it took me to walk from Kate Kearney's Cottage to Lord Brandon's. There was a freak cell of high pressure off the Atlantic coast, because of El Ninyo I suppose, and pissin down all over Europe, so we had the best of the weather. Blue sky, and light mist to lend colour to the stawns and the cloppin o' me horse's hooves annoyin me, so I walked through, leavin the jauntin car at Kate Kearney's. It was then I started to think that I would come out here.'

'But *why*, Jarvey? Can't you see how lucky you are to be born where you were? No one's ancestors come from here.'

'One gains the impression,' says Feidhlim, 'beautiful though it be, the best o' the Irish went abroad, leavin only dumbclucks. For example, on the back of the Iarnrod Eireann flier, you read the following: "When reading timetables, place a piece of paper across the page under destination station. Read across the table for the times of the trains stopping at your destination point. Read upwards to train column to find departure times for your destination." Did you know there's a ruins of a Royal Irish Constabulary barrack in the Gap o' Dunloe? It was put there to protect the Thomas Cook tours from London, in the nineteenth century, which was the world's first tourists.'

'As distinct from travellers,' says Adam. 'Jarvey, can I have a word?'

'A minute, Adam. A minute please. I'm tellin the people why I come out from Kerry, though I do miss the oak woods with the ivy and wood pigeons with their barred wings, and the constant sound of water, the grey slate and the pink sandstawn, the low cloud and red deer, the ruins of Innisfallen, the Castle o' the O'Donoghues, and the yellow birch leaves fallin and the web in the gorse, and the second flowerin o' the ling, the call o' the craws and the ducks, and the smoke from the oil and coal fires when the fires is lit at three p.m. But the sacred places of Ireland are the most beautiful places and overrun with tourists.'

'Well, where there's a tourist there's a livin to be had. How can a small Irish farmer survive, Jarvey? Christ, he's runnin at a loss now. Takes him thirty months to finish a beast on grass. Your grain-fed European beef is finished, in sheds, at twelve. It's all for export, too, so he'll need more subsidies to survive, yet the EU's callin for a thirty per cent cut. It's farmin makes no sense.'

'But the cost o' rehousin the rural unemployed,' says Feidhlim. 'And no jobs in the cities, Adam!'

'What a price, to reduce everything to cash.' Jarvey's eyes are glazed with wine. 'I never saw the Gap of Dunloe till that day I was there alone in the Gap, and the next day I was rude to an American tourist and lost me jauntin-car licence.'

'So you think Americans talk too loud, Jarvey?'

'What's that you say, Madam? Speak up.'

They've all drunk about a bottle of the French plonk and the savour of the marvellously flavoured entrée resounds still on the palate.

'That was a nice green salad,' observes Feidhlim, belching. 'Only greens Jarvey and me saw as boys was the mint in the mint sauce. We need farms for our tourists, Adam. And sports horses is worth a bob, too. Horses for racetracks.'

'All we know', says Robyn Kincaid, the wife of Wade Kincaid, 'is we liked our stay in Ireland better than anywhere, didn't we, Wade?'

'We did, because the people are so friendly.'

'And did you take the jauntin-car ride through the Gap of Dunloe?' inquires Feidhlim.

'We did.'

'And was it the driver's birthday?'

'Well, as a matter . . .'

'Aha! Jarvey here had three hundred and sixty-five birth-days every year, didn't you, Jarvey? And always puttin himself through a college, and come from a very poor family 'n all.'

'We do come from a very poor family 'n all,' says Jarvey,

'though I wear a coat and tie when I drive a jauntin car. But the lyin preys on your mind, it's true, and all your ill-gotten gains you must lose. I says the same to Father Carney, this arvo, when I witnessed the weddin.'

'What weddin?'

'That girl over there and that old man. They was wed this afternoon.'

'Good God, Shillinsworth must think he's young again. Have I got news for him. Yes, we'd like our daughter to visit Ireland, Jarvey. We're a bit concerned over her. She's in with this inner city crowd that digs up corpses and drinks the blood and practises group sex and injects opiates.'

'Don't be worried, Wade,' says Adam, 'it's nae but a stage they gang through. Come and have a game of pool with me, Jarvey. Have a game of pool while the Old Boys are guessin what Carney's dreamin of. I'd say he's fishin in Queensland.'

'When you was comin in,' says Adam, putting the arm round Jarvey's shoulder, 'did you notice a man wearin a black Stetson, black preacher's frock-coat and granny glasses? Cause that'd be Dud.'

Slap! A roar of laughter now from World Wide as Ursula dispatches a fly, and next thing they know she's running past, dragging Carol out for a game of pool. Though Ursula's headlights are no bigger than Carol's, she wears hers on high beam, whereas Carol, through low self-esteem, habitually wears hers on low.

'Looks like the girls beat us to the table, Jarvey. We'll talk and have a smoke in the loo.'

'If you want to know what Father Carney says, Adam, he says I should marry Billy Minogue, because he says 'tis the will o' the Virgin there be no priest in the Crooked Corner, or why else would Mary offer Billy, through me, this Carnal Redemption?'

'You mean you didn't see a man in a black Stetson, black preacher's frock-coat and granny glasses? Damn! I hope he didn't go out to Rugby. No Livin National Treasures out there.

If they was to see one, walkin down the road, God knows what they might do.'

Blap. The door to the men's room opens, as World Wide irrupts for a piss. He just drank his first ever bottle of wine, straight down, on a dare from Ursula.

'Ah!' he says, referring to an action he must take for granted, but for which Billy may long, 'that feels better. Listen to me, you pair! Who's lookin after me bears? Poor little bears mustn't be left untended. 'Smatter o' fact, I'm thinkin o' duckin out, only thing is, not sure if I can drive in the worst handlin car ever assembled. You said to tell you if I feel strange, Adam, well I feel strange. I feel excited and truthful.'

'Go back in and sit down. Wake up to your bloody self. You stink of marihuana smoke. You'd be the least truthful person in the whole o' Bobby McGees.'

'Don't you be insultin World Wide, Adam. 'Tis sure he was a great help on our fane, and all unpaid.'

'Huh. I suppose you realise that if Dud don't wanta batch there you have wasted that stone? There's a market for that stone. There won't be any Japanese weddins here, if those bears die.'

'Yes, but I have met my bride-to-be, through the buildin o' the fane.'

'Rather you than me, mate. You oughta stick with your vocation.'

'Ursula says it don't matter, in a city, what sex a person is, Adam. Catch up. And what about Paddy's miracle? Ever given that a minute's thought? Way Paddy got straightened up, though you dosed him on Valium syrup and put him to bed, so, that what with all this action goin on, everyone seems to have forgotten him? Well, I haven't forgotten him. Was that all for nothin, then? The miracle? Ever consider, had we not built the fane that Pat would still be bent in half? It seems to me that if we can cure him, we could have a Lourdes 'ere, Jarvey and me. So sit on this and spin, Adam, and stick yer Wonder from Down Under. Mike Hock's the hero here. He designed that fane! Dud Leahey's a jerk who can't even sing, which is common knowledge.'

'God, you're so purblind. The people who shine in later life, Duncan, are seldom those who impress at school. Take Shillinsworth. Look at the build on him! No wonder I can't recognise him. I recall him as a weedy little nerd, and there's bound to be a rational explanation for Paddy. What sort of Virgin would straighten Paddy, yet not spare a bear in his prime o' life? Eh? And the reason I put Paddy to bed, I had too much on me platter.'

'You killed them bears. You poisoned 'em.'

'Oh, there was two died o' their burns, ain't that right, Jarvey? Don't think it hasn't crossed me mind, Duncan, the tourist potential o' the pilgrimage. I've been to Knock. I've seen 'em diggin up sand on the beach at Iona and puttin it in bags to sell, but Jarvey'd be the first to admit that Paddy's an unusual Australian.'

'Why's that?'

'Because he never had sex in his life. You see, Duncan, this is not the Old Country. The Old Country's gone, mate. It's even gone from the Old Country. In the New Country, sellin Dud Leahey T-shirts and CDs makes more sense. I imagine the Catholic Church is finished, outside the Central Desert. When we come here from the Old Country – from The Dingle, in the case o' my people – we shrugged off superstition, or rather, had it thrashed out of us. There is no justice here in the New Country and no Hereafter neither. Well frankly, I hold the Catholic Church accountable. We oughta be treatin Dud Leahey like the Irish treat the German Head of State. He's that important to Yarrawongamullee. He's got first option on that fane.'

'We all oughta be more believing. I only know if Mike Hock hadda been a believer, he mightn'ta been on drugs.'

'Am I hearin right? I must say that's pretty rich, comin from you, Duncan Webb.'

'I'm talkin about 'ard drugs, aren't I.'

'Oh, I see. The kind you can't grow. Yes, of course. What you do with that syringe?'

'Eh?'

'That syringe you found in Mike Hock's backpack, the

night he passed away. That horse syringe. The one you've seen before. It's mine. I want it back.'

'Why? It's usin syringes over and again, that's given us all AIDS. Don't you know nothin?'

'Adam,' says Jarvey, 'is that not Patrick's voice? Is that not old Paddy's voice I hear no?'

'I hope not. But tell me what it says and I will tell you if it's him.'

'It says, "Don't tell me that you wet your pants again." '

'Oh Christ, they come to town. It never lets up, does it.'

The balance of power between the boys has shifted, now Patrick is back to his former height. He is taller now than Brother Joe, whom he steers towards the loo in the interests of presentability. Entering, they meet Jarvey, Adam and World Wide, on the way out.

'Adam,' says Joseph, 'you said I should come to the Reunion to learn, and here I am. Dud turned up?'

'Hush man! I was hopin he was in Crooked Corner. Hello, Kerry!'

'Who's lookin after me bears?'

Kerry, who brought in the old boys – that's the old boys not the Old Boys – is chatting over a cue. It takes Adam's breath away, the sight of three beautiful women. Wouldn't that be a bad omen, to see three beautiful women at once? Adam walks over to confer with Kerry, when Blue MacEwe bursts out of the lift, with the second course of his banquet, which has been grilling on the coals by the rails. Adam and World Wide won't be partaking. They go back to the Corner with Kerry.

Wonga pigeon, glazed in pork fat, one of forty or so to sit on each platter, directly over the image of the fane. Only men to be served. Billy isn't served. Keyring deals them from a laundry basket, confiscating the cutlery. Eat with your fingers, no fingerbowls. Rinse in Puligny-Montrachet, then suck. Squabs, all shot through the eye by Blue, sitting starkly on the platters.

No comment, no introduction. No veg. No salad, no sauce,

bar pork fat. No mention of the fact it's Wonga pigeon, hereabouts all but extinct. No real clue as to how to proceed, neither, till Blue appears in the kitchen door. 'Men's business,' he says, chomping on the squab he thrusts in his mouth. He saunters back to the kitchen in his 'Man from Crooked Corner' walk.

Yes, another coup. A fine meal, a protein meal. A meal to think about, in Sydney's MG Garage. The eroticism of hearing the bird bones broken in the mouths of the alpha males, who quickly fall, with the second bottle, into the spirit of the very dark Irish, in whose dwellings stoves are often the only items to be found in mint condition. Fingers are plunged in drinking chalices, wiped on besmeared linen. A good percentage of the platters have dunted, the minute the hot food hit them. The women are being driven half wild, with a sense of furious injustice, with a sense of libidinous desire, with both.

Two chairs are found for Pat and Joe. They are seated among barristers all of whom reek of chlorine, having done their mandatory daily laps in the Ballymeaner indoor pool.

'What's this here?' says Joe to Shillinsworth, using the voice of the hearing-impaired.

'Wild pigeon glazed in the fat of feral boar,' shouts Shillinsworth, 'and very gamey! Very crisp!'

'I'll have a glass o' that wine,' shouts Joe.

'Yes, I'll have one too,' says Paddy.

'Shorn has fun with them pigs,' asserts Joe, disrupting an *ange passant*. 'He had one sleepin in his bed, about the time he kept his hens in hessian sacks, and what about the last big boar he fattened, Bubba. Can you ever forget him? We spent a week buildin a crate to go over him, then manhandled him onto the ute, for Duncan's Tuesday pig-kill it was, but the bloody mongrel burst out of his crate and took off, never to be seen again.'

'This could be him,' says Paddy. 'I seen him hangin round, just the other day. Shorn overfeeds, and has to starve 'em, to gain their co-operation.'

'I seen him do his block at a pig when he couldn't find his

brand. Remember that? Put a rope around its neck and tried to drag it from the kitchen. Now you can't drive a goat and you can't drag a pig. So it went blue, started thrashing its head, got a cut lip and a bloody nose. Went into shock, tremblin. I says, you should never try to drag a pig, Shorn. Rinse this plastic garbage bin in diesel then shove it over the pig's snout, to back it up. They always go into shock to ruin the meat on purpose. They're very intelligent.'

'Please shut up,' says Carol. 'You're putting people off their meals.'

'No, he's not! No, he's not!'

'I'll have another glass o' that wine,' shouts Joe. 'Very nice, that wine. Bubba! Drink up.'

'And what about the time', says Paddy, attended now by every out-of-towner in Bobby McGees, 'when I was shiftin me Murray Grey and her two-day-old bull calf? Strong, that calf. Couldn't catch him to get his balls off. We had to put him in the pacer float, but we couldn't get the cow on the float, she wouldn't go. Too strong. Tried to winch her up, no. Put up the tailgate, I says to Shorn, drive off slow and she'll follow. Well I think I had another couple of beasts I was shiftin as well. Yes, that's right. Just as well them very dark Irish never took to my cattle. Well she panicks, near the Killaarney grid, forgets the calf and belts back up the fane. Any animal got in that fane, we always give it law, see. Fane was the place of refuge. Now get in the float and make the calf bellow, says Shorn, so I climbs in the float and the calf, that hitherto bellowed non-stop, you think I could get a squeak out of it? I punched it, I bashed it with me stick, I kicked it, I pulled its ears, I poked its eyes. Not a peep.'

'They're too tame, them animals o' Shorn's, Bubba. They know what they can get away with. An animal must have a fear o' man or else he's uncontrollable. Carrot without stick won't work. I think this *is* a wild boar, too. I can taste the worms.'

'If it's not a rude question,' inquires Dick, on behalf of all 'are you an old Anzac? How old are you?'

'Old as me tongue and older 'n me teeth.'

'He's ninety-seven,' says Paddy, 'and I'm ninety-six and never felt better. Joe took part in the world's last cavalry charge and cut off a man's head with a sword, but he won't march on Anzac Day.'

The old boys are at once surrounded by Old Boys and Old Girls, who share, in this broken-down world, a desire for carnal immortality. Details of exercise and diet are sought.

Kerry Gurney drives; Kerry Gurney, conveying two dogs, Ad Hock and World Wide Webb. Adam scours the road for any trace of the Wonder from Down Under, as World Wide teases one golden retriever by tugging on the frisbee in its teeth.

'Is it all right to speak in front of him,' says Kerry, swinging left past the House of Prayer. 'This man who tears my fencing down and empties my dams and tanks?'

'Why, is it about sheep?'

'Yes.'

'Why not? He's in on it. Found the syringe I give Mike to vaccinate'm. It was in the backpack. I searched the pottery, as you know, but Duncan, though he denies it, was there first.'

'I still got that syringe.'

'Adam, when I fed my sheep this morning I found some had been shorn.'

'Ah yes, sorry, Kerry. That was me. I needed fleeces to tend some burnt wildlife, so I had to send in the shearers to shear 'em. Tampon MacHugh and the Red Bullock boys and Shorn. I'da told ya sooner, but I been flat out.'

'You've a strange sense of priorities.'

'Yes, I think you might be right. I'm still livin in the New Country. Don't worry. I know what a fleece is worth. What choice did I have? I'll pay ya back. I am your sleepin partner.'

'Lucky maan. So ya still got sheep on Killaarney, Kerry, despite bein destocked for two clips?'

'Of course she has, Duncan. She's not about to exterminate the breedin flock which last year fetched the highest price for any bale of superfine wool in the world. She'd keep a breedin cell that give the Golden Bale. I had this good suit o' mine made up from the wool o' that Golden Bale, didn't I, Kerry.

We're not talkin here of ordinary wool, Dunc. Ordinary wool was sellin, last week in Yennora, at eighty-five prices. Well that's thanks to your million-bale stockpile forcin down demand.'

'Thought they was freezin that stockpile.'

'They don't need to freeze it, Duncan. Those bales are like blocks of cement, as is, after eight years in the tri-packs. I was lookin at a few recently. To do anything with 'em at all, you'd have to heat 'em up and flail 'em out.'

'Where are these sheep on Killaarny then?'

'Pens in the old shearin shed. Oh Jesus, they're beautiful animals, Duncan. Most beautiful sheep you ever saw. Shorn knows they're there. Let her concentrate on the drivin. I'll clue you in. See, I encouraged a few select clients to ignore the Department of Ag as regards this OJD nonsense, which is all a storm in a teacup. Because Killaarney is officially destocked, I have to spirit the wool away.'

'And is that where Mike Hock come in?'

'Yes. Because except in the case of emergency, of the kind we just sustained, I want hand clippers on superfine fleeces. Mike did all me shearin. He was always the best shearer here and I knew I could trust him, as blood runs thicker than water.'

'I don't believe there's anything wrong with my sheep!'

'Well that's right too, Kerry. Stress-free sheep, no problem. A valuable stud bloodline, built up over many generations, and all they can suggest is to send 'em to a boy like Duncan here, belt 'em on the head, or more likely, consign 'em to Omar O'Hara, in Goulburn, to slit their throats.'

'Cruel, these Arabs, ay. When Omar was workin here, we had that run-in. I cut me finger and he was complainin there was blood drippin everywhere. What's a bit o' blood in here, I says. This is a killin room in an abattoir! Put a bandaid on it, says he. You just come back from Asia. I dunno what ya get up to. Fark, I says, ya sound like me bloody missus! Then it was on. He had my hammer and I had his shiv, and that's when they shanghaied him to Goulburn. I can't belt a sheep on the head any more, Adam. Them days is over.'

'I'm glad you see it, Duncan. You'll never work as a slaughterman in the New Country now, if you can't pray to

Mecca. Why, I'll bet you wouldn't even know which direction Mecca was in. Forty-three million sheep and lambs in this state and they close Knocklofty meatworks. I can't *believe* the things they do here. Mortality from OJD is less than fifteen per cent and the test is only thirty-five per cent accurate, yet Kerry is asked to surrender her flock. Well, as if. Quite apart from the brutality, think of the drop in the value of Killaarney's pastoral leasehold, if Kerry were to sell.'

'I won't be selling, Adam. I keep telling you, I won't be selling. Apart from the odd stud ram from you, we haven't purchased sheep here since nineteen fifty. How could we be infected?'

'It's preposterous. And now they put the quarantine on.'

'What's this bloody OJD?'

'Mycobacterium paratuberculosis. Stress-triggered, Duncan. That's where drought come in. See, they pick it up from infected pastures, but we bit the bullet, didn't we, Kerry? We imported live vaccine. They're so short-sighted they won't allow it in, so I had to swallow some condoms, to bring it from New Zealand, but that was all right. When you consider what superfine wool is bringin. And Mike Hock, we think, innoculated 'em the night he died. Well that's the hope. Did you find vaccine in that backpack, Duncan? It's most important you speak the truth here.'

'That's rich, comin from a man who couldn't lie straight in bed. Why would I tell you anything? You're nothin but a bloody shark.'

' 'Cause if you don't I will tell the coppers where you grow your featherduster heads.'

'Oh, all right then. It's true I found an empty condom.'

'You're sure it was empty?'

'I think I'd know an empty condom when I saw one, Adam.'

'He's tellin the truth here, Kerry. I can always tell. It does make sense. See, Duncan here thought the police was after Mike on account of drugs. He only acted as he did to protect his fire captain. You know what I think? I think Mike accidentally give himself a hit of OJD. Needle stick. I mean, a ram makes a move at a wrong moment, it can happen. And I know he knew the consequences, too, as we'd discussed them, in the context of the risk I was takin, bringin the bloody stuff in. Your calf or forearm muscles have to be completely stripped out. Why, if a condom hadda burst in me, I'da been booked in for a rebore.'

'Poor Michael,' says World Wide, 'poor Mike Hock! It was just about here, I seen him runnin in. I was drivin the Bush Fire Tanker. And to think he was probly sayin to himself, "This is the last run I shall enjoy." '

'Well you're assumin needle stick to his calf. What if he hit himself in the forearm? In that case he's thinkin, "I better get them platters and goblets made up for the Pat's School Reunion." '

'So you killed your own cousin in the course o' one of your crooked, dirty deals. Why, you're nothin but a shark.'

'Wasn't my fault he had the infarction.'

'Yeah? When he had nothin left to live for? Let me out, Kerry! Stop this people mover. I want to be alone, to consider the company I keep. Is it still a criminal offence, I wonder, to consort with criminals?'

'Drive on, Kerry! Don't panic, Duncan. Everything turns out for the best.'

'Bullshit! My head feels funny. I dunno where I am. I wanta go home and consider my future.'

'But you don't have one, and no more does Knocklofty, if them bears die or Dud don't front. Now shut up and sit down. We're comin to a church.'

Still no sign of the Boy from Oz back at Bobby McGees, although Feidhlim keeps one eye upon the lift for his appearance. The company, all of whom have now been told, in whispers, that Shorn is aboriginal, are moving slowly towards their third bottle of Puligny-Montrachet.

'Was that a Scot?' inquires Joe as Billy walks by with a bottle of plonk. 'It looks a bit like Billy Minogue would look if he wore a kilt.'

'Billy', says Jarvey, 'is a girl born, and could I put this question, can she still be a member of the Fire Brigade when we come back from our honeymoon?'

'I don't know he's to marry,' says Molly, who moved in with the old boys. 'I can't think of him as her, and he needs permission to marry, and I won't have him marryin. He was to remain single and work for me. That was to be my kickback.'

'We can do as we please,' explains Ursula Shillinsworth née Mulcahy. 'We don't need permission.'

'Oh, we'd make it difficult for her,' admits Joe, 'if she's a girl. True, there's no law against it, and I have seen girls in other brigades, but we don't want them in ours. So we'd shun and ignore her, belittle her and mock her, I suppose, and humiliate her best we could, generally making things most unpleasant until such time as she got the message.'

'That', says Ursula, 'would invite action under Equal Opportunity Legislation, and perhaps, Joe, as a card-carrying redneck, you could explain to me just what it is you fear in having a woman in a brigade. Or a priesthood, for that matter.'

Joe, sipping from his goblet, might not have heard Ursula, who's sitting on his left, while Carney, subliminally triggered by the mention of the word 'priesthood', stirs and yawns.

'I had a terrible dream,' he admits, looking quite affrighted. 'Yes, I dreamt I was at a banquet which was not unlike this banquet and to my left was Bernardo O'Higgins, the Liberator of Chile, and to my right was Bigpella Bill, Nambawan Man Bilong Papua. And both looked resentful, and Bill Skate turns to me and says, "Where is my father?" And I saw at once the tragedy of the Irish in exile: Lawlessness and Miscegenation.' He promptly falls asleep again, as it was time for the whiskey at the dinner in his dream.

'And what would you have done,' says Molly to Carol, 'as you've three of your own? He ups, he would have been no more than four, declares himself a boy and says he won't wear a dress, but thanks to that support group he now loves the ballet, and the theatre, and the opera, and the Three Tenors, and wants to be a hairdresser, when he's to be a publican! I recall the very day he declared as much, he had the scissors in one hand. It was the day after the day everything went right for Mike Hock. Mike never spoke a word to me that day. Oh, they give him a terrible time at school, Billy, terrible, but his mind was made up, see, and no amount of bullyin and beltin from me or others could make him see sense. So we moved to this New Country from the Western Division, that we could start again, with him posin as a boy. And now, after poor Mike Hock find all that money for the operation, he's gettin married as a girl, is he? Well he won't be a girl, not a proper one. He's like the East German athletes now, he knows he could never have children. He'll be neither one thing nor the other. He'll have the erectile appendage between point nine and two point five centimetres. Although they'd rather dig a hole than build a pole, I s'pose. Oh, there's times I wish I were out of it, I do. The world's gone mad.'

'Most hairdressers are girls, Molly.'

'Oh no. Our Billy wants a string of his own salons. He wants to be able to *afford* to see the ballet and the theatre and the Three Tenors.'

'I wonder when this next course is coming,' whispers Oblong to Feidhlim Foley.

'I'm not the cook,' replies Feidhlim, 'and you're on the Old Boys' Committee. But I do see a man diggin a feck of onions, this arvo, so be patient, please.'

'It has to do, I'm sure,' says Joe eventually, 'with the effects of Death on the Sexual Urge. The Urge, in the male, responds to the deathly threat by goin up or down, and the former, which is what you want in a fire-fighter, can be a distraction on a fire ground, if there's pretty girls about.'

'He's right,' observes Shillinsworth as Ad Hock storms from the lift well and heads for the kitchen. The company listens to hear what he says, as World Wide, wearying, resumes his seat.

'You black bastard,' roars Adam, in a slur all can attest. 'You drunken mongrel. You miserable, irresponsible swine. You prick. You heathen. You knocked them bears for yabbi feed, without a thought for Yarrawongamullee.'

'I can't think to what you allude,' replies Blue. 'I'm endeavourin here to prepare me Burger from Hell. Fuck off and leave me be!'

'I'm not sayin I don't appreciate all you've done here,

Shorn, but I just come from the Crooked Corner, where I see a note on the fane porch, purporting to be from your drinkin buddy, and may I quote ya? I'll quote ya. "As the bears is fully recovered I released them to the wild, and have tidied up the fane, puttin the hay and chaff in the slab hut. There may be needles among it, so go easy when you feed it to the stock. Have stashed fleeces, pendin satisfactory outcome on Native Title claim to Killaarney. Am goin down The Hole." Signed, Aloysius MacHugh. Now I put it to you, Shorn, the success of your entrée has gone to your Irish tonsure. No way were them bears fit to be returned to the wild, and those are my fleeces. Did you send a message out?'

'Puttin him on the abo.' Ursula smiles. 'Cobber done the runner.' The company concur.

'Is it a criminal offence,' whispers World Wide, 'keepin a corpse on ice, Ursula? 'Cause that's what's preyin on Adam's mind. He got a copper on ice, in a tub. It wasn't my idea.'

Adam emerges from the kitchens, his arm round Blue and a smile on his face.

'May I share my feelings with you?' he inquires of the Old Boys and their partners. 'I dunno when I ever had a better feed, and if I seem a tetch testy, it's only because I had planned a surprise for yez, which is unaccountably delayed.'

'We only ask for a Fair Go,' pleads Blue. 'A Fair Go and access to Our Country.'

'I shall procure for you justice,' says Shillinsworth, pricked to the depth of his liberality. 'What is this about a policeman, Adam. Have you done something illegal?'

'I've done nothin I'm ashamed of, Dick,' says Adam. 'Is there wine left for me? Ta. Siddown, Shorn. Take a break, come on. Oh, he's a cook and a half. Yes, if I seem a tetch testy with this boy, it's only because they light these fires. Local darkies o' the Kamilaroi lighted a fire on Blanket Flat, which has all but destroyed our local breedin colony of koala bears. Yes, it's tragic, but that's all right. That's OK. I'm and he's OK. We're OK and they're OK. Shorn was just doin what come natural.'

'*No!*' says Ursula, torn between her love for koala bears and a desire for reconciliation.

'We never lit that fire,' says Blue. 'If you must know, I'm a Bush Fire captain.'

'Dick! If Adam knew Shorn was a Bush Fire captain, isn't he guilty of a libel?'

'Well I'm not sure, Ursula. In my experience, Bush Fire captains light more fires than anyone.'

'Whyncha tell Dick why that copper was out here,' says World Wide, 'copper ya got in that tub. Don't believe a word Shorn says, anyone. He's a lyin mongrel. When I asked him why Mike was out the Corner, he never once mentioned sheep.'

'I always had a mouthful o' tie wire. No good fightin 'roos, mate. No fence'll stop 'em. They'll go straight through any fence they could as easy clear.'

'None o' your abo talk there, to justify yer slack fencin.'

'Concealing the death of a policeman is a serious offence,' cautions Shillinsworth. 'Be careful what you say here, Adam. It could cost you your house.'

'But what if I'm in the right?'

'Why would that matter?'

'He better come clean, ay,' says World Wide. ' 'Fore he does, let's get one thing straight. It wasn't abos lit that fire, it was your man, Harley Christian. Copper that size woulda sent up a shower o' sparks all through them Tubbercurry esses. Always scrape your runnin board on a Heritage Springer when cornerin. Joe will tell you sparks like that can often ignite a fire. The fire actually started in the forest and spread back down to the Flat. See, Shorn woulda waded along the Flat with a torch, lightin ti tree, 'cause that's his form.'

'I hope yez are not tryin me on,' says Adam. 'Don't spoil your honeymoons. I was the first to inform young MacEwe here he was a Kamilaroi, and let me assure you, as Deputy Mayor, we're backin his every land grab. We won't tolerate racism, from these plutocratic Gurneys and it's *vital* we reclaim the lost art of didgeridoo construction. We don't want didges that look like them didges in the presbytery. Seen 'em? What a sight. All covered in dots and dashes. What we want,

Shorn, is kangaroos, the Three Sisters, Ayres Rock and the Opera House.'

'Local coppers woulda twigged you had sheep in that shearin shed,' says World Wide. 'That's why you had 'em send out Harley Christian, to investigate them missin steers. Don't think I haven't seen that CB in your Merc tuned onta the police channel. Don't think I don't know you play golf with the local superintendent of police. Why, you're nothin but a shark. You knew that Harley was stayin in town. Ah yes, I see it all. As to them steers, I noticed the ones up there now are the ones that got stolen. There's that white one with that one black ear; you fucked up there, my friend. You wouldn't recycle and sell 'em, again and again, now would you, Ad Hock?'

'Name's not really Hock,' says Paddy. 'Started out as Himmelfarb. Cheapjack Joseph Hock was born Imre Himmelfarb, in Pannonia. Jew, passed himself off, in the Colonies, as Irish.'

Now convinced all present are agin him, Ad drains his goblet and plays his trump card.

'You look pretty fit there, Dick. What time would you run in the City to Surf?'

Ursula bursts out laughing. 'He can't break the hour!' she says. 'Couldn't break the hour.'

'And what about you then, Ursula? I gather you'd run a fast time?'

'Oh, Ursula's a wonderful runner, Adam. Fifty-seven, was it, darling? Fifty-four?'

'Fifty-eight thirty-seven. Yes, I admit I was pretty chuffed.'

'I'd be chuffed too,' says Oblong. 'Best I could manage was seventy-four!'

'I run as a gorilla this year,' claims one Old Boy. 'Yeah, me too,' claims another.

'I had a bad run,' admits Shillinsworth. 'Eighty-seven, worst I ever done. Mind you, I tore me cruciate at Christmas, but Ursula and I first met in the City to Surf. I had change in me pocket and she sang "Jingle Bells" as she ran by, in the sweetest voice. Not sure I should have run at all this year. Do I seem to people to be limping?'

'I know a good knee man in Gordon.'

'Yes, I go to the Sutherland Centre, Wade. He does the Sharks and the Kings.'

'Then what would you say', says Adam, 'of a time of forty-one twenty-seven? That's the time Mike just run. Mike Hock, or a close associate. Oh, it's a long and complicated tale, but I see I have you attention. Yes? Billy, fetch us another bottle of the Puligny-Montrachet.'

'Puligny-Montrachet. Damn!'

'Thought you mighta picked it, Dicky, never mind. I'll try you on somepin German next time.'

To the rapt audience of wealthy, hard-working, ultra-fit and motivated Old Boys – to them that hath shall be given – Adam recounts how two gorilla suits were hired out from Bally-meaner Party Hire, and of how suspicion fell upon Mike, given they were hired in his name and never returned. He tells of the visit to Yarrawongamullee, for the Ministry for Sport, of Harley Christian, and of how Harley came to an illegal grief, colliding with the Gucci 'roo. At first, the Old Boys determine to savour the full horror of this thought and choke on the notion that the dreaded class bully was the man they envy most in all this world. The man who made the platters was the runner in the suit, who broke the rules and won the crown and fled the scene. God, it's all too much, there can be no justice, and whether through drunkenness or, more likely, sap van Olifant making its way up the food chain, a few Old Boys start to sob like Young Boys again, overcome with bitterness.

'The bloody place was hell, Ursula. Carney and Mike Hock between 'em, they made my life sheer hell. Mike Hock singled me out on the stairs, I don't know why. I shall never know why. He made me feel I was the most worthless worm on the face of the planet, and all Carney ever give us was cuts of the cane and threats of damnation. Yes, that's you I'm talkin about! You up there, you bloody rogue, you monster! I had to catch a late bus, every day of my school life, to avoid Mike, because he'd throttle me, with me own tie, if ever he caught me walkin out. Oh, I'd hide in the loo till he'd gone. Hide in the loo, like a prisoner in a cell. I did years. Then I'd have to feed the cows and churn the cream in the dark when I got home. And you wonder why I never speak of my childhood, or visit the old bastard. Well now you know!'

'Mike Hock, as a boy', explains Joe, 'had his heart set on bein a prize fighter, but no one in this district would fight him and he wouldn't go out of the district for a fight. And no one ever come here that could fight, present company excepted. By the time he took up runnin he was too old to make an impact, but I think he enjoyed shearin sheep, till such time as the Heartier Rowans undercut him, usin the wide, electric comb. Mike always made his fencin timber with an axe, the way my father done, but though his posts were twice as good as anything else on offer, they were three times the price. O' course, he was there when O'Mara got cooked, and all who was there when O'Mara got cooked was never the same again.'

'See, that's what Carol don't understand. *I* was there when O'Mara got cooked. See, that's what you don't understand, Carol.'

'Who else from here was there when O'Mara got cooked? There was you and me, Bubba, and Shorn from the Crooked Corner, O'Mara and Duncan and Mike Hock from Knock-lofty and that was it, I think.'

'Was there no Critical Incident Debriefing?'

'Ar forget it, Ursula, for God's sake. Forget O'Mara for the time being. Who wore that other gorilla suit? Can't you people understand the implications for Sydney Two Thousand?'

'We're not into runnin round, Dick. We're got more important things to do.'

At the mention of the phrase 'Sydney Two Thousand', which is a licence for printing money, Ad Hock takes a gulp of wine and the goblet he drinks from dunts up, pouring wine down his Golden Bale suit. He turns and hurls it at the lift well, Pannonian-style.

'Duncan was in the pottery the night Mike Hock died and he's responsible for this duntin, although he'll deny it. Oh, they'll all dunt up 'fore the night's out. Don't bother takin 'em home.'

'I admit I went to the pottery, Adam. I only wanted to protect Mike Hock. I'd just got it outta Carol that Harley Christian was moonlightin snoopin, spyin on men doin lawful business, for the pay of jealous women. Well Mike Hock had enough problems in regard o' women. I admit he was my hero. No one ever licked Mike Hock. He was the only friend I had left, thanks to them drug and alcohol counsellors, warnin my mates to never associate with me again, if they wanted to stay out of gaol. If you blokes hada give Mike a fair go at school, he'da conquered the world. Yez wouldn't give him a fair go! He told me that. I went there, as a man will, for a friend, when a copper's askin questions, but he was pottin like a fiend, and told me to fark off, he was too busy to see me.'

'Fine work in these platters,' says Doblander's wife. 'I could unload them, I'm sure, in my gallery. Notwithstanding the dunting.'

'Take'm,' says Adam. 'Take the lot. It works out for the best.'

'So I went out and sat in me car, ay, fell asleep, and when I come to, he was dead. Farct. But he was still wearin the backpack, hadn't had time to remove it, so I opens it up, to find an empty condom and a syringe. Well, I took his shoes and sandals. I don't want anyone, here or anywhere, pinnin anything on Mike Hock.'

'You actually had my syringe in your car when I stopped to lend you assistance and you never said a word?'

'Musta done.'

'What size were these shoes, Dunc? Was there one pretty new Nike jogger among 'em, size twelve?'

'Don't matter a damn, Dick. 'Cause it wasn't Mike won that race. I asked him, of course.'

'He'd deny it, wouldn't he,' says Ursula.

'Nup. He was never a lawyer. He never consorted with lawyers. Never told a lie in his life. Wouldn't lie to women, which was another reason he couldn't get ahead. See, that's what Carol understands too well, but I don't blame Mike. I blame meself.'

'What did he say', persists the quondam Royal Commissioner, 'when you asked who wore the other suit?'

'Never asked.'

'You expect me to believe that?'

'I don't care if you believe it or not! I'm not in a bloody witness box! I got more important things to worry about, mate, like findin a job. And when you're dealin with a man who holds a grudge against the world and never tells a lie, you do get a bit careful what you ask, if ever you're in a hurry.'

'Had to be a man of Our Dreaming.'

'I expect Shorn's right. Bound to have been some darkie. Remember how, Joe, when O'Mara got cooked and they all come rushin out o' The Hole, when they smelt the cooked meat, they was all wearin shoes on just the one foot? Geez, they could run up a hill, ay. Like a lizard up a rough-barked tree. Like a monitor up a turpentine.'

'What's this Hole, Duncan? May I just add, for an unemployed man, Duncan dresses beautifully? I think Carol's a lucky woman. *I'm* not sorry for Carol!'

'Well thanks, Ursula. I do me best. Oh, it's tiger country, mate, down the bottom o' Killaarney. Right on the edge o' the Wilderness. Great big canyon, goes down for ever. Bit of a local secret, even so. Runs into the Little Kowmung. Heritage Springer down there now. Seems prone to lightning strike. Often get a bit o' smoke driftin up. We was doin a burn got away, eh Joe. Oh, I blocked a lot o' this stuff off, over the years. Had to. See that's what Carol don't understand. See, that's what you don't understand, Carol. Adam knows more than he lets on, too. Ask Adam about The Hole.'

Adam sharpens a match as a toothpick.

'We have a mutual friend down there, me and Mike Hock, it's true. I never actually met him. He's alone down there, far as I know. Name's MacYew. Just MacYew. Him and me communicate by drawins on cave walls. He moves a few head o' stock about, from time to time, over the rough country. Gets paid in cans o' condensed milk. It was me introduced him to Mike, as Mike was after the cocopop pine. That's a pine only grows down The Hole, got bark like a cocopop. This is back in

Mike's wood-carvin days. There's only a dozen pine left now. Dry rainforest species.'

'Used to be hundreds of 'em down there, when Bubba and me was boys. I think all them dams on Killaarney has dried up The Hole, from what it was.'

'We'll be fillin 'em in,' says Blue. 'We intend to fill in the dams and pull out the fences, in consultation with the Gurneys.'

'What's the time now, Duncan? Midnight? I'll tell yez the full story. Yes, I can, as I'm over the New Country. I think I'm over Australia. I've put the boot in, I've deplored it bein put in by others, and I've copped it myself. See, as Mike Hock and Dud Leahey discovered, you can only beat your head against a brick wall so long. I'd say Mike ordered that second gorilla suit for young MacYew.'

'Dud Leahey!' says Dick. 'Now there's a name I haven't heard in years. What become o' Dud Leahey? I haven't seen him. Is he here tonight, Adam?'

'No, he never come,' says Adam. 'Appears he had more important fish to fry. He lives in America, these days, Dick. Greenwich Village and Wyoming.'

'Well that's a long way to come.'

'Oh, he's unknown in Gillette. They never heard of him in Sheridan. Our committee provided him a return air ticket, for tonight, which he accepted.'

'He had such a lovely nature as a boy. I recall him on the school bus, Ursula. There was only Dud and me left on the bus, after the Red Bullock turn-off.'

'Fancy.'

'I don't recall him at all,' says Oblong. 'Can't put a face to the name.'

'Look, here he is in the school photo. See?'

'No, that's not him, Dick. This is him here. He never stuck out at school. He had a weak personality. Liked to think he could sing, but he can't. He hung round with Mike Hock, real smarmer. No musical talent to speak of. I been listenin to a CD he made, tryin to see what they see in it.'

'What, he made a CD?'

'Won a Grammy. Not that that means anything. Likes to call himself "The Boy from Oz", "The Wonder from Down Under", "The Livin National Treasure".'

'Don't believe all you read, Adam. Those who know us well often think us less than candid, but there's nothing we can do about the press. They get it wrong.'

'I recall him now,' says Oblong. 'Didn't we all hate him? I felt the warmth of his smile at ten paces. I wanted nothing to do with him.'

'Wise choice, Oblong, for your malignity would have been no match for Dud's charms. He was a good mate of Mike Hock, Ursula, yet I'd say it was one of those friendships, of the kind we discussed on the way up, that persist, with a kind of perverse pride, when all common ground has gone.'

'If indeed it existed in the first place.'

'If indeed it existed in the first place.'

'I can't think what Mike saw in him, to tell you the honest truth. My cousin had more talent in his little finger than Dud in his whole entire bottleneck.'

' "Fame, Whose Loud Wings fan the Ashen Past to Signal Fires"!'

'Yes, that's true. But when everyone sends you a card, you only notice those who don't, and you assume they hate you, but the fact is, they may just be unaware of your win, or they may not know what to say, or they must just assume you're sick of being praised. Right now, we have a problem. The Hamburger from Hell has gone cold and I won't nuke it in a microwave. And I can't reheat it. I wonder why Tampon went down the Hole? Tampon, he says, says he: You must never go down to the end of The Hole if you don't go down with me.'

'Are you a success then, Dicky? Because all you ever do is complain.'

'I wouldn't complain with a wife like you,' says World Wide. ' 'Pon me soul I wouldn't.'

'What, is Carol asleep there, Duncan? Yes, I see she is. The fact I complain is assurance success has not gone to my head, She-bear. Pass us that bottle. Give us that bottle. You see, Blue, nothing has changed for you, but something *has* changed for them. You now realise no one believed you, when you assured them of your eminence, so far from being delighted by their congratulations, you are distrustful of your associates, who always seemed to concur when you assured them of your brilliance. And of course losers, who comfort fellow losers, see it as betrayal if a loser gets up, and some losers take that pretty hard and need to be comforted all that much harder by those whose role in life is comforting losers.'

'Oh, for Chrissake, Dick, shut up! You're making a fool of yourself. And me. I wish I'd never married you.'

' 'Ear 'ear.'

'Not'in makin sense no,' says Jarvey. 'All t'e people fallen asleep wit' t'eir heads on t'e tableclot', look about. All passed out no. Only Joe and Paddy and Shorn, and Billy and Mrs Minogue, and World Wide Webb, and Adam and Dick Shillinsworth, Ursula Mulcahy, and Oblong Donlan and Feidhlim, me brother, and me. Tat's all tat's left conscious.'

'Well I could feed yez at my place, I guess,' says Blue. 'We could eat traditional there.'

'Let's go,' says Ursula, rising. 'Am I the only one at this table feels the pull of The Hole? Oh I wish, in a way, I were out there now, headin down the Hole with Tampon.'

'The Hole exerts a pull,' asserts Joe. 'Never was truer words spoken. We all feel the Pull o' the Hole, from Crooked Corner to Blanket Flat. When Bubba and me was boys, our da would sit us on the edge o' The Hole, first fastenin a piece of rope about our waist, to secure us from the pull. He'd make us sit there, day upon day, just studyin the way the mist swirled up, maintainin that if we understood that mist, we could interpret the smoke from any fire – and fires always come up The Hole, Midsummer's Eve, Hallowe'en and Beltane – as smoke will always follow the same pattern as a mist follows. Learnt our fire-fightin down The Hole. See, MacEwe o' The Hole lights two bel-fires, each Beltane, in his camp below, and drives stolen cattle between, in a belief it prevents their repossession.'

'But our trainin couldn't save O'Mara, Joe.'

'That's true, Bubba. We couldn't save O'Mara. We slipped

up there. I wouldn't mind headin back to the Corner. I'm about ready for bed.'

'Gimme a drive in yer WRX,' pleads World Wide. 'Ursula and me could mount a search for the bears, on the way out.'

'It's gone midnight,' pronounces Billy, grabbing Jarvey. 'I want to announce an engagement.'

Carney wakes, as they walk to the lift, and runs after them, begging alms for Pat's.

22

The drizzle clears. The constellations are now visible, if inverted, Orion become a saucepan. The fire on the Blanket Flat, holed up in some blackened stump, plots, on behalf of what's left of the eucalypt forest against what's left of the rainforest, plots, on behalf of what's left of the hunter against what's left of the pastoralist.

'Mind you,' says Adam to Dick, as he drives back to the Corner, using for the purpose his daughter's new boyfriend's van without so much as a glance towards the ruined Merc, 'you could be Australian of the Year and yet remain an American citizen. Like the Head of the World Bank.'

'He's a Jew, Adam.'

'Oh yes. Well I know I'm fed up with parochiality, whatever I may be. I was never a mason. I did what I could for this shire. It's time some younger man took the reins.'

'You give my Lord a Crown o' Thorns,' says Carney from the back seat. He's mumbling about the need for a crusade to drive the Islamites from the Christian enclaves of Irian Jaya and East Timor.

'I'm not sure we ever met,' replies Adam. 'But I'd give one to you, had I one to give.'

'Shorn says we can keep the 'orses, Adam.'

'Great news, Jarvey.'

'Yes, he says we could have the top paddock on Killaarney.'

'How very generous.'

'With the grove of oaks and shamrock? If I was to build a five-rail, black-painted iron fence, with Billy, and tear down the shearin sheds, and seal the dirt tracks with bitumen, save for the practice paceway, and put a few Angus vealers on, and build an artificial lake, with artificial islet, and move me little fane down, stawn by stawn, from the hill, why I'd have a Muckross Park.'

'So you would. Where ya goin on yer honeymoon, Jarvey?' inquires Feidhlim, changing the subject.

'Joe give us his Ansett tickets to Melbourne for first September.'

'That's tomorrow. Will you marry tonight?'

'Well Father Carney is here and Billy's mother has no objections, if Billy keeps workin in the pub. We'll marry again, legally, when Billy turns eighteen. There's just the one problem, as we see it. The fane is unconsecrated.'

'No, it's not,' says Joseph. 'Adam, the Jew, took off the cross and hurled it to the devil. It's down behind the fire shed. I'll show you where.'

World Wide drives as he's never driven, as Ursula and Blue strive for balance in the rear. Webbie is half minded to drive on to the tubs on Tubbercurry Road.

'Do we look for the bears yet, Duncan? Do their eyes shine in the dark?'

'Not half so bright as yours, I shouldn't think, me dear. Adam reckons Shorn had 'em thrown in his dam, ay.'

'Well, that's crap! Tampers'lla stuck 'em up some tree somewhere. Where's the nearest manna gum? Probly better off, in the open. Always dyin in them Japanese zoos.'

'That's because they can't keep their paws off 'em, Blue. Kill 'em with kindness, ay. Adam wants to build a koala park here, Ursula. Says I could be in charge.'

'Stop at the shed a minute, mate. I wanta see if the Blitz is there.'

'Think Mike give himself a needle stick, Blue?'

'I know he was up the shed that night.'

While Declan Carney and Molly Minogue confer on Billy's immediate future, Adam hunts for the Celtic cross behind the fire shed. The platters are back at Bobby McGees but they won't be needed. While Ursula vies with World Wide, throwing doughnuts on the tennis court – a process whereby a turbocharged vehicle can spin in a stationary position – Blue goes out to the shipping container that looms behind his rear shed, returning with a brace of rock wallaby, somewhat stiffened.

'Oh, there's still some o' them down The Hole then,' says Paddy, 'for that's the only place you'd find rock wallaby here. We used to live on them and pumpkins.'

'These are the last,' admits Blue, ripping off bargeboards from his house to light the fire. 'Maybe a few right down the bottom, under the falls, who knows. None left at Jenolan Caves. National Parks put a sign up at Yerranderie, askin walkers to report any they saw, but no one sees any. See, they got no toenail. They can't escape from foxes. Yeah, it's a shame to see'm go, Paddy, but I thought I'd mince up the few that was left, for me Hamburger from Hell. That's when I thought Dud'd be here. Wouldn'ta bothered for this crowd. All right, so Dud can't sing or play, but he sure is joyous in his outlook.'

'That's the main thing, Shorn. Ruined the evening for everyone, didn't it, Dud not turnin up.'

'I'll just singe'm and we can eat 'em rare.'

'Always hang 'em in winter to set the tail fat.'

The company huddle around the coals, as Blue burns bridges in the form of Hardiplank, which tends to melt, rather than burn, like plastic on cotton overalls.

'Do what Ted Turner done for the buff on his property in Montana, Shorn. Pull out the fences and let the native animals roam free. Then you'd have a game park. You could train 'em, and charge photographers admission. I'm lettin me house in town, you know. I'm not sellin, as yet.'

'What's that, Adam? Where ya goin?'

'Try me on Double ewe Double ewe Double ewe, Aussie Ad Hock, Wyoming, dot com. I'm persuaded the US consumer is the sole remainin engine of world economic growth. I wanta warm me hands on him.'

'We will pull out them fences, Adam. Tampon's probably pullin 'em out now. He built the fences and Keyring dug the dams. Oh, it isn't gonna be easy. What a fencer that Tampon, ay. Never heard o' pliers. Cuts tensile wire with his teeth, and you know how, when you're diggin a posthole, you've always got dirt left? Not Tampon, mate. He has to chase for extra dirt, every post he tamps. Christ, he can tamp. You'd be hangin for a smoke, but he'll Tamp on.'

'Are we going down The Hole when we finish this meal?' Ursula wipes her hands in her long hair. 'From what I gather, it's this MacYew won this year's City to Surf, Dick. I'm so longing to meet the man who won the City to Surf. I shall probably throw myself at him. At long last, an Aussie to put in against a Kenyan from the Rift. More haunch, please. The thought of those two in their gorilla suits, Dick, heading through the Wilderness, then jogging across the Cumberland Plain.'

'I suppose they'd longed to see the beach they'd heard so much of, Ursula, and felt, being shy, or in Mike's case, obtuse, they wanted to do it on a day, and in a fashion, that wouldn't attract undue attention.'

'Shy, them very dark Irish,' says Joe. 'Shy and very aggrieved.'

'Tell 'em about O'Mara,' says World Wide, staring in the fire. 'It's bound to come out. Then she'll know why we leave'm be. You wouldn't throw yourself at a MacYew.'

'No! We made a pact of silence and you was party to that pact. But we could speak about the time Patrick and me first saw MacEwe o' the Hole. No pacts back then, but with the devil, and circumstances was similar.'

'What a night,' whispers Jarvey to Billy. 'See how the shadow of the Celtic cross there is movin over the persimmon?'

'That persimmon's comin out, sport.'

'No, Shorn! You'll not touch me persimmon!'

'O'Mara walked with a bounce,' says Joe. 'He never had much to say. He'd just come up to you, with a smile, and wait to hear what you said. He just about left the ground with every step he took.'

'Oh, shut up,' says World Wide, 'you're makin me ill, Joe. You was party to the pact.'

'Yes, but they only took his legs. That's what I was comin to.'

'They did come scramblin up,' says Paddy, starin in the coals of Blue's house fire, 'like they did when O'Mara got cooked, only there was more of 'em, back when we was boys. See, they react to the smell o' burnt meat. Poor men, can't help 'emselves.'

'I can still smell O'Mara. See, that's what Carol don't understand.'

'It was Hallowe'en,' says Joe. 'I'll tell this. Four in the afternoon. We only had sacks and shovels back then, or rakes. No custom-built fire-fightin gear. Dad was with us, I recall, Dad and all the men from Crooked Corner, forty or fifty or more. It was necessary, back then, each Hallowe'en, to burn a break around The Hole, because that was the day MacEwe extinguished and rekindled all his fires, and they was prone to get away. Suddenly, a bolt of lightning struck The Hole, causing a big downdraught, which sent MacEwe's sacred Samhain flame racin up the slope towards us. Some lower down got caught up. Bubba and me was runnin up fast as ever our legs'd take us, while all below was terrible confusion, screamin, smoke and fire. Suddenly, from out the smoke, appear a few men, with boots on one foot, some of the type you wouldn't want to meet on a very dark night indeed. But some was only very dark, and one was small and white.'

'T'at was him. T'at was MacEwe o' T'e Hole.'

'So it was, Paddy. T'at was him. T'ey was all carryin knives and forks where we had hoes and shovels, and they had napkins under their chins, where we had muslin smoke scarves, so a pitched battle broke out, when we saw what they was doin to our burnt, as distinct from cremated.'

'What was they doin, Joe?'

'Of that, Me Lord, I dare not speak. You'd form a low impression of the Irish. You'd think us tarred with the same brush as Pearce, the cannibal of County Monaghan, who, in his escapes off MacQuarrie's Harbour, ate the arms and legs of seven of his cobbers. MacEwe was more selective. His boys only took the thighs. Yes, they took the calves, quads and thighs. And Bubba here chases one, see, and trips him up with his hoe, and raises the hoe, and bends over him, and strikes off your man's head!'

'God, a massacre, Dick. Here. Is it known to history books?'

'And Paddy never straightens up, afflicted with arthritis, until the day we pull him out of Jarvey's little fane.'

'It's a miracle. She forgive me for me murder, so She did. I prayed to Her night and day. And the fire Joe and me has been burning on our hearth, all these years, was taken from that very flame. I'll go across the road, now, and extinguish it.'

'And will the strangers hold their tongues for the sake o' the Irish reputation?'

Joe looks hard now at Ursula Mulcahy, then at Molly Minogue, and at Oblong Donlan and Dick Shillinsworth, although the last two are a bit put out, as they don't regard themselves as strangers. They was at Pat's.

Silence. It may seem MacYew's, and The Hole's, privacy is assured. The bonk of a pobblebonk frog, disputing the dam with any yabbi left. Just the glowing of coals and the tearing down of rock wallaby sinews with teeth.

'But here's not two hundred kilometres from Sydney's CBD!'

'T'at's roight, Molly.'

'We had a licence to print money.' Adam sighs, thinking of Sydney Two Thousand. He'll get over it.

Blue tosses another length of Hardiplank on the coals.

'Yez don't belong here,' he tells them. 'The weather is tellin you that. El Ninyo is makin this New Country unsuited to Irish farmin. So don't dud us very dark Irish. We're the Future of the Nation.'

It's hard to know how to reply. To think of a response may take time. As we cogitate, let Blue MacEwe drink another glass of cheer while World Wide rolls a small number; let Carney make preparation for something that could never be, a Christian wedding; let Molly conjure up poor Mike Hock, who understood, in his final hours, the Mystery of the Round Tower, of which there are sixty-five left, in part or in ruins, on Hibernia; let Billy caress Jarvey, who must now leave the Land of Fairies to train harness horses to win harness races; let

Oblong dream of cocopop pine, in his own backyard for its preservation, as Adam hums the chorus of 'The Fane of St Fiacre' by the Grammy-winnin Wonder from Down Under.

And let a bear glint from a manna gum, let a mopoke owl call from beyond the umpire's chair, on the tennis court, as a steer on Killaarney bellows at the rising crescent moon, while satellites shine down on Crooked Corner.